Project Cost Overrun

Causes, Consequences, and Investment Decisions

Cost overrun is common in public- and private-sector projects. Costs tend to grow, plans fail, and financial problems follow, but how can we approve the right projects if we cannot estimate their true cost? This book, for academics in project management, management accounting, and corporate finance, as well as for managers in the public and private sectors, offers a new way of thinking about the causes and consequences of cost overrun for firms and society. It demonstrates that there is a logic behind cost growth and overrun, identifies projects and situations that are more vulnerable, and examines the effects of increased costs. It further identifies the negative and positive consequences of cost overrun, analyses how and why preconditions for cost overrun differ when the logic governing private firms dominates versus the logic of the political sector, and explains why cost can sometimes be of lesser importance to decision makers.

Esbjörn Segelod is Professor in Business Administration at Mälardalen University, and was previously at Gothenburg and Uppsala Universities. Most of his research has focused on the appraisals, assessments, and processes associated with investments in major firms, entrepreneurship, the economic aspects of software development, and accounting history. He has previously published nine books, three as editor.

Project Cost Overrun

Causes, Consequences, and Investment Decisions

Esbjörn Segelod

Mälardalen University

CAMBRIDGE
UNIVERSITY PRESS

CAMBRIDGE
UNIVERSITY PRESS

University Printing House, Cambridge CB2 8BS, United Kingdom

One Liberty Plaza, 20th Floor, New York, NY 10006, USA

477 Williamstown Road, Port Melbourne, VIC 3207, Australia

314–321, 3rd Floor, Plot 3, Splendor Forum, Jasola District Centre, New Delhi – 110025, India

79 Anson Road, #06–04/06, Singapore 079906

Cambridge University Press is part of the University of Cambridge.

It furthers the University's mission by disseminating knowledge in the pursuit of education, learning, and research at the highest international levels of excellence.

www.cambridge.org
Information on this title: www.cambridge.org/9781107173040
DOI: 10.1017/9781316779675

© Esbjörn Segelod 2018

First published 2018

Printed in the United Kingdom by Clays, St Ives plc

A catalogue record for this publication is available from the British Library.

Library of Congress Cataloging-in-Publication Data
Names: Segelod, Esbjörn, author.
Title: Project cost overrun : causes, consequences, and investment decisions / Esbjörn Segelod, Malardalen University.
Description: Cambridge, United Kingdom ; New York, NY : Cambridge University Press, 2017. | Includes bibliographical references and index.
Identifiers: LCCN 2017030646 | ISBN 9781107173040 (hardback)
Subjects: LCSH: Project management – Cost control.
Classification: LCC HD69.P75 S4195 2017 | DDC 658.4/04–dc23
LC record available at https://lccn.loc.gov/2017030646

ISBN 978-1-107-17304-0 Hardback

Contents

v

Figures

Tables

Acknowledgements

My interest in cost overrun, and its causes and consequences, derived from an interest in corporate finance and cost–benefit analysis, as well as the observation that textbooks and articles on these subjects disregarded the problem of estimating the costs and revenues needed to make the calculations proven theoretically correct. The figures and the probabilities, when such were used, put into our calculations were assumed to be correct, although they were seldom based on reviews of implemented investments. We did not seem to learn from experience, which made the link between theory and practice weak.

An opportunity to research the area opened up in 1982 when I, as part of a larger research programme designed by Göran Bergendahl and Lennart Hjalmarsson, received the assignment of finding out the true cost, in real monetary value, of two nuclear power reactors at Barsebäck, which the owner, and funder of the research programme, the South Swedish Power Company, had constructed. It turned out to be time-consuming work due to all the calculations that had to be made, but it offered the opportunity for very informative discussions with former project managers, and the power company later asked me to review two more of their major investments in new power plants.

These experiences led me to apply for funding to study investment planning and deviations in major construction projects in both the private and public sectors, which were reported in my doctoral dissertation and book published in 1986. Having defended my dissertation, I left the cost overrun area and devoted my research time to other issues. Most important to the present book are three other empirical studies of investments in industry. The first was a study of the way some major ventures in new areas had been initiated and implemented, the second a study of investments and investment processes in major industrial groups, and the third a similar study of intangible investments and investment processes in major service groups.

In 1979–80 Göran Bergendahl and I had had an assignment for a government committee on the organization and finance of nuclear waste to propose a system for its financing. The committee resulted in the creation of the Swedish Nuclear Waste Fund, an organization for which I would undertake a few assignments in the years to come. It was probably these earlier experiences that, in 2003, led Per-Anders Bergendahl and Peter Rosén to ask me to review the cost development for the nuclear waste programme on behalf of a new government committee on the financing of nuclear waste. This gave me a reason to review the literature on cost overrun published since I left the area in 1986. To my disappointment, I observed that there had been a great number of new publications and studies in the area, but many of them were just replications, often without reference to similar earlier studies. Surprisingly few radically new ideas had been advanced, and it was still a fragmented area of research. This made me think: It seems time to summarize what we know about cost overrun, its causes, and its consequences, before embarking on any major new study of the subject matter.

Later, when time permitted, this allowed me to sketch out a book summarizing what research has taught us about cost overrun, its causes, and the consequences to firms and society. It led to an application for funding to Ragnar Söderberg's Foundation, without whose generous financial support the book would never have been written.

Many other organizations and people have contributed to this book. Of great importance has been my team of supervisors back in the early 1980s, namely Göran Bergendahl, Bertil Gandemo, Thomas Polesie, and Ulf Peter Welam, and also Lennart Hjalmarsson, who granted me access to the Swedish State Power Board.

Further, I want to thank my colleagues Gary Jordan, Leif Carlsson, Jan Löwstedt, and Svante Schriber, who all have given me constructive comments on the book's manuscript.

Another group of contributors of great importance is, of course, all of the managers who participated in my research, as without their help my studies of investments and cost overrun could not have been made. They are many, but I will refrain from listing them all as they do not appear in earlier studies, the reason being that some of them gave me interviews and help only on the condition that their names were not revealed.

I am also thankful for the useful advice I received during finalization of my manuscript from Valerie Appleby, and James Gregory, David Moore, and Paula Parish at Cambridge University Press, three anonymous Cambridge University Press reviewers, and Leanne Johnstone and Kate Kirk for language editing. It has been a pleasure to work with you.

1   Introduction

In 2003, Canadian Northland Resources started to explore an iron ore deposit close to the Finnish–Swedish border. The company was listed on the Oslo Stock Exchange in 2006, and moved from Canada to Luxembourg in 2010. Total capital investment for an iron ore mine producing 5 million tonnes a year was estimated at US $694 million in September 2010,[1] and the payback period of the mine was projected to be 4.9 years, or a net present value after interest and taxes of US $463 million at a discount rate of 8 per cent. Less than a year later, in May 2011,[2] these figures were updated to a net present value of US $934 million.

Plenty of investors were found, and Northland Resources started to construct the mine, but costs began to grow. In 2013, the company announced[3] that the total cost had increased by US $425 million. More money was needed to finish the project and the company had to ask for an out-of-court restructuring. An agreement was reached with debtors and creditors, and an injection of new capital made it possible to continue the project, but by June 2014 the company had to stop all payments and propose an informal reconstruction.[4] In October of the same year, the company had to seek permission to continue the reorganization[5]. But it was too late. Declining iron ore prices forced the company to file for bankruptcy[6] on 8 December 2014. The venture, which had begun in 2010 needing an estimated capital investment of US $694 million, ended with an open mine shaft and the receiver estimating total liabilities minus assets at more than US $1.5 billion.[7] However, this sum does not include losses accrued on public sector investments in roads, housing, and other forms of supporting infrastructure, nor any other private investments that had been made as a result of the project.

New mines have a tendency to exceed their budget. Another major new iron ore mine, the British[8] Anglo American's Minas-Rio project in Brazil, had a cost overrun that resulted in Anglo American recording an impairment charge of US $4 billion[9] in its 2012 earnings. A coincidence? Unlikely. A study of 63 international mining projects recorded an average cost overrun of 25 per cent.[10] Mining projects tend to become more expensive than anticipated.

We have all heard of projects that exceeded their initial cost estimates. The rising costs of large public projects, such as new roads and railways, public buildings, new military aircraft and naval vessels, and events such as the Olympic Games, often feature in the press. Olympic Games between 1968 and 2012 show an average cost overrun of more than 300 per cent, with a median of 150 per cent.[11] The Channel Tunnel incurred a cost overrun of 80 per cent, the Trans-Alaska oil pipeline was 12 times more expensive than originally estimated, and the Sydney Opera House 14 times more costly than initially expected. More recently, the US Air Force F22 Raptor aircraft became so expensive that the number to be built was reduced from 650 to 187 and substituted with the cheaper F35 Lightning II aircraft, which itself has been delayed and costs increased by more than 50 per cent.

Delays and cost overruns affect both public and private sector projects, although the latter rarely come to the public's attention. A review of 35 studies[12] of major projects did not find a single study where major projects had not, on average, exceeded their budget. Other studies have shown that cost overrun is no smaller today than 100 years ago.[13] We do not seem to learn. Still others have shown that cost overrun varies by type of project and the organization planning and implementing the project. Technology and management matter. Anyhow, as Table 1.1 illustrates, cost overrun is the norm.

Delays and cost overruns are endemic. Still, there are plenty of questions to be answered. Where and when do cost overruns tend to occur? Are certain types of project more prone to cost overrun than others? Are larger projects more likely to increase in cost than smaller ones? Does the length of the construction period affect cost overrun? Is cost overrun less of a problem today than in the past? What are the drivers of time and cost overrun? Are they to be found in the technology, in behavioural biases, in politics, or in the control system and the way projects are organized? Does deviation in cost appear at random, or can the logic behind deviations be modelled and foreseen? What happens in projects and firms when costs increase? What are the consequences of overrun on firms and society, and are there perhaps both negative and positive effects of overrun? These are some of the questions we will try to answer in this book.

A number of studies into the causes of cost overruns in the development of new military aircraft and missiles were carried out in the 1950s in the USA. These studies emphasized the process of developing new knowledge. The number of publications on cost overrun expanded quickly thereafter, especially during the 1970s when inflation reached

Table 1.1 *Average cost overrun according to a few studies of cost overrun*

Year of study	Type of project	Number of projects	Average cost overrun in %
1971[14]	R&D projects in two US pharmaceutical firms	75, 69	78, 111
1983[15]	US public sector military projects	244	127
	US public sector civilian projects	200	92
1985[16]	Turkish public sector construction projects	394	44
1990[17]	Indian public sector projects	133	82
1990[18]	R&D projects in Swedish engineering firms	91	80
1992[19]	Canadian computer software projects	89	33
2002[20]	Transportation infrastructure projects	258	(27.6)
2008[21]	Mining and smelting projects	63	25 (14)
2008[22]	Korean road projects	138	28.6 (10.7)
2011[23]	Swedish rail projects	65	(21.1)
2014[24]	Norwegian road projects	434	10.06
2014[25]	Nuclear reactors	180	(117)
	Hydroelectric dams	61	(71)
	Thermal power plants	36	(13)
	Wind farms	35	(8)
	Electricity transmission projects	50	(8)
	Solar farms	39	(1)
2014[26]	Major oil and gas projects	205	59

Note: Figures within parentheses are in estimated constant money value.

double digits. Today, there are many studies across a wide range of sectors, including electric power, road, mining, major public sector infrastructure, construction projects in both the private and public sectors, new industrial plants and processes, product development projects in pharmaceutical and engineering companies, computer software projects, and new weapons system programmes. There are case studies of problem-ridden projects, postal surveys mapping managers' theories and attitudes to cost overrun, laboratory experiments with managers acting on cost data, theoretical papers, and statistical studies of groups of projects. The study methods vary, but the causes of cost overrun identified are generic.

Many studies argue for or test whether a single variable can explain cost overrun. They claim, for example, that projects overrun their budget due to the estimators being overoptimistic, or not being entirely truthful in order to get their project approved, or the fact that the lowest tender is most likely to have underestimated the real cost. These single variable causes often advanced in academic journal articles are certainly relevant explanations in experimental situations and for specific projects, but many of these studies disregard the fact that major projects involve many actors, several sub-processes, and stretch over many years, as well as the importance of control systems for project cost estimation and implementation. Projects are planned and implemented in a context.

An important factor is that major projects and programmes are not planned in detail at approval, and that project planning is a learning process. It begins with a vague vision that must be specified before it can be realized. This requires testing of ideas and alternative solutions, and inevitably means that the plans will change, sometimes radically. When an investment project that was estimated to cost $100 million turns out to cost $150 million five years later, the two projects being compared are almost certainly not exactly the same, as important changes will have been made as the project progressed.

There has also been a tendency to disregard earlier studies by claiming that they do not apply to the type of project being studied currently, and references are only made to studies of similar projects. However, as we will show, experiences from different types of projects are very similar. There is a logic behind cost growth and cost overrun.

The ability to predict future costs is a prerequisite for meaningful investment planning and appraisal. If the cost of certain types of project tends to increase more than others, then we will allocate more funding to such investments than intended. Cost overruns affect the direction of investment, and possibly also the volume. This is a fundamental bias that is not mentioned in textbooks on capital budgeting, corporate finance, and corporate governance, where estimates are usually taken for granted. How to calculate the payback, net present value, and internal rate of return of an investment has become a compulsory subject at all business schools and in engineering management. We teach the pros and cons of various capital budgeting techniques and supply figures for students to exercise their numeracy. It is seldom mentioned that costs tends to increase and market goals take longer than anticipated to achieve, but if we cannot make reasonably good estimates how can we make the right investments?

We need to know more about where, when, and why deviations tend to occur, what the consequences are, and how to deal with deviations.

There are, as we will see, systematic biases in estimates. For instance, comparisons between budget and outcome of investment projects show that deviation in cost varies more for small than for large projects, and correlates with the length of the construction period, project complexity, advances in new technical knowledge, and changes in the project. There are also systematic biases in the way costs are estimated and how organizations handle cost overrun, and major public sector projects often have multiple goals and are initiated, planned, and implemented in a highly politicized environment. There are significant differences between private and public sector projects. A better understanding of these factors is important for investors, project managers, corporate finance, and the allocation of resources in organizations and society.

Investments in fixed assets are designed and have their costs estimated by engineers. They have the technical knowledge to make the choices that determine the economy of the investment, which is why their knowledge is of course essential to the quality of cost estimates. However, deviations between plan and outcome are also studied by accountants, economists, sociologists, psychologists, and political scientists. This book builds on research from several of these disciplines, so our first task is to define the terms used, as their interpretation differs somewhat from discipline to discipline.

When we talk about *cost overrun* we mean that the cost has exceeded a budget or contract, and we measure this *budget overrun* as the difference between approved budget and final cost. A *cost underrun* is the opposite. In this context, we can also talk about *time overrun*, and *time underrun* relative to a time schedule. The term 'overrun' is used differently in industry and in studies of public sector projects. While a cost increase prior to an approved budget would not be labelled a cost overrun in private industry, many studies of public sector projects use the term cost overrun to denote a difference between early cost estimates, sometimes the very first estimate, and final cost.

We will also talk about *cost increase* or *cost growth*, with the opposite being *cost decrease*; here, we mean an increase in cost between two estimates where the first estimate is not necessarily an approved budget or a figure stated in a contract. The term *cost growth* is used in the project management literature.[27] A term used in social science to denote an unanticipated increase in cost between two estimates is *cost escalation*,[28] and its opposite is *cost de-escalation*. However, as 'cost escalation' in project management literature is used to denote a price increase in specific goods or services (i.e. a relative price change), we will not use that term to avoid confusion.

While traditional project management literature focuses on planning and implementing projects to approved budget and goals, we will view cost overrun from the perspective of the firm and society. Thus, an investment project becomes only one of many investment options open to an investor, and what is of interest is the cost of a project to the firm or society as a whole. We term this a *business economist perspective*.

This book consists of six chapters and three appendices. In Chapter 2, we discuss the problem of measuring cost overrun and define our variables. Chapter 3 deals with what happens when cost increases above budget, and the negative and positive consequences of cost overruns to organizations and society. In Chapter 4 we present a model of cost overrun and growth based on results from earlier studies of the subject, and the assumption that estimators base their estimates on facts and update their estimates as new information becomes available. Cost growth becomes a consequence of the way project cost estimators and planners resolve economic-technical uncertainty. We further develop this model in Chapter 5 by adding on the dimension of political decision making and the resolution of political uncertainty versus economic-technical uncertainty. The results and conclusions of our analysis are summarized in Chapter 6. For a review of the literature, see Appendices A to C.

Chapter 2: We start our venture into the realm of cost estimates and deviations using four examples to illustrate the many problems of estimating the correct cost of an investment project, the appearance of cost overrun, and actions taken when cost increases. The first example, an investment in a new press section in a paper machine, shows that it is not always a simple task to estimate the correct cost even when a tender offer exists. The next two examples involve investments in a paperboard machine and two nuclear reactors, and illustrate how the cost of individual budget items can increase even though the total budget does not.

When costs increase, the first thing project management does is to search for savings to meet the budget. The paperboard machine example illustrates how savings can often be made by postponing parts of the investment or by selling and leasing back parts of the project, savings that usually become future operating and investment costs. The final example deals with one of the largest construction projects being undertaken currently: the management of nuclear waste. This project is planned and cost estimated in a highly politicized environment, and our example shows how costs and assumptions made in the costing process can be affected by political decisions. We will use these examples to illustrate problems associated with establishing the size of a cost overrun, and how important it is to avoid comparing apples and oranges. We will return to these examples and the problem of measuring deviations later on in the book.

Chapter 3: When costs increase, project management first uses up the contingencies built into the budget, then tries to make savings by choosing cheaper solutions and/or refraining from implementing some of the plans. They may also postpone parts of the investment or let somebody else finance parts of it and lease these back. Not all postponed parts will be implemented in the future, but postponement typically means that the investment outlay is reduced by increasing future investments and leasing fees. Choosing cheaper technical solutions can also mean higher future operating and maintenance costs, but may not, as the trade-offs between investment and operating cost made when choosing technical solutions is mostly driven by technical standards and practice. The budget can be met more easily if the project is divisible and can be implemented in stages, resources are reversible, and goals and ambitions can be re-negotiated.

The ultimate consequence of cost overrun is bankruptcy, but this is rare. Much more common is that the cost overrun places a financial burden on the firm that reduces the firm's financial flexibility and ability to take advantage of future profitable investments opportunities, acquisitions, and business deals when these appear. It can of course also threaten jobs and affect a firm's image and reputation.

There are also positive effects. Cost overrun might, under some conditions, increase total investments and savings. It makes us invest more in categories of investments that are more prone to exceed their estimates than initially planned, and less in projects that are less likely to exceed their cost estimate. This reallocates investment funds from investments in maintaining towards renewing existing product portfolios. Cost overrun can thus contribute to renewing firms and society, and this is probably the most important positive effect of underestimating the true cost.

We will also identify four types of investment project where there is a tendency to underinvest if we know the real cost of implementation at too early a stage, namely infrastructure projects with the potential to open up new markets for exploitation; radical innovations creating business opportunities for exploitation; new ventures opening up new products and markets for exploitation; and projects benefiting from changing value systems. These are all types of projects where underestimating their real investment outlay can sometimes be balanced by similarly underestimating their true long-term benefits. A key question here is to what extent the firm can appropriate profit from its investments, or whether other firms and the economy at large will reap the benefits. There is a considerable knowledge spillover, especially from R&D and intangible investments.

Chapter 4: In this chapter we show that cost growth can be explained by how we make estimates and resolve uncertainty as the planning and implementation process proceeds and we receive more accurate information. The outcome of the process depends on the technology, prior knowledge, the learning during planning and implementation of those involved, and the way the process is organized.

When project planners launch an idea they cannot specify in detail exactly what has to be done to implement their idea. The learning process as the project develops means that they might discover additional works that have to be carried out, and therefore have to make changes to the original design. The project can increase in scope, and its design can be altered. The cost of making such changes increases with the amount of resources spent, as resources already spent on the earlier design cannot be fully recovered. It does not cost much to make design changes while the project is still in the planning process, but when the project is being implemented it becomes increasingly expensive. The need for such unanticipated changes drives cost.

Implementing an idea is a process of learning. The idea always comes first. Then a plan has to be formed showing how this idea can be implemented. Based on that initial plan, a cost estimate can be made, and this will gradually become more reliable as the project planners form a more precise image of the project and what is needed to implement it. Changes in the original plan and additional work will often be necessary as uncertainties are resolved, and some types of project require more changes than others, depending on previous knowledge and the need to develop new skills and knowledge.

These observations make it possible to formulate a model based on the way uncertainty can be resolved. Therein, we distinguish between uncertainty that will be resolved during the planning process, termed dynamic uncertainty, and static uncertainty, which is always present and will not necessarily be resolved. Uncertainty associated with standard houses and other projects which can be planned in detail and implemented can be resolved using existing knowledge; R&D projects require the acquisition and development of new knowledge for uncertainty to be resolved. Static uncertainty derives from things we cannot control, such as changes in market prices, or what other actors in a development or production chain do, and we must remember that what is resolvable uncertainty for one actor might not be so for another.

We then take a closer look at cost overrun as a consequence of static uncertainty such as price changes, and the importance of regulation, standardization, and utilizing economies of scale. The cost difference between standardized and unique projects has been widened, and it seems that estimators tend to underestimate the long-term above-inflation cost growth that some types of projects experience.

Finally, we study the trade-offs between expected risk, return, and the cost of resolving uncertainty, and show that there are situations in which it is not optimal to resolve uncertainty prior to the decision to invest, either because the expected return is so high and so dependent on early operation that it is risky to wait, or because the cost of resolving uncertainty is too high in relation to expected return.

Chapter 5: Profit-maximizing organizations seek economic efficiency, and are governed by the logic of economics. Politics is partly governed by another logic, as politicians have to align their decisions and acts to the norms and values of voters and society. We therefore review the consequences of these two different logics for estimates and cost overrun.

Our original model concerns the resolution of economic-technical uncertainty. While economic-technical uncertainty derives from lack of information, political uncertainty derives from disagreement among stakeholders. The solution to political uncertainty is to form plans that are acceptable to a large enough majority of stakeholders so that the decision can be approved. Good decisions have to satisfy both the logic of economics and the logic of politics. In extending our model in Chapter 5, we discuss alternative ways of resolving political uncertainty, and show that political uncertainty has to be resolved before economic-technical uncertainty can be fully resolved.

The control systems by which proposals and estimates for new projects are reviewed before they are approved, and then monitored during implementation, are important for the accuracy of cost estimates. All organizations, private as well as public, have such control systems, and when project estimates turn out to be too low, this indicates that the system has not worked as intended. We therefore compare the way major companies control investment cost estimates with the control systems found in the public sector. In principle, there are many similarities, but the preconditions for these means of control to function well differ in many respects, and we will analyse the consequences of this.

Chapter 6: In this chapter we draw together the pieces of our endeavour in the land of estimates and deviations. We do that by first discussing situations in which the cost of the project becomes less important due to the compromises that have to be made to secure funding, or because a project exhibits symbolic power or is the result of a strong personal goal. Decisions to spend resources on projects may not be motivated solely by economic reasons, but by emotions and instincts, such as an individual's need to boost their self-esteem in the face of death. We then briefly discuss explanations for cost overrun, summarize what we have learnt and return to the issue of the effects of cost overrun on the return on investments.

Appendix A: The study builds on an extensive review of the literature and what we can learn from earlier studies of cost overrun and growth. Appendix A gives an overview of studies in this research area. There are a great number of studies into time and cost growth and budget overrun, the most common being case studies and statistical studies of groups of projects, and these demonstrate that cost overrun is the norm. There are projects that are implemented to, or below, estimated cost, but taken as a group it is difficult to find a study showing that the final cost on average is not underestimated. There are a few examples, but they all derive from one single organization. We will also see that this applies to a range of projects, including construction, R&D, and computer software projects, to older studies and newer ones, and to public and private sector projects.

Appendix B: In Appendix B, we formulate the conclusions from earlier studies, conclusions which led to the development of the model in Chapter 4. We show that estimates tend to rise over time, that they tend to increase more in the beginning of the planning process than later on, and that the outcome of smaller projects tends to vary more than for larger projects. We will also learn that estimates become less reliable the longer the time between two estimates, that cost overrun co-varies with time overrun and external and internal changes, and that some organizations are better at estimating costs than others.

Appendix C: The model in Chapter 4 assumes that the estimator has access to gradually more accurate information, and the ability to identify and choose the alternative that maximizes his utility. In Appendix C, we relax these assumptions and assume that estimators are limited in terms of information, cognitive ability, and time to process information. Decisions are based not only on reasons, but on a mixture of emotions and reasons.

There are a great number of explanations in the literature emphasizing the importance of emotions in cost growth and overrun – for instance, that investors appropriating funding are overoptimistic, do not consider what is spent as sunk cost, and know less than those requesting funding. We will review the more prominent of these explanations: optimistic bias, self-serving bias and anchoring bias, path dependence, and information asymmetry.

2   Project Planning, Cost Estimates, and Deviations in Major Projects

When talking about cost overruns, most of us probably think of an increase in cost between an approved budget and the eventual cost of a finished project. However, the estimate on which the budget or the decision to invest is based is seldom the first cost estimate for an investment. Many years may have passed since the very first estimate, and numerous investment appraisals may have been undertaken before final approval. Costs also tend to rise between the first estimate and the one that the formal investment decision is based on, and then again after the decision to invest. Occasionally, costs fall, but the opposite is far more common.

A construction project, and in principle other types of project, can be divided into four phases. First, the concept or idea phase, in which the project will be specified and its feasibility reviewed. This usually results in a first estimate of the investment outlay.

The planning and design phase comes next, in which an appraisal suitable for an investment request is made. This involves choosing the optimum technical solutions, estimating the costs of these technical solutions, and compiling an investment request according to the company's standard practice, which may involve following an investment manual or protocol. The investment request involves a project budget and schedule, a financial plan, a description of the proposed alternative, and its present and future known options, risks, and flexibility.

If approved, the third phase is implementation of the project, beginning with more detailed design work and procurement. Project costs are monitored regularly during construction, and the final cost is reported when the project is finished.

The fourth and final phase is the running-in period, during which additional investments may be necessary to trim the machinery and achieve the intended product quality and quantity. It can take time to reach the production capacity and product quality specified, and hence following up these parameters generally occurs after six months to two years.

In the planning and design phase, work is focused on those parts of the plant that are vital for it to function. Peripheral parts are usually designed

11

only when the formal investment decision has been taken. Tender offers can be requested without engagement to help estimate costs, but formal tenders and procurement cannot be initiated until approval has been granted. Major investment projects are typically not specified in detail when they are approved, meaning that additional specifications and new trade-offs have to be made during implementation.

The largest cost increases are likely to occur early in the planning phase, i.e. between the first and second estimates, one reason being that the first estimate is usually very approximate, having been made long before all the consequences of the investment have been identified. Sometimes, the first estimate is simply set low enough to allow the investment idea to be investigated. Then, as the investment is investigated further, planners become aware of new problems and needs, and changes and additional items make the estimated costs increase.

When building a new plant or machine, a major risk is that the plant or machine will not work as intended. If a new plant cannot be commissioned as quickly as planned due to technical problems, additional interest charges will soon consume all future profits and make the plant unprofitable. All work on project planning therefore is directed towards ensuring that those parts of the plant that are essential to the production process will work as intended. Consequently, buildings and other parts of the investment that are more peripheral to the production process tend not to be costed more accurately than as a lump sum at the time of the investment decision. Also, environmental regulations may make it necessary to plan certain parts of the project in more detail to meet such external requirements.

A cost estimate usually includes a budget item to cover unspecified contingencies and unforeseen costs that experience tells us are likely to appear later on. It is frequently about 10 per cent of the investment outlay – sometimes more, sometimes less, depending on who has done the estimate and what is permitted. This buffer can be easy to identify under the term 'contingencies', or it can be partially or totally hidden in other budget items. Some senior managers and boards do not approve unspecified budget items such as contingencies, and in these cases we have to assume that the buffer has been hidden under other headings. It is generally very difficult to specify the exact size of this buffer, as experienced project managers are skilled at making budgets easier to meet by including buffers in their estimates and plans. In response, some senior managers make cuts in the project budget before it is approved to create pressure on costs and increase cost-consciousness. They prefer to approve a budget that they know is tight, and are prepared to have to approve additional funds if project management cannot meet the budget.

When the investment decision has been made and the project is being implemented, costs are monitored and, in a similar way as before the decision to invest, major surprises frequently turn up in the beginning of the implementation process. When a quarter, or at the most a third, of the project budget has been spent, project management should have a rather good idea of what the final cost will be.

The four examples in this chapter illustrate the importance and difficulties of estimating the true cost overrun. The first shows that estimating the correct investment outlay is not always straightforward, even when a tender offer exists. The next two illustrate how cost deviations can be large for individual items in a project budget, even when the project comes in roughly within budget, and highlight different actions taken to counteract cost increases. The fourth case illustrates how costs can be affected by political decisions. We will return to these examples and the problem of measuring deviations throughout the book.

A Press Section Example

Let us start with an example[1] demonstrating that it is not always easy to establish the correct investment outlay even with a tender.

A paper-making machine consists of three sections: one where the wet paper web is formed, a press section where the web is pressed and drained, and one where the web is dried. In our example from a Swedish paper mill, the press section was the bottleneck, and production was expected to increase substantially if a new unit was installed. The investment was also expected to save energy, as the new press section would deliver a drier web to the drying section. Comprehensive pre-studies were conducted to choose the optimal press section, a few suppliers were invited to tender, and one supplier was selected. The supplier selected quoted a press section at a preliminary price of SEK 39 million. The quotation was accepted and the company board made a preliminary decision to invest.

The preliminary decision was followed by technical and commercial negotiations between specialists from the mill and the supplier. The terms for delivery and a great number of detailed plans and technical drawings were agreed, including for a building, electricity supply, electronics, piping, hydraulics, and pneumatics. However, in developing an investment request, project management had to decide what to include in the budget, and that turned out to be a non-trivial issue for a number of reasons:

– The final price for the press section was not SEK 39 million as in the preliminary quotation, but SEK 38.5 million after negotiations, not least because the price varied considerably depending on the terms of payment.

- Several suppliers were involved and it was difficult to define delivery limits.
- The cost of financing the investment was covered by the discount rate. However, the investment was financed through a bank loan and the bank required collateral. As a press section is considered to be part of the building, a cost appeared of 2 per cent of the loan for the mortgage, or SEK 700,000.
- There were also costs for pre-studies. These are sunk costs and should not be taken into account, but it can be problematic to decide what is sunk cost and what is part of the basic investment.
- Investment requests have to consider all future costs and savings resulting from the investment. In this case, changes had to be made in the foundations of the building for the press section and pumps, and electrical, piping, hydraulic and pneumatic equipment had to be purchased and installed.
- The budget also had to cover the necessary insurances, training for operators, costs for dismissal and pensions for operators made redundant due to the new equipment, start-up costs, costs for adjustments, rejects and reduced capacity, and capital cost for increased capital requirement in the operation.

The board based its decision on a preliminary price of SEK 39 million. When all further payments resulting from the investment had been added, the total projected outlay rose to SEK 45–50 million, a cost increase of 15–20 per cent.

As this example demonstrates, it is not always easy to correctly estimate the investment outlay, even in cases where the investment is well defined and of limited size.

To avoid cost overruns, project managers have to take care to identify and assess all the consequences of the investment decision. In theory, if sufficient time and resources are spent on project planning prior to the decision, it should be possible to estimate the investment outlay with the required precision. However, it may not always be wise to do so, as will be shown, as this may require choosing low risk or costly solutions that do not offer the same functionality as choices made later, when better information has been acquired.

A Paperboard Machine Example

Tables 2.1 and 2.2 show the budget and outcome for Frövifors Bruk AB's investment[2] in a new paperboard machine at Frövi, about 250 kilometres west of Stockholm, in the late 1970s. Frövifors Bruk was at

Table 2.1 *Cost deviations for the Frövifors' paperboard machine project, part I*

	Approved budget	Adjusted budget	Outcome	Deviation from approved budget in %	Deviation from adjusted budget in %
Fuel processing	10	11	13	30.0	20.0
Pulp line	64	82	90	40.6	9.8
Power block	115	108	148	28.7	37.0
Paper machine	543	507	561	3.3	10.7
Water and drainage	10	19	20	100.0	5.0
Plant area, storage	22	29	34	54.5	17.2
Contingencies	47	55	–	–	–
Total	811	811	867	6.9	6.9 (−0.5)

Notes: All figures in million Swedish krona. A cost overrun of 6.9 per cent in current monetary value corresponds to an underrun of −0.5 per cent in real monetary value.

Table 2.2 *Cost deviations for the Frövifors' paperboard machine project, part II*

	Adjusted budget	Outcome	Deviation in %
Unclassified	71	81	14.1
Buildings	214	256	19.6
Machinery etc.	345	344	0.0
Piping	52	71	36.5
Electrical equipment	56	85	51.8
Instrumentation	18	30	66.7
Contingencies	55	–	–
Total	811	867	6.9 (−0.5)

Notes: All figures in million Swedish krona. The cost of buildings (+19.6 per cent) was adjusted upwards between the first and the second estimate which is why the total cost overrun for buildings became about 30 per cent. A cost overrun of 6.9 per cent in current monetary value corresponds to an underrun of −0.5 per cent in real monetary value.

this time a company in the ASSI group; today Frövifors is a part of the BillerudKorsnäs group. The paperboard machine that the board of the ASSI group decided to invest in back in 1979 would create the largest liquid packaging board and cartonboard production line in the world.

There are two estimates in these tables. The first, the approved budget, is the estimate that the board approved and upon which it based the decision to invest. The second estimate, the adjusted budget, was presented six months after the board's decision to invest, when design work had proceeded further and tenders had been received. The plant was procured part by part from different producers after inviting tenders, and the project was led by a project management team from the company, aided by consultants.

As is evident from Tables 2.1 and 2.2, deviations in a project budget can be large even when the project overall does not show any large cost overrun. If we go one step further and subtract inflation to correct the payments made, the cost of the plant is reduced from an overrun of 6.9 per cent to an underrun of −0.5 per cent. In other words, the project becomes less expensive than anticipated. To an outsider who does not have access to the figures in the tables, it appears to be a project implemented as approved. Nevertheless, the cost of electrical equipment had increased by 51.8 per cent and instrumentation by 66.7 per cent between the second estimate and the review, and costs of water and sewage drainage treatment works had increased by 100 per cent during this time. Hence, certain budget items showed major cost increases even though the project as a whole met the budget.

To meet the budget, the project managers had to not only use up the lump sum included for contingencies, but also to save SEK 45 million by cutting some of the smaller investments, and by selling and leasing back certain buildings included in the project. In addition, they managed to purchase the paper machine for SEK 20 million less than expected due to the depressed state of the market. If we include these savings of about SEK 65 million, we can see that they reduced the cost overrun from 14.7 per cent to 6.9 per cent. To what extent suppliers made profits or losses on their work is unknown, but rumour suggests that some of them made losses and that a few smaller ones went bankrupt.

The saving of SEK 65 million and the shifting size of deviations for different budget items show that many new and significant trade-offs were made during implementation. Such deviations between plans and reality constantly appear and have to be managed, meaning that new specifications, choices, and trade-offs have to be made. Plans cannot be followed uncritically. Project management have to adapt them during implementation.

Table 2.1 shows a common pattern. The cost deviation for the most important part, the paperboard machine, is small, in spite of the fact that the subsystems that made up the machine were procured from different suppliers. This can be explained partly by the fact that project planning had focused on ensuring that the paperboard machine would achieve the planned production capacity and product quality as soon as possible, and partly because the risk of cost increases was transferred to the sellers through price clauses. Similarly, the relatively large deviations between the estimate that was approved by the board and that made six months later can for peripheral parts be explained by the fact that the more detailed design needed to cost them accurately was not developed until after the investment was approved.

Major companies with substantial fixed investments usually have a written protocol, an investment manual, which specifies the way investments should be evaluated, the decision process, and who is responsible for what. These investment manuals may also contain an instruction stipulating that additional funds must be requested and approved if the cost growth exceeds 10 per cent; in some companies the cut-off figure is 5 per cent. This becomes a limit that those responsible for the project are reluctant to pass, and the project managers in our paper machine example managed to avoid this by reducing the overrun from 14.7 to 6.9 per cent.

If the cost overrun turns out to be small, then it may be possible to manage the budget with the help of what has been allocated for contingencies. If that is not sufficient, savings can usually be made on the quality of certain parts, postponing other parts, or selling and leasing back warehouses and other buildings. Although these measures decrease the investment outlay, they often lead to higher future additional investments, and higher costs for maintenance and operation. Similarly, there is often an unwillingness to return unused funds, so if there happens to be a surplus, project management will find a use for it.

From a technical point of view, the project was very successful as the paperboard machine achieved planned production capacity and product quality faster than earlier similar projects against which it was benchmarked. However, finance caused problems. Frövifors Bruk AB belonged to the ASSI group and finance was handled at the group level. To finance the new paperboard machine, ASSI took a loan in US dollars when one dollar was SEK 4.20 and the lending rate 6.5 per cent. Some years later, when the dollar had recovered, the Swedish currency had been devalued and the interest rate had reached 12 per cent, wherein the cost of finance had increased by more than SEK 300 million. Unfamiliar with taking loans in a foreign currency, ASSI had not covered the loan for exchange rate fluctuations. If we add SEK 300 million to the budgeted SEK 811 million, we have a cost overrun of 37 per cent.

Another issue is cost in relation to production capacity. Engineers have a tendency to specify new plants, perhaps especially in the process industry, at a higher capacity in normal production than stated in the investment request because they want to make sure they can reach the targets. This sometimes means that the excess in production capacity becomes higher than the cost overrun. In the Frövifors case, we know that they reached planned production capacity faster than in those earlier similar projects against which it was benchmarked. This is very important since a one-month delay for an investment of 1 billion at 12 per cent interest rate costs 10 million.

Was the new Frövifors plant a successful project that became operational faster than similar projects and had a small underrun of −0.5 per cent in real monetary value? Or was it a project with a cost overrun of 14.7 per cent in nominal monetary value, or even a project that cost the owner 37 per cent more than anticipated? It is not always easy to establish the investment outlay, nor is it easy to establish the actual cost overrun, not least since plans have to be adjusted and changed as they are being implemented. Calculating cost overruns depends on what we measure and how the measurements are made.

A Nuclear Power Plant Example

A review of the two nuclear power reactors at Barsebäck on the south Swedish coast close to Copenhagen further illustrates where cost deviations appear. Tables 2.3 and 2.4 are based on a review[3] made on behalf of the owner of the reactors, Sydkraft AB, the South Swedish Power Company, today a part of E.ON AG. The two reactors, Barsebäck 1 and 2, cost slightly more than SEK 700 million each in monetary value as of December 1971, payments on interest excluded. The cost overruns of the two reactors were 24 per cent and 45 per cent in nominal terms, payments on interest excluded.

Adjusting payments made with the help of Statistic Sweden's monthly consumer price index to correct for inflation and discounting these payments to December 1971 gave cost overruns equivalent to 6.6 per cent and 1.7 per cent in constant monetary value. Inflation was the single most important cause of cost growth and, as a consequence of rising interest rates, interest payments were higher than anticipated. The timetable was kept to, and it took about five years from the board's decision to invest to commercial operation.

The cost overruns in this example are very unevenly distributed. For reactors and turbines, price clauses transferred the risk and responsibility for possible cost increases to the suppliers, which explains why the cost for these two parts just about followed the consumer price index. Similar settlements were in place for the waste disposal plant, but it became more expensive than anticipated due to the need for additional work. So too for nuclear fuel and for building works. However, the cost of construction work increased as the buildings were designed and procured after the decision to invest. The cost of nuclear fuel fell due to lower uranium prices.

Table 2.3 *Cost deviation for Barsebäck 1*

	Estimate	Outcome	Deviation	Deviation in constant monetary value in%	Deviation in current monetary value in %
Reactor facility	230,927	224,078	−6,849	−3.0	26.2
Turbine plant	84,703	86,455	1,752	2.1	45.0
Building works	101,246	133,243	31,997	31.6	66.7
Equipment	2,279	3,383	1,104	48.4	75.6
Waste plant	8,990	12,066	3,076	34.2	88.4
Additional equipment (including electrical equipment)	11,583	28,776	17,193	148.4	234.8
Nuclear fuel	115,304	91,913	−23,391	−20.3	15.0
Spare parts	4,408	7,557	3,149	71.4	105.4
Project initiation and planning	2,231	2,844	613	27.5	12.1
Temporaries including support measures	3,594	15,259	11,664	324.6	400.2
Administration	30,738	50,170	19,432	63.2	114.6
Insurances	2,088	1,419	−669	−32.1	0.8
Operation and maintenance	8,700	18,032	9,332	107.3	184.1
Taxes	3,248	1,043	−2,205	−67.9	−67.9
Contingencies	24,244				
Total, excluding interest payments	634,283	676,238	41,895	6.6	22.3
Additional items included in the budget and/or follow-up	8,000	29,200			
Total, excluding interest payments	642,283	705,438	63,155	9.8	24.0

Note: All figures in kSEK(million Swedish Crowns).

Items for temporaries were the most severely hit. These included support measures (324.6 and 66.5 per cent), additional equipment, including electrical equipment (148.4 and 27.7 per cent), spare parts (71.4 and 158.0 per cent), and operation and maintenance (107.3 and 148.5 per cent). The costliest element of the project apart from the reactor was the building works (31.6 and 33.0 per cent). In absolute terms, building works accounted for about 50 per cent of the total cost overrun. The fact that building works and temporaries were hit hardest is not surprising, as these elements were planned after the decision to invest had been made. Cost

Table 2.4 *Cost deviation for Barsebäck 2*

	Estimate	Outcome	Deviation	Deviation in constant monetary value in %	Deviation in current monetary value in %
Reactor facility	263,484	260,016	−3,468	−1.3	31.7
Turbine plant	97,243	97,137	−106	−0.1	47.9
Building works	90,863	120,813	29,950	33.0	71.4
Equipment					
Waste plant					
Additional equipment (including electrical equipment)	22,670	28,957	6,287	27.7	77.5
Nuclear fuel	110,731	90,818	−19,913	−18.0	18.3
Spare parts	3,000	7,740	4,740	158.0	290.5
Project initiation and planning					
Temporaries including support measures	7,692	12,807	5,115	66.5	125.8
Administration	31,280	35,033	3,753	12.0	51.4
Insurances	1,926	1,374	552	−28.7	9.1
Operation and maintenance	4,400	10,935	6,635	148.5	267.5
Taxes	2,000	775	−1,225	−61.3	−41.8
Contingencies	20,000				
Total, excluding interest payments	655,289	666,405	11,116	1.7	42.5
Additional items included in the budget and/or follow-up	–	50,193	–	–	–
Total, excluding interest payments	655,289	716,598	61,309	9.4	44.8

Note: All figures in (million Swedish Crowns).

estimates are based on plans and drawings, and it is only when you have carefully worked out all the details of these plans that you know what to include in the estimate. Inevitably, as project planning proceeds and the plans become more detailed, you discover more work that needs to be done, and hence total cost increases.

The cost overruns for temporaries are much lower for the second reactor, B2, Table 2.4, than for the first one, B1, Table 2.3. This indicates that B2, which was built in tandem but with a lag of two years, benefitted from learning acquired through building the first reactor. According to the project managers, this cost-reducing learning effect could probably have been utilized even better if the time lag between the reactors had been a little longer.

Ten years after the decision to construct these two reactors was made, the cost of producing electricity at this nuclear power plant turned out to be twice as high as assumed in the initial investment request. Luckily, the production costs in fossil-fuel power plants rose even faster due to the very sharp increase in oil prices during the 1970s. The cost of new nuclear power plants also rose very rapidly after these two reactors had been procured due to increased safety requirements, and rumours suggest that at least a few of the manufacturers and suppliers involved took losses because these were the first nuclear power plants they worked on and they wanted to secure a position on this new expanding market. Overall, the Barsebäck nuclear power plant turned out to be a very good investment for its owner, Sydkraft AB.

From the paperboard machine and nuclear power plant examples, it should be clear that it is not always easy to describe or calculate the extent of the cost deviation. Firstly, the risk of cost growth may have been transferred to the supplier through a price clause or other form of con-tract, in which case any change in cost will turn up as a deviation for the suppler. Secondly, there is often room for redistributions and savings in project budgets, but such measures may increase future operating costs and necessitate future additional investments. We must therefore suspect that the true cost often differs from what is reported, and that both overruns and underruns may be larger than announced.

A Nuclear Waste Programme Example

Nuclear power and the production of electricity became a highly political issue in the early 1970s. During the 1950s and 1960s, there seems to have been a consensus on replacing dirty coal with oil, but when OPEC more than tripled oil prices, oil became uneconomical to burn. Growing envir-onmental concerns blocked any further expansion of hydroelectric and coal power, nuclear power became expensive due to increased safety requirements, and oil power became too expensive due to OPEC price increases. Some believed we would run out of oil by 1985. There was a need to use energy more efficiently and to find new ways of producing it. Nuclear power was seen as a saviour by some – partly because there is plenty of uranium in Swedish alum shale – and as a threat by others. Thus, the nuclear waste programme offers an example of cost estimation in a highly politicized environment. Important assumptions have been (and still are) imposed by external actors, and are an outcome of political processes.

Nuclear power is a capital-intensive technology with large negative salvage values, since it requires very large investments to deal with spent radioactive fuel and reactor parts long after the reactor has been shut down. It has been estimated that the cost of R&D, investment, decommissioning and nuclear waste on the one side, and the cost of operation and management on the other, each accounted for roughly 50 per cent of the total cost for the French nuclear power programme from 1970 to 2000.[4] Recent studies of plants in operation gives even higher investment costs.[5]

By 2004, 122 new nuclear reactors had been given permits in the United States. The cost of decommissioning these was estimated at the time at US$ 33 billion, and the cost of management and disposal of radioactive waste from operations and spent nuclear fuel at US$ 58 billion,[6] making it one of the largest construction projects ever undertaken. Similar nuclear waste projects were planned in many other countries that used nuclear power. Sweden, for instance, had 10 commercial reactors still in operation (originally 12), and the total cost of dealing with radioactive waste was estimated at about SEK 80 billion[7] in 2004, a figure equivalent to approximately $10 billion. Ten years later, in 2014, when close to SEK 50 billion had been spent, the estimated remaining cost had increased to SEK 100 billion,[8] i.e. US$12.5 billion, a considerable increase in estimated future cost.

Swedish operators started to make allowances for these costs when they commissioned their first plants, assuming that these funds would not be taxed until they were used some 30 to 70 years in the future. This aroused the attention of the tax authorities and opponents to nuclear power, who calculated that allowing these companies to postpone taxation for so many years would make nuclear power self-financed. The issue prompted one government committee to investigate technical solutions,[9] and another to study the organizational and financial issues.[10]

The committee investigating organizational and financial issues[11] recommended a solution in which the operators of nuclear power plants should take responsibility for the management of the waste their reactors generated. The operators chose to assign this task to a jointly owned company, SKBF (Swedish Nuclear Fuel Supplies Co.), later SKB (Swedish Nuclear Fuel and Waste Management Co.).

SKBF and SKB developed a programme to transport radioactive waste in a specially constructed ship from the reactor site to SKB's facilities, where it would be separated according to its radioactivity and half-life. Short-lived low- and intermediate-level operational waste would be disposed of in a final repository suitable for that type of waste (SFR), in bedrock 50 metres underground. Spent fuel would be stored in a central interim storage facility (CLAB) for 30 years, by which time its radio-activity would have diminished by 90 per cent. At this point, it would be easier to handle and could be transported to an encapsulation plant to be encapsulated in copper canisters. These would then be placed in a deep repository for spent fuel embedded in bentonite clay at a depth of about 500 metres in 1.9-billion-year-old bedrock. The repository was expected to isolate the spent fuel for at least 100,000 years, by which time it would be no more harmful than natural uranium.

The committee on organizational and financial issues ordered a first cost estimate for this programme. It came in at a little under SEK 45 billion (monetary value January 2014), and was soon followed by an updated estimate. When SKBF sat down and made their first, more thorough, review of the total project, the cost came to about SEK 100 billion (monetary value January 2014), i.e. approximately 100 per cent more than had been foreseen only four years earlier. This prompted efforts to find more economic solutions in order to bring costs down significantly over subsequent years, a trend that was halted in the late 1990s as the construction of the deep repository came closer. Figure 2.1

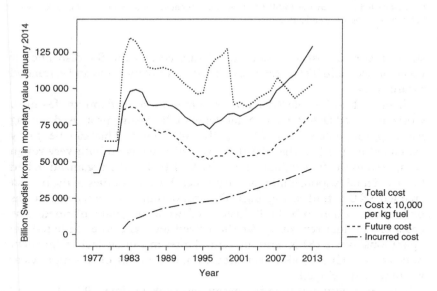

Figure 2.1 Incurred and estimated future costs of the Swedish nuclear waste programme

Table 2.5 *Incurred and estimated future costs of the Swedish nuclear waste programme*

	SKBF 1982	SKB 1996	SKB 2004	SKB 2013	1982– 2013 in %	Remaining cost in %
Transportation	5,840	3,034	3,153	4,827	-17.3	53.0
CLAB	12,232	13,080	13,533	19,391	58.5	45.0
SFR	6,218	3,117	3,595	8,116	30.5	52.8
Reprocessing	8,702	9,646	9,845	9,845	13.1	0
SKB adm., RD&D	6,508	6,341	13,061	23,073	254.5	42.1
Encapsulation plant	9,210	7,448	7,761	12,856	39.6	96.0
Decommissioning of nuclear power plants	21,848	15,353	17,455	22,705	3.9	100.0
Deep repository	18,217	16,564	19,186	28,894	58.6	82.5
Total cost	88,774	72,720	87,305	129,707	46.1	64.9
whereof incurred	3,967	22,638	31,063	45,543	—	—
whereof future cost	84,807	50,082	56,242	84,164	—	—
Remaining cost in %	95.5	68.9	64.4	64.9	—	—
Total tonnes of uranium	7,269	6,380	9,448	12,564	72.8	—
Cost / tonnes uranium	12,213	11,398	9,241	10,324	-15.5	—

Notes: All figures in million Swedish krona (MSEK) and monetary value January 2014. Total cost according to SKB 2013 is estimated to MSEK 129,707. Including the new risk premium total estimated cost increases to MSEK 148,963. Estimated use of uranium 1982 unknown; 7,269 was the figure used in 1983.

shows incurred cost and estimated future cost of the Swedish nuclear waste project, and Table 2.5 gives a breakdown of incurred and estimated future costs.

Figure 2.1 and Table 2.5 allow us to identify some common features. Costs increased fastest in the initial stages of the costing process, doubling from approximately SEK 50 to SEK 100 billion. This can be partly explained by the fact that the first two estimates were both very rough compared to the first estimate made by SKBF after the organization had been assigned responsibility for the project. Further studies of the project enabled SKB to find cost savings. The cost of transportation decreased as only one boat had to be built, instead of two as originally planned. The costs of the final repository for short-lived low- and intermediate-level operational waste (SFR) and the central interim storage facility for spent nuclear fuel (CLAB) also decreased as new methods of storing nuclear waste were developed.

The exact design of the programme has evolved since 1982. It started with the intention to first prove that nuclear waste could be stored in a deep repository,[12] with a detailed design and location coming later. The programme consisted of several sub-projects, and the total cost covered both investment and operation. In the mid-1990s, investments made up about one-third of incurred costs, and today investments, demolition, and operation account for roughly one-third each of estimated future costs. The repository for short-lived low- and intermediate-level waste (SFR) experienced cost overruns, which was not unexpected as there were no prototypes, but the total cost of SFR did not increase as this cost overrun could be balanced by lower operating costs. The difference between next year's budget and outcome is usually small, but when comparing costs over longer time periods, individual items vary considerably, with some budget items increasing and others decreasing.

However, when more detailed plans were made for the deep repository and decommissioning of the nuclear reactors, costs started to rise again. These rising costs prompted SKB to spend more on research, development, and demonstration (SKB adm., RD&D) in order to find more cost-effective solutions, and so the budget item SKB adm., RD&D in Table 2.5 rose by 250 per cent from 1996–2013. This created worries, and new government committees[13] reviewed the financing of nuclear waste, leading to changes in the financing system. In 2007, there were also changes in the way risk was to be handled in calculating future costs.

Early estimates of the cost of decommissioning and handling of nuclear waste assumed that there would be 13 nuclear power reactors built in Sweden, each with a lifespan of 30 years. Nobody knew for certain what the economic life of a nuclear power reactor was, but 30 years was chosen as it was the same as for fossil-fuel plants. It was considered cheaper to reprocess spent fuel and so some fuel was reprocessed, but this cost advantage disappeared when uranium prices dropped in 1979–80.

The partial nuclear meltdown at Three Mile Island in Pennsylvania in 1979 was a contributing factor in a non-binding referendum on the future of nuclear power in Sweden in 1980. The result of this referendum led to parliament voting for only 12, rather than 13, reactors to be built, and that all of these would be closed down by 2010, after which it was assumed that nuclear power would have been replaced by renewable energy sources. As the last 2 of these 12 were to be commissioned in 1985, the economic lifespan of the reactors was set to 25 years, and this would therefore be the lifespan used in SKB's future estimates. It was also decided that spent fuel would not be reprocessed but encapsulated and buried in a deep repository. The Chernobyl meltdown in 1986 resulted in a ban on planning for new nuclear power plants in addition to the 12 reactors already approved.

Ten years later there was still no alternative to nuclear power, so in 1993 SKB began to estimate the cost of disposing of nuclear waste over both 25 and 40 years of operation. However, 25 years remained the reference case even though the oldest reactors had already been in operation for 21 years. The location of the two reactors at Barsebäck, reviewed in the previous section, was strongly criticized due to their proximity to Copenhagen, and the political decision was taken to close them down in 1999 and 2005.

Thus, the number of nuclear reactors was reduced to 10. In 2000, SKB made 40 years their operational reference. Later, in 2007, this was extended to 50 years for some reactors and 60 for others. Previously, the plan had been to dispose of encapsulated waste in a deep repository so that it was impossible to recover, but now it was considered better to make the spent fuel recoverable. In addition, the ban on planning for new nuclear power reactors was lifted.

Three out of four Swedish nuclear power plants are located close to major population centres. One reason for this decision was plans to use excess heat from the cooling water in the reactor for heating, and thereby reduce use and dependence on fossil fuel. This plan was never realized because of opposition to nuclear power, along with criticism that this would make nuclear power more profitable and result in the country becoming more reliant on it. The excess energy from the cooling water is instead lost, and remains the largest producer of non-harvested energy in the Swedish energy system. This situation, and a tax on nuclear energy introduced in 1984, have made nuclear energy less profitable.

Political decisions have also influenced assumptions about the number of years reactors should remain in operation and therefore the amount of spent fuel produced, the way reserve funds can be invested, the way spent fuel should be managed, the design of the deep repository, and the risk premium to be used in estimates; also, political priorities have changed over time. These externally driven changes in assumptions have of course affected the cost estimates presented in Figure 2.1 and Table 2.4. The system costed in 1982 is not the same as the one costed in 1996 or in 2013.

Table 2.5 shows the total tonnes of spent uranium estimated to be produced in Sweden. In the very first pre-1982 estimates, it was 9,000 tonnes, which was reduced to 7,269 when the economic life of the reactors was reduced to 25 years, and then to 6,380 when Barsebäck was closed down. But it increased to 9,448 tonnes when SKB made calculations based on 40 years of operational life, and then 12,564 tonnes when SKB was allowed to calculate based on 50 or 60 years in 2007. Dividing the estimated cost of the programme by the amount of uranium gives a decreasing cost per tonne of uranium. In constant monetary value, the estimated total cost of the programme per tonne of uranium has decreased by 15.5 per cent since 1982. In Figure 2.1, the declining curve represents total programme costs divided by the assumed amount of spent uranium multiplied by 10,000.

Another external factor that raised estimated future cost was the decision in January 2008 to add a premium for uncertainty and risk. This raised the future estimated cost in 2015 by almost 21.8 per cent, from SEK 82,740 to SEK 100,750 billion. The risk premium is used to calculate a fee to cover the risk of there not being enough funds reserved, or the reactor owner being unable to cover cost increases. One might describe it as an insurance against unanticipated cost growth.

These two changes in assumptions – extended life and the risk premium – were imposed externally and are the two most important factors behind the estimated cost increase between 2004 and 2014. Correcting for these changes, cost growth during 2004–14 decreases from 67 to 10 per cent. A new method of calculating costs and risks since 2007 may also have contributed to some of this 10 per cent cost growth. Political decisions have driven cost, but this is not reflected in the media, which simply cite costs increasing to new heights without explaining the complicated reasons behind this. Blazing headlines sell more newspapers.

Cost estimates serve two purposes. They are estimates of future payments, and they form the basis for estimating the fee operators of nuclear plants pay to the Nuclear Waste Fund (NWF), which in 2013 reported a capital fund of SEK 53 billion[14]. These fees are determined by the estimated cost of the programme and the return received by the NWF, and the way the latter is allowed to invest its capital has changed over time. Operators wished to invest in stocks, and legislators in more secure assets. The most recent government ordinance regulating the waste fund dates from 2008.

The situation is unstable. The 2014 estimates soon became obsolete because E.ON and Vattenfall, which owns most of the Swedish nuclear reactors, decided to wind up four of the oldest reactors in 2015 as they had become uneconomical. The reasons advanced were that the Fukushima meltdown in 2011 has made expensive investments in older reactors necessary, political decisions to subsidize wind power and increase taxation on nuclear power, a nuclear tax[15] based on installed capacity instead of production, and low and volatile energy prices. When the wind is favourable for wind power, prices fall below the production cost of base-load energy. Reduced service life and low return from the NWF due to low interest rates and because the fund has not been allowed to invest in bonds and stocks led to the Swedish Radiation Safety Authority recommending an increase in the nuclear waste fee from SEK

0.022 to 0.038 per kWh in 2014, and in 2015 to SEK 0.055 to 0.067 per kWh[16] – an increase of 150 to 205 per cent.

However, in June 2016 five out of the eight parties in the Swedish parliament reached an agreement,[17] with the stated goal of creating an energy system with 100 per cent renewable energy by 2040. The agreement included the abolition of the tax on nuclear installed capacity, the possibility of replacing ten nuclear reactors if investors wanted to do so, increased subsidies for wind power, and several other measures. The agreement prevented the premature decommissioning of nuclear power plants, a source of energy not regarded as renewable, but did not resolve the uncertainty of the composition of the future energy system, necessary for the industry to make major capital investments in new nuclear power plants or in energy-intensive industrial plants. This ambiguity was probably a precondition for agreement as both proponents and opponents of nuclear energy can argue that they are the winner of this agreement. Thus, the agreement resolved political uncertainty but not economic-technical uncertainty, and SKB and the NWF will have to revise their estimates once more.

In 2009, 32 countries were operating nuclear reactors. They have different funding systems[18] and ways of handling spent nuclear fuel.[19] Some major users of nuclear power, such as France, Japan, Russia, and possibly also China, have chosen to reprocess; others, such as Germany and the USA, have chosen to dispose of waste in a repository. Former Eastern bloc countries have reprocessing agreements with Russia, and some West European countries with France. Some countries have chosen to take on a leadership role and develop reprocessing or deep repository technology, while others have chosen to be followers, storing spent fuel in interim storage facilities and hoping that others will develop the necessary technology.

The Swedish programme has been deemed successful in that it has managed to develop a complete programme for the management of nuclear waste, the so-called KBS programme. KBS stands for Nuclear Fuel Safety, and its focus on safety solutions rather than the disposal itself has been credited[20] for its success. The KBS-3 method developed by SKB is now being implemented in the Finnish repository built at Olkiluoto. In 2010, the Finnish parliament ratified the government's decision-in-principle by 159 votes to 35 and a construction licence was issued in 2015.[21] Construction is expected to start in 2016, and operations in 2023.

The process has not yet come as far in Sweden, where support for nuclear energy is weaker. Consensus for the technology has been sought throughout the process via consultations and referrals. One of the actors is the Swedish Society for Nature Conservation, a coalition of non-governmental environment organizations, which is financed by fees from the reactor owners and which reviews the solutions suggested by SKB. Not unsurprisingly, the organization is against the KBS method and recommends studies of deep borehole disposals, an alternative under consideration in Germany and the USA. SKB's application for permits from 2011 and plans to start construction in the early 2020s are still under review.

It has been even more difficult to reach consensus in the USA. The US National Academy of Science recommended the deep repository solution as long ago as 1957.[22] The Department of Energy started to study the construction of such a repository in 1978. Work was intensified when Congress adopted the Nuclear Waste Policy Act of 1982 in 1983.[23] The project has experienced severe time and cost increases as estimated costs have grown from US$ 2 billion in 1982 to US$ 5.5 billion in 2001.[24] The fight against the chosen solution was conducted largely in the courts. In 2002, President George W. Bush approved the continuation of the Yucca Mountain nuclear waste repository project in Nevada, but in 2008 in his presidential campaign Barack Obama promised to close down the Yucca Mountain project, and did so in 2011. Which way the USA will choose is now unclear. In the meantime, US nuclear plant operators store spent fuel at sites in 35 states. However, to store spent fuel in basins for a few decades is not necessarily a bad alternative as it gives time for radioactivity to decline.

These experiences from Finland, Sweden, and the USA, as well as the solutions chosen in other countries, illustrate the importance of the political culture and means of conflict resolution to the progress of national nuclear waste programmes. A process that is acceptable in one country is impossible in another. The one trait most programmes seem to share is time delays, but these can be an advantage as delays give planners ample time to search for safer and more economical solutions. It also gives them time to develop and negotiate technical solutions that can win acceptance, and also be technically and economically sound.

The Difficulties of Measuring Cost Overrun

One can of course make it simple and say that the cost of a project estimated at 100 million that eventually costs 150 million has increased by 50 per cent. To know that 50 per cent more finance is needed is all the finance people need to know, but to know what we are getting for that extra 50 per cent, we need to know what we are comparing. The question is whether the two estimates we compare are based on the same project, or if we are comparing apples and oranges. The examples given above show that this is not a simple question to answer, and allow us to identify five principle sources of error when establishing the size of a cost overrun. We need to know:

- which cost items should be included in the investment amount,
- whether estimates represent the most probable outcome,
- whether we should view cost from the perspective of the project or the firm,
- whether we should consider changes in the project, and
- whether estimates and payments have been adjusted for price changes and inflation.

Firstly, it is often difficult to establish exactly what to include in the investment budget. It depends, as our press section example illustrated, on what is considered as sunk cost, when payments are made, and whether start-up costs, cost for adjustments, rejects, training of operators, loss of production due to construction, increase in working capital, or interest should be included. In principle it is easy, but in practice it is not unusual to miss out one or more cost items, and sunk cost is history. Investment decisions should be based on anticipated future payments due to the investment, not on what has been spent. Observe, however, that all that has been spent need not be sunk cost to the organization if what has been learnt or developed can be sold to somebody outside the organization,[25] or reused in the organization.[26]

It is also important to compare outcome with approved budget and not with earlier estimates, although this happens quite often when it comes to public sector projects, because early cost estimates may be discussed in the media long before a final proposal is approved.

Secondly, as the nuclear waste case exemplified, inputs into cost estimates made in politicized environments can sometimes be determined and changed by actors outside the firm. In this example, internal estimates had to be adjusted to align with externally imposed assumptions. Thus, the cost estimate need not represent the most probable estimate the estimators would have made had they been able to base these on their own assumptions.

Thirdly, what should be regarded as the cost of a project depends on whether we focus on the project budget or the cost the firm, or indeed society, has incurred for the project. In the Frövifors case, finance was handled by head office and, due to borrowing in a foreign currency, the cost of the finance to the group increased by some SEK 300 million. Should this 300 million, which project management had no control over, be added to the investment outlay? Furthermore, how the group prices capital can affect the cost of projects implemented by subsidiary companies. Similarly with human resources, machines, and materials used in the project but owned by the company. In reviewing projects, one must ask oneself what is the correct price to put on in-house resources used, as one not uncommon way of managing the budget is to manipulate the cost of in-house resources.

Finance is usually not handled by project management. In private companies, it is centralized to the finance function, and in public companies sometimes to the owner as the owner can borrow at a lower rate. Therefore, cost estimates often do not include interest costs during the period of construction. One might therefore suspect that cost growth in some cases reported in the media can be partly explained by the inclusion of interest costs in the stated final cost of the project but not in earlier reported cost estimates.

Sometimes, it can be informative to take yet another step and view cost and outcome from the perspective of the stakeholders that are involved, such as employees, suppliers, investors in supporting infrastructure, and taxpayers. To what extent has the project achieved the stakeholder's expectations?[27] There are winners and there are losers – sometimes mainly losers, as in the Northland Resources example in Chapter 1, where public and private investors found it difficult to recover investments made based on the assumption that the mining venture would succeed.

Furthermore, in measuring cost overruns we also have to decide whether we should compare approved budget with reported cost, or with the review made six months to two years after the new plant or machine has reached full production. One should observe here that full production capacity in some types of technology may exceed what was specified in the original request for investment. A building will not have more square metres than what was approved, but it is not uncommon in the process industry for the production capacity after a few years of operation to surpass that specified without, or with only small, additional investments. One might then argue that a possible cost overrun should be related to the outcome in production capacity at normal production. The Frövifors plant was designed to produce 160,000 tonnes per year, but was prepared to be tuned up to 200,000 tonnes with only minor investments if there was market demand. The Scanraff refinery built on the Swedish west coast in the 1970s was designed to produce 7.3 million tonnes per year, but produced 10 tonnes only four years later. Similarly, a new bridge, road, or railway can have fewer or more travellers than anticipated. The list of investments in which output can differ from what was stated in the decision can be made long.

Fourthly, as the Frövifors case illustrated, it is often possible to meet the budget by making savings in the project. One can postpone part of the project, let some other actor implement parts of the investment and lease these back, and choose parts of lower quality. These are all measures that will typically increase the future costs of operation and investments. Choosing a simpler design does not necessarily increase future cost, but choosing lower quality often means shorter lifespan and higher costs of operation, and sale-leaseback will reduce investment but increase operating costs. If such savings are made, the project implemented will not be exactly the same as the one approved.

Changes in a project can lead to cost increases both directly, due to the price of inputs increasing, and indirectly through an increase in the scope of the project. We can also separate *anticipated* and *unanticipated price increases*. Project cost estimates usually contain a reserve for anticipated increases in price. In Tables 2.1, 2.2, and 2.3, there were buffers intended to cover anticipated price increases. When this buffer is insufficient, we have an unanticipated increase in price. Thus, it is only unanticipated increases in price that can cause cost overruns. Therefore, let us, as in Figure 2.2, distinguish between *an increase in price* and *an increase in scope*. The price of goods and man hours used in the project can increase between approved estimate and post-completion review. If the increase was foreseen in the estimate, we talk about anticipated price increase, otherwise it is unanticipated price increase. Similarly, if we use up more goods and man hours than anticipated in our budget, we have *an unanticipated increase in scope*.

Furthermore, we distinguish between price changes, i.e. changes in the price of different types of input, and inflation measured as a consumer price index based on the value of a basket of different goods. It is important to distinguish between changes in the price of individual inputs and the general price level, and there is a covariance between these two variables in that prices tend to become more volatile with higher inflation. Thus, high inflation does not only mean that the value of money decreases faster, but also that it becomes more difficult to forecast the future prices of goods and man hours.

This leads us to our fifth and final point: price changes and inflation. Estimates and appraisals can be made in both constant and current money value. An appraisal in constant money value can, in times of high inflation, make it easier to visualize the effects of the proposed investment, and in certain situations it can also be easier to make such an appraisal without having to estimate an uncertain level of inflation. However, payments are always in current money value, which is why an appraisal using current money values always has to be made to evaluate

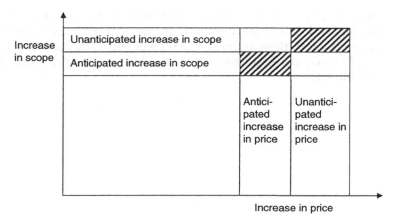

Figure 2.2 The relation between anticipated and unanticipated increase in prices and scope

the effects of taxes and different financial alternatives. A cost increase can be due to inflation, but to know that, we need to know price clauses and terms of payment, as well as what has been budgeted for in anticipated inflation – data which only the firm making the investment can give us access to.

Comparing projects becomes still more difficult if costs are in different currencies. According to the so-called purchasing parity theorem, or the international Fisher theorem, there is a perfect correlation between inflation and the value of a currency, between exchange rates and inflation rates. If the inflation of one currency is higher than another, this will lead to the value of the same currency decreasing. Tests of the international Fisher theorem show a fairly good correlation between exchange rates and inflation for connected economies. However, for less well-integrated economies, the connection is weaker. To see this, we can observe how the value of the US $ relative to the Euro, British £, and Japanese Yen has gone up and down without this being fully reflected in the inflation rates of these countries. Other factors such as productivity growth, the state's budget deficit, and the economy's place in the business cycle also affect the adjustment of the exchange rate to the level of inflation. Even the Big Mac Index (i.e. comparing the price of a Big Mac in different currencies) might sometimes give more reliable figures.

From this we learn that it is not simple to calculate a cost deviation correctly. We should be aware of this when we read about cost overruns and cost growth in the press, and in studies based on data collected through various official sources. If one compares a large enough number of projects, these sources of error will hopefully cancel each other out, but one can never be certain. Establishing the true figure is not elementary.

What Do Organizations Do When Budget Overrun Threatens?

The first thing project managers do when a project threatens to exceed its budget is look at what savings can be made to avoid having to request additional funds. Savings can be made by various means, including lowering goals or specifications, postponing certain parts of the project, and letting somebody else finance the parts of the project which can be leased back. What can be done depends on the technology and whether or not the goals and specifications can be re-negotiated. However, large savings often turn up as future investments.

The project budget usually contains a reserve for anticipated additional costs. This buffer may be found in a budget item termed contingencies, or distributed and hidden in other budget items, or both. Some managers do not approve unspecified budget items, but there is always some buffer for activities not yet specified. It is not unusual to have an official buffer of 10 per cent of total investment, although it can differ substantially from case to case. A mail questionnaire[1] gave an average of 9 per cent under contingencies for 57 major private sector construction projects, and 6.3 per cent for 74 major municipal construction projects. However, the contingencies budget item varied from 2–15 per cent for private, and 0–20 per cent for public projects, so one must assume that some of these projects had buffers built into budget items other than contingencies.

Project management is usually required to request additional funding if project costs increase by more than 5 or 10 per cent. However, project managers can do a lot to avoid having to do this. If the buffer is insufficient, additional savings can usually be made by choosing cheaper solutions and lowering ambitions. Savings can also be achieved by delaying parts of the investment that can be postponed to a later date, and by outsourcing. This explains why reported cost overruns of 0–5 per cent are rare, because outside this range there is a tendency to either meet the budget or request additional funding.

The ability to make savings to meet the budget was illustrated by the Frövifors case. The Frövifors machine was estimated to cost SEK 811 million and ended up at SEK 867 million, a cost overrun of 6.9 per cent, or, in real monetary value, −0.5 per cent. An exceptionally good result – or was it? The budget was met by using up the SEK 55 million allocated for contingencies, postponing investments and leasing buildings worth SEK 45 million, and a harsh business climate allowing Frövifors to purchase the paper machine for SEK 20 million less than anticipated. However, many of those parts of the investments that were postponed or leased would later reappear as future investments and leasing fees.

On the other hand, if project costs decrease, it is as Parkinson's Second Law states, '[e]xpenditure rises to meet income',[2] it is always easy to find uses for spare funds. Funds approved for projects are seldom repaid. At the same time, it is difficult for those approving a budget to know exactly how large the buffer is, and experienced project managers argue for a high budget threshold to make it easier to meet the budget. To counteract this, senior managers might consider it better to approve a tight budget and be prepared to have to approve additional funds if needed, to ensure that funds are put to efficient use.[3]

The ability to absorb cost increases in order to meet a tight budget can be illustrated by the construction of Karlshamn Power Station's three oil-fired power plants, a major project built on time and on budget. It consisted of three units of 340 MW each, taken into service between 1969 and 1973. Detailed planning started in 1964, and construction began in 1966. The plant was to be jointly own by several power companies. The South Swedish Power Company was to build it and applied network planning and systematic cost controls for the first time. The first block was estimated at SEK 170 million, excluding interest during construction. Ninety percent of total work was procured and performed by subcontractors governed by contracts with price clauses, and anticipated price increases were considered in the budget.

When reviewing the project, the project manager[4] spoke with pride about staying on budget and how hard it had been to do so. Savings were made on mechanical equipment and buildings. Numerous changes had been required along the way as costs increased, forcing project managers to choose not necessarily less good but simpler technical solutions.

The plant was built at a time when inflation was low and stable, around 3–4 per cent per year, before the oil shock of 1973–74 gave us double digit inflation and taught us the necessity of considering the difference between nominal and real monetary value in project reviews. On behalf of the South Swedish Power Company, the author used the consumer price index to express payments made in real monetary value. It turned out that the project manager had not only been able to keep within budget, but had also made savings roughly equivalent to the actual rate of inflation, i.e. 3–4 per cent savings per year, which came as a big surprise to him, and probably also to many others before the double digit inflation of the 1970s. It seems like the economist Erik Lundberg[5] was right when he proposed that a low level of inflation is beneficial in that it can create a pressure to make savings and economize on investments.

The opportunity for savings can further be illustrated by the differences between high and low estimates during a budget period. Project management for the nuclear power plants at Barsebäck presented the budget for the next year in October or November, a first forecast in March or April, an updated forecast in October–November in connection with the budget for the coming year, and finally the outcome for the previous year in February. Comparing these estimates shows that the estimated cost increased in the range of 7–17 per cent in real terms from October to April during the years in which the two Barsebäck nuclear reactors were constructed. The project managers explained that this pattern was due to the budget being lowered following careful scrutiny. The first quarter forecast was higher as it was not subjected to the same scrutiny as later budgets, and it might have included ambitions that were not approved in the budget, along with a buffer for unforeseen events. The third quarter forecast was lower than the first partly because most work planned to take place over the year is already done by then, and partly because the moment of truth when the budget must be met is approaching.

The same cyclical type of inverted U-shaped curve has been observed in several Swedish municipalities. After the first quarter, budget estimates often exceed the approved budget. This tends to create concerns and initiate pressure to cut costs, which in the end leads to a situation where the budget is met, more or less. The explanation for this is essentially the same as for the Barsebäck example.

To what extent additional funding is appropriated or savings have to be made in a project also depends on the availability of capital, the expected profitability, and the perceived importance of the project. An extreme example of the latter is the construction of the Trans-Alaska Pipeline System, which joins the oilfield at Prudhoe Bay off the northern Alaska coast with an oil terminal at Valdez in southern Alaska. The pipeline was constructed in 1974–77 after the first oil crisis in 1973. It opened up a major new oil field for exploration in a time of record high oil prices, when the US had become increasingly dependent on oil from the Middle East, and OPEC had issued an embargo on exports to the United States.

The estimated cost of this project rose from US $863 million in 1968 to US $9,300 million including interest payments[6] – i.e. the project became 12 times more expensive than originally estimated. However, the cost of the pipeline, US $9,300 million, should be compared to an estimated profit of US $44 to US $100 billion during its lifespan.[7] Thus, the important thing for the company was to get the pipeline into operation as fast as possible to pump oil from the new oilfield at Prudhoe Bay. It was economically feasible to push the project forward, partly because the state allowed the company to deduct most of the cost increase, and it was politically motivated because of the urge to reduce US dependence on OPEC oil. The economic return for an early start was so high that there was no need to spend more on planning ex ante to avoid cost overruns.

Whether a firm will abandon or put more money into a project is affected by how vital the project is considered to be to the future of the company. Organizations are usually much more willing to save projects that are within their core area of business. When the auto-maker Volvo encountered problems with its new Dutch 343 model, no one, it has been claimed, called for the car model to be withdrawn. Instead, the company invested very large amounts to solve the pro-blems, and succeeded.

Ventures in new areas, be it through acquisition or internal develop-ment, are much more at risk when they turn out to suffer from cost overruns and announced plans do not materialize, as they have yet to prove that they are a future core business.[8] Unfortunately, ventures in new areas are also more likely to encounter cost overruns simply because organizations have less experience and competence in managing projects in the new area than in their core business.

To sum up, when costs increase, project managers use up the buffers that exist in the budget, try to make savings by choosing cheaper solutions, and refrain from implementing some of their plans. They may also postpone parts of the investment or let some-body else finance parts of the overall project and lease these back. Not all elements that are postponed will be implemented in the future, but postponement and outsourcing mostly mean that the investment out-lay is reduced by increasing future investments and leasing fees, and this is why leasing should be regarded as an investment. Choosing cheaper technical solutions can also mean higher future maintenance and operating costs, but not necessarily, as the trade-offs between investment and operating costs made when choosing technical solu-tions is mostly driven by technical standards, norms, and practice. Next we will see that the budget can be met more easily if the project is divisible, i.e. it can be implemented in stages, assets are tradable, and goals and ambitions can be re-negotiated.

Divisibility, Timing and Cost Overrun

Industry has long been able to increase profitability by exploiting economies of scale and scope in various parts of the value chains.[9] Economies of scale exist when the cost per unit of output decreases as the scale of a production plant or machine increases; economies of scope appear when a firm's total cost of production decreases due to, for example, a machine having alternative uses or increasing productivity in other parts of the firm. Economies of scope offer an explanation as to why flexible manufacturing methods, mergers, and acquisitions can decrease a firm's total costs.

Cost increases prior to the decision to invest may have been partly caused by a decision to increase the size of an investment in order to achieve better economies of scale or scope, and thus make it more profitable in the long run. A good example of the former is the Frövifors paperboard machine. The first estimate was SEK 300 million for a machine that could produce 70,000 tonnes per year. This specification was subsequently increased to 100,000, 150,000, and finally 160,000 tonnes per year, at an estimated cost of SEK 881 million, as the board became convinced they needed to aim for economies of scale and build the largest paperboard machine in the world.

Building larger plants to reduce the cost per unit output is also a common practice in the public sector. Smaller utilities and municipalities cooperate both with each other and with private interests to build larger, more cost-efficient facilities for, e.g. energy production and district heating, water purification, waste treatment, and transportation.[10]

Economies of scope refer to situations where the average unit cost can be lowered by co-producing different products or services. Such co-production of services is common in the public sector, where projects are often designed to meet the needs of several interest groups. Examples are abundant, especially in smaller municipalities that have to offer a wide selection of social services on a limited budget. A new school can be built with an auditorium that can be used as a civic theatre and a meeting space for organizations in the evenings; a new rest-home for the elderly can be co-located with other services offered to the elderly, such as health care; a stadium or cultural centre can be constructed for multiple uses. This use of economies of scope often also offers an increase in economies of scale.

A third strategy is to reduce the financial burden by implementing investments in stages, in what is referred to as 'stepwise construction'.[11] It can be easier to finance such an investment, and it may also be more profitable if it can be expanded when market demand increases. This is another common strategy in both the public and private sectors. The

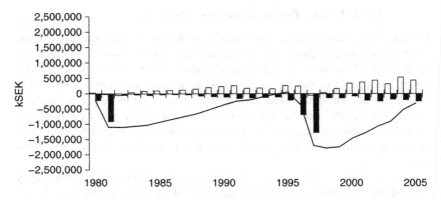

Figure 3.1 Cash flow for the Frövifors case 1980–2005
Note: The figure is based on Frövifors Bruk ABs annual reports and shows Frövifors Bruk's operating income before depreciation (white bars) minus investments (black bars).

Frövifors machine had a capacity of 160,000 tonnes per year but was prepared for an increase to 200,000 tonnes when the market for an additional 40,000 existed. New commercial and residential areas are often developed or renewed in stages, and schools, sport facilities, energy, water, and sewage facilities designed in a way that enables them to be enlarged if demand should increase. If an investment is divisible in this way, i.e. it can be implemented stepwise, then project management can control cost increases during implementation by, for instance, building a smaller plant. This inbuilt flexibility can help project management to meet their budget.

The use and effects of economies of scale and scope and stepwise construction can be illustrated by comparing the cash flows from the Frövifors carton paper machine plant and the introduction of natural gas in the south of Sweden by Sydgas. The cash flow from these two cases can be reasonably well calculated as they were implemented by separate companies and, as has been claimed, transfer prices between these and other companies in the groups were fair. Frövifors Bruk AB was owned by ASSI AB and Sydgas AB by Sydkraft AB.

In the Frövifors case, the owner ASSI built the largest paperboard machine in the world to maximize economies of scale, and co-located a pulp plant to increase economies of scope. Figure 3.1 shows the cash flow and investments of Frövifors Bruk AB in current monetary value. The currency losses made by the owner ASSI AB are not considered in this cash flow.

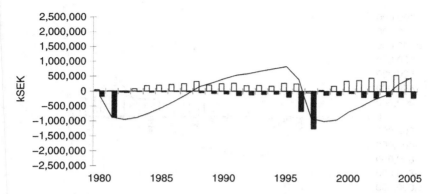

Figure 3.2 Adjusted cash flow for the Frövifors case 1980–2005
Note: The figure is based on Frövifors Bruk ABs annual reports and shows Frövifors Bruk's operating income before depreciation (white bars) minus investments (black bars). Figures have been corrected for lower than expected price level.

The Frövifors machine was calculated to have a payback period of 7 years, but project management estimated 9–10 years to be more realistic. Figure 3.1 indicates that payback actually took 12 years. The main reason was that the new machine represented such a huge increase in supply that it, together with ASSI's aggressive pricing policy, halved the profit level on paperboard products. This is a problem associated with economies of scale and the introduction of major new machines in low-growth markets. Prices would have stayed higher if the machine had been postponed for a few years. Adjusting for this in Figure 3.2 by increasing the operating income by 100 per cent during the first 7 years gives the new plant a payback period of approximately the 7 years stated in the request for investment.

New plants in the process industry often have considerable development potential and paperboard machines are no exception. The Frövifors machine was designed to produce 160,000 tonnes per year, but could be upscaled to 200,000 by small additional investments, making it possible to increase the speed of the paper line. The technical limit of the machine was anticipated to be 275,000 tonnes per year in 1979, but new technology became available and in 1995 the company decided on an investment programme to increase yearly production to 375,000 tonnes. However, the higher production levels could not be achieved without first solving some very costly unanticipated teething problems. This caused a deep fall in revenues in the late 1990s, not because of the investment, but because production was down; it is far from common, but it has happened before in the process industry when scaling up production.

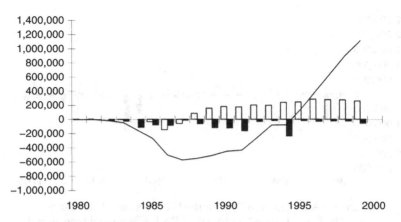

Figure 3.3 Cash flow for the Sydgas case 1980–99
Note: The figure is based on Sydgas ABs annual reports and shows
Sydgas' operating income before depreciation (white bars) minus
investments (black bars).

In 2005–6, Korsnäs bought Frövifors Bruk AB for SEK 3,650 million.
By that time the machine was producing 400,000 tonnes per year and
plans had been made to increase production to 450,000 tonnes. In 2012,
Korsnäs merged with Billerud to form BillerudKorsnäs, and in 2014 the
board decided to invest SEK 900 million to increase capacity to 550,000
tonnes per year,[12] an increase in capacity of 244 per cent above the
original investment, and one that will make the Frövifors machine once
again the largest cartonboard and liquid packaging board machine in the
world. The cash flow for the machine might indicate a failure, but one
must remember that a paperboard machine can function for 100 years if it
is maintained and updated with new technology, and if no revolutionary
new method of paper production or alternative material is invented.
Thus, there is plenty of time to re-coup the initial investment.

In 1978, Sydkraft proposed constructing a Swedish natural gas pipeline
network that could handle the import of 1,200 million cubic metres of gas
per year from Germany. The proposal was rejected by the government
then in power. Shortly afterwards, the same government advanced a
smaller project of 400 million cubic metres of gas to be delivered from
Denmark, starting in 1985. This proposal was adopted in 1980 and
became an integral part of Swedish energy policy, and in the same year
Sydkraft decided to implement this smaller project. It was calculated to
have a payback period of little more than 10 years and, as can be seen in
Figure 3.3, Sydkraft managed to achieve the target; however, as we will

also see, this was only possible after adjusting the size of the project and re-negotiating purchase prices.

The fall in oil prices at the beginning of the 1980s led to a deterioration in the financial prospects of the project, and this was before work on the plant had even started. The primary reason was that the margin between the oil price in Sweden that determined Sydgas's revenues and the purchase price for gas had declined. The state-dominated Swedegas, which purchased the gas from Denmark, had signed an agreement in a situation when gas prices were high and were expected to increase, and had neglected to make sure that there was a re-negotiation clause in the agreement. At the same time, the previously high oil price had led to energy-saving measures that were beginning to take effect, leading to a decrease in demand.

These changed conditions meant that Sydgas had to pay greater attention to the heating sector and to smaller consumers of gas, which increased the cost of constructing the gas network. An agreement in 1983 for the state to become a 50 per cent joint owner of Sydgas, to provide guarantees for the company's loans, and to introduce tax concessions for gas as an energy form offered some relief. In 1987, Sydgas demanded re-negotiations with Swedegas, and succeeded in achieving a reduction in purchase prices. A year later, an agreement was made for the state to pay its share of accumulated losses in the form of a new injection of capital amounting to SEK 202.5 million, and that it would transfer its shares in Sydgas to Sydkraft AB.

The project approved in 1980 can be seen as the first part of the earlier project proposal of 1978. The approved budget was exceeded, but it is uncertain by how much, and the project grew in size. According to the original plan, the company should have reached 400 million cubic metres by 1991; in reality, they were to deliver 500 million cubic metres that year. Thus, the project was successful, but the risk of not being able to meet the target was much smaller compared to the Frövifors case, as a gas network is scalable. There are large buyers and smaller ones. If costs rose, Sydgas could balance this by building only those parts of the network that were the most profitable, with the possibility of extending the network at a later date. The project could be divided and the decisions to construct extensions could be made when the market exists. A gas network is divisible, a paperboard machine is not.

A further example of the flexibility offered by projects that can be implemented in stages can be seen in the renovation and redesign programme of Kvarnsveden paper mill. The Kvarnsveden paper mill was established in 1898–1900. Eighty years later, the plant was planning for its 11th paper machine, having become, after 80 years of investments, a mixture of old and new systems with a not very rational layout. A major renovation and renewal programme was therefore approved to make the plant more efficient and economical to run, and to provide a basis for future expansion. The first stage was investing in a new paper machine, estimated to cost SEK 800 million. Some of the new investments were necessary to meet increased environmental requirements and the product quality required by customers. The investment programme was successful, although it was a very complicated project and stretched over several years in order to minimize disturbances to production. However, project planners had taken plenty of time to go into the details, as the first proposal was presented 10 years before the programme was approved.

The investment was originally estimated at SEK 900 million. The project consisted of several sub-projects which the proposal to the board estimated at SEK 1,089 million over a 5- or 10-year period. In addition, a baseline of the minimum necessary investment was estimated at SEK 306 million over a 5-year period. Thus, if SEK 1,089 million was approved, it should be possible to meet this budget by minimizing unnecessary sub-projects up to a cost overrun of 256 per cent.

The board decided to postpone a new office building and warehouse, whereby the approved budget became SEK 806,965 million. This estimate did not include interest expenses or cost of production disturbances. An offer for a boiler already existed when the decision was made, but the rest of the project was procured after the decision to invest and at fixed prices.

Three years later, when most of the work was done, its total cost was estimated at SEK 771,994 million, i.e. a cost underrun of −4.3 per cent. Despite this overall figure, there were cost overruns on individual budget items. Machinery, which accounted for a third of the budget, increased by 6.4 per cent, and painting and insulation of pipes by 22.4 per cent, all covered by a reservation for contingencies of 7.7 per cent, and smaller savings on items such as electrical installations and equipment, and consultants.

Renovation projects are prone to grow as it is difficult to know exactly what has to be replaced and renovated before the object or structure to be renovated has been dismantled. However, in this case several factors made cost increases less probable. Firstly, meticulous planning was vital to minimize production disturbances due to the renovation programme. Secondly, the approved budget was possibly generous as the owner, the Stora group, wanted to avoid the severe cost overrun experienced in their last major investment, a new pulp mill at Skutskär. (The extent of the overrun is unknown, as the pulp mill was constructed during a time of high inflation, but in nominal terms cost estimates increased from 250 million to 400 million at approval, and then 800 million when finished). A third and important reason, which must have provided a safety net, is that the programme consisted of many different sub-projects which could be postponed. Projects such as the Kvarnsveden and Sydgas cases are divisible. They can be implemented in stages and the amount of work performed can therefore be adjusted to some extent according to what the budget allows.

The savings made are of course dependent on the importance project management and the firm attach to meeting the budget. If the company financial situation is strained, it becomes more necessary to balance cost growth with savings than if the opposite applies. This becomes more important in larger projects as these impose a larger financial burden and risk until revenues start to flow as planned, and the pressure for savings might be less strong for projects that are considered to be of strategic importance to the future of the firm than for peripheral projects. On the one hand, we have the liquidity and willingness to supply additional capital. On the other hand, we have project-specific factors which make it more or less possible to balance cost increases with cuts and postponements. This allows us to identify the following three factors in adjusting costs to meet budget:

- project divisibility;
- asset tradability;
- goal re-negotiability.

Project divisibility. has to do with whether a project can be implemented in stages – so-called stepwise construction. If that is the case, the budget can be met by postponing elements of the project to later dates. The Frövifors, Sydgas, and Kvarnsveden cases all exemplified the importance of divisibility to the ability to make savings to avoid cost overruns. Cost overrun is easier to avoid if parts of the project can be postponed. If divisible, project managers can even plan in advance which parts of the project should be postponed if costs increase, and which parts should be implemented first when new finance exists.

Asset tradability. In several of our examples, project management was able to meet the budget by allowing somebody else to construct buildings that were then leased back. A precondition for this is that the part of the project that is leased can be separated from other parts of the investment and 'sold' to another actor, thus it has to be a tradable asset. However, more and more goods and services have become tradable, so many parts of a project can now be outsourced and leased back.

Goal re-negotiability. It becomes much easier to meet the budget if it is possible to renegotiate goals and requirements. Strict requirements have contributed to cost overruns in, e.g. nuclear power plants, where the smallest change in the design has to be approved by the supervising authority before it can be made, and new weapon systems, since the next generation of weapon system has to outperform the previous one. This also means that an important trade-off in project planning is between what to specify ex ante and what not to specify in order to allow the flexibility to act on new information when it appears.

Consequences of Cost Overruns for Organizations, Individuals, and Society

The ultimate consequence of a severe cost overrun is, of course, bankruptcy. Many new ventures fail because the predictions of their success are far too optimistic, and there is no shortage of established firms that have, for instance, paid far too much when acquiring firms they did not know much about. Cost overrun can bring down the most highly reputed company. A well-known Swedish example is Uddeholm and their investment in the KM7 paper machine.

Uddeholm was founded as an iron works in 1668.[13] Iron production used up enormous amounts of charcoal, and over time Uddeholm became a substantial owner of forest and later a producer of pulp and paper. Uddeholm as a group eventually consisted of several forestry and steel companies. In 1974, the group recorded sales of SEK 2,267 million and decided on an ambitious SEK 1,300 million investment programme for 1975–77. A major part of this investment was a board mill, including a new paperboard machine, KM7, at Skoghall with a production capacity of 110,000 tonnes per year; a thermomechanical pulp plant, estimated at SEK 247 million by the consultant company Jaakko Pöyry; and a back-pressure turbine. Uddeholm made their calculations based on 7 per cent inflation and the group board approved a generous budget of SEK 325 million for the pulp and paper project and SEK 109 million for the turbine.

In 1977, the follow-up report to the board showed that the total cost of the paper machine was SEK 470 million and the turbine SEK 155 million. The board authorized a consultant to find out the causes, and the consultant reported:

To sum up, and with certain simplifications, the main difference between appropriation and outcome can – apart from the cost of interruptions and 'other items' – be attributed to the following three reasons, which unfortunately are so common that they can be termed classics:

1. Insufficient time and limited resources for pre-planning, resulting in an incomplete and partially inadequate basis for the allocation decision.
2. Decisions during construction to make self-motivated changes and additions, which resulted in cost increases without a corresponding increase in appropriation.
3. Higher price increases than anticipated.[14] [Author's translation.]

However, this was not all, or even the worst. The paperboard machine had serious teething problems and had to be rebuilt. This increased costs even further and caused a liquidity crisis. The Uddeholm group had to strengthen its liquidity and was saved by a conditional government loan of SEK 600 million. Later, in 1978, it had to merge its forestry divisions with Billerud, retaining only a 30 per cent share in the new, jointly owned company. The total cost of KM7 after repairs and reconstruction has been estimated at SEK 612 million in 1977 monetary value[15]. Adding the unanticipated costs of low production, poor quality, and rejects during start-up brings the total estimated cost to SEK 1,138 million – a cost overrun of more than 200 per cent.

Eventually KM7's teething problems were resolved, and Skoghall is today a part of the Stora-Enso group, producing close to 300,000 tonnes a year, almost three times as much as planned in the original investment appraisal. Uddeholm's steel division was restructured, the last mine wound up, and Uddeholm delisted from the Stockholm Stock Exchange. The remains of the steel division are today found in the Austrian steel group Voestalpine AG. Cost overruns brought down a 300-year-old company that was previously recognized for its technical competence.

A well-known international example is the Rolls-Royce RB211 engine, which in 1971 brought down both Rolls-Royce and the Lockheed Corporation commercial airline business. Cost overruns on the engine project forced the Conservative government to nationalize Rolls-Royce to avoid bankruptcy. It allowed the completion of the RB211 project, a new generation of turbofan engines that transformed Rolls-Royce into a major supplier of commercial jet engines. The RB211 jet engine was delayed for two years, which seriously hurt Lockheed's new commercial airliner, TriStar, as the RB211 was the only engine suitable for this new aircraft, and contributed to the fact that Lockheed later withdrew from the commercial airline business.[16]

Another, more recent, example is the Swiss company ABB's acquisition of the American company Combustion Engineering in 1990. The latter had more than 100 orders for a new generation of commercial turbines that were expected to deliver 58 per cent electric power efficiency. But this improvement in turbine engineering was never achieved, causing ABB to incur huge indemnity payments to those who had ordered the turbine. This, along with very large asbestos claims filed against Combustion Engineering, contributed to bringing ABB close to insolvency.[17] The turbine business, and its problems, was sold to French company Alstom in 2000, which in turn contributed to the French state having to step in and save Alstom in 2004.

The ABB, Rolls-Royce, and Uddeholm cases are all examples of how unanticipated technical problems can cause such significant cost overruns that they force major companies into bankruptcy, or, as in the ABB case, force them to sell off substantial parts of the group. It has sometimes been claimed that cost overruns have made projects like these unprofitable, but that can be difficult to prove. Rolls-Royce needed state funding to complete the revolutionary RB211 jet engine, but the engine and the technology behind it came to form the basis for engines still produced today and made Rolls-Royce a major player in the jet turbine industry. Combustion Engineering's turbine problems were not solved, at least not in time, but the paper machine Uddeholm constructed is today a profit generator for its current owners.

Bankruptcy is the ultimate consequence of cost overruns. Two less final but potentially negative consequences of cost overruns are that they impair the investor's future financial capacity and can have social implications for those involved. The three consequences of cost overruns are summarized in Table 3.1.

Bankruptcy. The Uddeholm machine might have brought a company to bankruptcy, but one does not disassemble and move a large paper machine once it is built. That is too expensive. Nor do you close down a new machine with teething problems. There will always be another company willing to take over and finish the project, so the machine can become a good deal for a later owner. Also, the decision to build it was a good deal for those working at the plant and for economic activity in the region. The community gets its new plant and employment, even if the owner changes. Similarly, the RB211 project became a good deal for Rolls-Royce, British industry, and society once it had been completed.

It is very different when an easily moveable investment, such as a new computer software program, a web-based business, or a new technology project, is hit by major cost overrun. The juridical location of such

Table 3.1 *Possible consequences of cost overrun, part I*

	Investing firm	Society
Mainly negative consequences		
Bankruptcy	Examples: Uddeholm; Northland Resources	Society had to financially support Uddeholm, and clean up after Northland Resources.
Impaired financial capacity	Examples: ABB; Alstom; ASSI; Lockheed; Rolls-Royce	Society had to financially support Alstom, ASSI, Lockheed, and Rolls-Royce.
Social consequences	Can affect a firm's organizational memory and the future of employees associated with the project.	

intangible assets can easily be moved to another geographical location. When it comes to structures that are costly or impossible to disassemble and move, such as major plant, or constructions such as mines, bridges, and buildings, there will almost always be some new investor who, by regarding spent investment as sunk cost, will be willing to complete the project. Hence, cost overrun is a loss for the initial investors in the project, but not necessarily for the next investor, the employees, or the local economy.

Losses can sometimes be transferred to the public sector and taxpayers. That happened in the Trans-Alaskan pipeline case, as the company was allowed to offset losses by carrying them forward against future profits. The risk for taxpayers is evident in projects with large negative salvage value such as mining, oil, and nuclear energy plants. Taxpayers may have to pay for cleaning up after mining projects if the company cannot cover the cost of restoring the area, as will probably be the case with the Northland Resources iron ore mine mentioned in Chapter 1. For nuclear power, fees are set aside to cover decommissioning and the management of nuclear waste. There is also insurance to cover accidents, but this can prove too small should a meltdown occur. Thus, when companies cannot manage the risks, society and the taxpayers are sometimes forced to step in.

Bankruptcy can have consequences not only for the firm that closes but also for other firms and local society. Investors, creditors, suppliers, customers, and taxpayers can all risk losing money, but Billerud, which took over Uddeholm's ailing machine, was a winner. The company got a new paper machine at a discounted price.

Impaired financial capacity. Only a few projects are so large relative to their investor that they can induce bankruptcy, but many projects can force firms to borrow more money and possibly have to ask their owners or government for a capital injection, as Frövifors' owner ASSI and Rolls-Royce had to do. Cost overruns also contributed to the fact that Lockheed had to ask for a loan guarantee from the US government to avoid bankruptcy in 1971, and ABB had to ask its shareholders for SEK 19 billion or 40 per cent of the value of its stocks in 2003. These events strongly affected the future growth and profitability of these firms. They almost certainly displaced other profitable investments and impaired both firms' financial capacity, reducing their financial flexibility and ability to take advantage of profitable investment opportunities, acquisitions, and business deals when these appeared. Such constraints hamper future growth and profitability and may very well be the most important consequence of large cost overruns in major investments and projects.

Social implications. Cost overruns can also have social implications for both firms and individuals. The cost overrun on Stora's paper mill at Skutskär, and the turbulence and doubt over the company's ability to handle major projects that resulted, meant that the board asked project management to supply their most pessimistic estimates for the Kvarnsveden investment. Memories of cost overruns can be long-lived, and affect the business confidence of those involved.

Consequences for the individual vary by organization and by type of investment. A cost overrun of 20 per cent on an investment in machinery can lead to inquisitions and sermons, while a similar cost overrun on a marketing campaign can pass unnoticed. Many firms invest much more in markets and marketing campaigns than in production equipment. Funds for marketing campaigns are allocated on rules of thumb of uncertain validity, and deviations become more acceptable when it is difficult to measure the result. Accountability tends to be focused on that which can be measured.

A new strategy is usually associated with a shift in power. If the cost of a venture in a new area grows, it is usually the manager most closely associated with the project, or the entrepreneur, that has to take the blame. Opponents can use unfulfilled promises to gain influence and change the strategy. When major projects within existing business areas grow, the consequences may be minor. If the manager responsible is important to the organization, a way to maintain working relations must be found, along with the acceptance that failures do happen. Thus, ventures in new areas are not only more prone to cost overruns, they also stand a greater risk of losing support if their costs increase.

On the other hand, the political cost of overruns need not be too high. Many record-breaking and iconic buildings, Olympic Games, and other major events have never been unpopular, despite being partly financed by taxpayers' money. In some cases, such glamorous – but expensive – projects have in fact boosted the careers of those associated with them.

Positive Effects of Cost Overrun

In an article with the provocative title 'Entrepreneurial error and economic growth' published in 1952, John E. Sawyer[18] drew our attention to the fact that underestimation of the actual need for capital and the real problems in some larger infrastructural projects may have contributed to economic growth.

Sawyer gives examples of a number of ex post profitable projects for which an underestimation of total investment is balanced by a corresponding underestimation of demand. Large investments opening up new resources for exploitation are an example, such as the railways in the USA, which made expansion into the West possible during the pioneering years, and a number of canal and other railway projects in the USA and Europe. The effect is more evident for the American railways, as they were built to open up new regions for exploitation, while European railways were often built to accommodate existing traffic. These were projects where very large-scale and indivisible investment had to be made before any return could be expected.

He describes a typical case in which the entrepreneur had heroically struggled to assemble sufficient capital to begin the project. This was in itself sufficiently difficult to lead Sawyer to assume that the project would never have got off the ground, or would have been started at a later date, had the real costs been known. Once the project had got started and exceeded all limits in terms of time and money, the original investors felt obliged to provide far larger funds than they had originally intended, either because they believed in the project or because they felt under pressure to recoup some of their initial investment. Had they not been willing or able to do this, there were fresh investors who could be attracted by the low residual costs, and by the hope that the project could be swiftly completed and the cycle could start all over again.

Sawyer's ideas have been developed further by Albert O. Hirschman[19] in a study of development projects supported by the World Bank, a study in which he concludes that project planners and probably the World Bank as well would never have got involved in these projects if they had known in advance all the difficulties that had to be overcome if the projects were to be successful. But they also had an overly pessimistic view of the investee countries' abilities to deal with problems when they appeared. Hirschman concludes that complete knowledge of the problems ahead would have had a negative effect in many cases and hampered the search for solutions, which not only saved the project, but also enhanced the overall value.

Since we seem to underestimate our creative abilities, it is obviously also desirable that we underestimate future problems, so that the effect of these tendencies is balanced out. Underestimation compels us to resort to our creative ability, and Hirschman terms this the principle of The Hiding Hand.[20]

Another and more well-known group of projects for which underestimation of the costs and the market potential seems to occur regularly are long-term R&D projects with a significant component of basic research and radical innovation. Sawyer exemplifies with the development of nylon, and Christopher Freeman[21] with synthetic rubber, PVC, the transistor, the computer, and the use of computer software to control industrial production. Early market estimates and the full potential of almost every major innovation in synthetic materials and the electronics industry have been underestimated. Due to the uncertainty related to the long-term consequences of such radical innovations, argues Freeman, there is a tendency to underinvest in such projects, and a corresponding over-investment may very well exist for short-term R&D related to product and brand differentiation.[22] This is a major argument for government support for basic research and radically new innovations.

These, and other studies by the author,[23] allow us to draw the conclusion that there are at least four types of project in which there is a tendency to underinvest if the real cost of implementation is known too early in the process, namely:

- infrastructure projects opening up new markets for exploitation,
- radical innovations creating business opportunities for exploitation,
- new ventures opening up new product markets for exploitation, and
- projects benefiting from changes in the value system.

For these types of projects, underestimation of the real investment outlay needed may sometimes be balanced by a similar underestimation of their true long-term benefits, and we will discuss them in due order. Observe that although the examples are fixed indivisible investments, the principles illustrated apply also to intangible investments and investment programmes.

Infrastructure projects opening up new markets for exploitation. This group includes projects that open up new markets by drastically reducing the cost of transportation, such as the investments in canals and railways that aroused Sawyer's interest. In these cases, the owner's optimistic forecast of the investment outlay was balanced by an equally unforeseen income created by the economic growth following the opening up of new geographical regions for trade and exploitation. The real cost could have been forecast more accurately in many of these cases had project planners spent more resources on planning prior to the decision to invest. However, that might also have postponed implementation and hampered economic growth as a consequence. Accumulating more accurate information can hamper action.

Radical innovations creating business opportunities for exploitation. This type includes the long-term R&D projects into fundamental and radically innovative ideas, which Freeman and Sawyer discussed. Underestimating the actual time and resource input necessary for such projects can be balanced by an equally unanticipated market potential. For example, IBM did not anticipate the computerization of society. They saw only a market for scientific and data handling functions for large corporations and public organizations. The list of radical innovations for which so-called spinoff effects have been unforeseen or underestimated can be made very long.

New ventures opening up new product markets for exploitation. Some projects are intended to renew the product portfolios of established firms by developing the new knowledge, skills, and processes necessary to establish the firm in a new business area. The time and resources needed to do this are typically underestimated, and these ventures are often linked to entrepreneurial managers within mature organizations. Such companies develop routines for evaluating and assessing what are for them traditional investments, which is why they often become good at handling such investments, but the system might fail for investments where they lack previous experience, and hence cost overruns and failures are common in these types of projects.

In a study of 13 major ventures in new areas,[24] unanticipated technical problems, and time and cost overruns were common. In these examples, there were always one or more entrepreneurs pushing the project. As the projects were ventures into new areas, practical experience was lacking, and the available information was vague and open to multiple interpretations. These situations are vulnerable to opportunistic entrepreneurs, who are typically good at piecing together fragments of information to create a seemingly coherent and attractive vision, but usually ignore the missing puzzle pieces and underestimate the problems that these may create and the resources that may be required. These underestimates led to the projects taking longer and requiring more resources than initially anticipated, but the mistakes are not usually malicious, rather the results of mixing facts and hopes:

It's typical for large investment projects that they are usually more expensive than planned. You are getting involved in new areas. Those championing a particular line of research have to overcome opposition too. That leads them to highlight positive aspects of the project. In some cases, the board is aware of cost excesses in these projects, but it too has problems in thinking of all the difficulties which might crop up.[25] (MD, champion of the development of a new steel process)

It's not the case that there have been deliberate miscalculations – I don't think that's the case – but calculations have been made as optimistically as possible, and we have perhaps done that for the next line I've calculated. There is probably a considerable risk that people think they are able to bite off more than they can chew.[26] (MD, champion of the implementation of a new plastic fabric process)

The real problems were quite clearly underestimated in many of the 13 ventures studied. One might well wonder whether these projects only got off the ground due to an entrepreneur's ability to formulate and win support for an unrealistic vision. Would senior management have even bothered to examine these project ideas if they had had full knowledge about all the problems that would emerge later and have to be solved if the venture was to succeed? Eight of these ventures were wound up or divested, and would not have been initiated if the board had foreseen the problems. The remaining five were still in progress and must be described as successful, but would they have been started with more knowledge? The question was posed to key actors and the collective answer was clearly 'no'. Technical or market problems had been so challenging that they would never have tried to overcome them if these obstacles had been foreseen when the ventures were approved. The real investment outlay had proved to be too high, a joint-venture partner with economic problems had had to be bought out in one of the cases, an airplane had had engine problems, and a new plant experienced running-in problems. Market estimates had in many of the cases proved incorrect, and expected market positions had been much more difficult to achieve than anticipated. Lack of knowledge[27] and miscalculations seem to have been a precondition for these 13 ventures getting off the ground.

In contrast, when the project managers for 35 major investments in new plants were asked[28] 'What would have happened if the first rough calculations had shown capital expenditure equivalent to the real capital expenditure of implementing the project?', only two of the respondents answered that the project would have been stopped. These were, with a few exceptions, expansion investments in existing business areas. Two might be an underestimation, as these answers were collected through a questionnaire instead of personal interviews, but it clearly indicates that ventures in new areas requiring the acquisition and development of new technical and market capabilities would stand a much bleaker chance of being approved if all problems could be foreseen. It seems like ability to foresee cost growth and other problems would make organizations invest more in existing areas of knowledge, and less in new areas.

Projects benefiting from changing value systems. Fourthly, we had projects in which cost growth was balanced by a change in the value assigned to the project. The Sävenäs waste incineration plant in Gothenburg can serve as an example of such a project. It would never have been considered if its cost had been correctly estimated ex ante. It would have been replaced by another garbage dump which, when the plant was taken in service, nobody would have wanted.

The Sävenäs project began in the mid-1950s, after managers from a municipal dump company attended a conference on waste management in West Germany. The amount of waste was increasing year by year and a new dump was needed, but the question was where it should be located. The managers discussed the situation on the way home. Since the amount of waste was unlikely to decrease, this meant that more and more land would be needed for dumps, until someone came up with an idea: 'Why can't we burn it? We could burn it and sell electricity and hot water.' The group stopped at an autobahn restaurant, brainstormed an innovative system for collecting and burning waste in a plant producing electricity and hot water for central heating, and made a first cost estimate on a table napkin of SEK 18 million.

Back in Gothenburg, they presented their ideas to the politicians on the board. The board liked the idea and included it in the long-term investment budget. The public found out about the investment because local newspapers wrote about the new plant and its estimated cost of SEK 18 million. However, as we know, new technologies for which no prototype exists often generate unforeseen problems, and developing this proposal was no different – not least because it was the first large-scale, low-emission waste incineration plant of its kind.

The more the team learnt about waste incineration plants, the more their cost estimates increased. At the time of the decision to go ahead, when they had received offers, estimated cost had increased to SEK 65 million, which made it difficult to gain a political majority for the decision. The politicians hesitated. The amount it would cost was not the key problem, the issue was that the public 'knew' that costs had increased from SEK 18 to 65 million, which made the incinerator difficult to defend. An additional dump would be cheaper.

Despite the difficulties, the plant was finally approved. Unfortunately, it turned out that burning large amounts of waste while keeping emissions of toxic substances low was difficult. The solution was to keep the fire at a certain constant temperature throughout the hotbed, which required more complex engineering, and the final cost jumped to SEK 120 million. But this is still not surprising, considering that there was no previous example of such a plant.

If the politicians had known that the bill would end up at SEK 120 million when they had to decide whether or not to proceed, there would have been a new rubbish dump instead, and the incineration solution would have been delayed until public opinion demanded better environmental solutions. But the project went ahead, and coincidentally was finished just as public opinion was becoming more concerned about cleaner environments. It is difficult to measure the economic outcome of environmental investments, but we can say that changing attitudes regarding the value of a clean environment compensated for increasing costs. The Sävenäs waste incineration station is in no way unique. Neither is it difficult to find projects for which values have changed in the opposite direction. Nuclear power is a good example of this. Once hailed as a clean replacement to dirty oil and coal, and a solution to increasing energy demand, its reputation has long since been tarnished.

Four types of projects and decision situations have been identified where projects that turned out to be profitable were only implemented because actual costs were underestimated. What these four project types have in common is that they all involve the development of radically new and innovative ideas. In such situations, it is usually difficult for a decision maker to imagine the full potential of the new technology and venture. The risk of failure is high and the market potential and spinoff effects are difficult to foresee, and sometimes underestimated. There are no prototypes and previous experiences are of little use – and can in fact restrict the ability to interpret new situations.

In the previous section we identified three consequences of cost overrun and growth that usually had a negative impact on the investing firm, other firms, and society, namely bankruptcy, impaired financial capacity, and negative social consequences. Some of these effects might be positive for certain actors (e.g. Billerud received a new machine at a discount price), but there are also effects that in most cases are mainly positive for both firms and society. These are situations where cost growth can be offset by positive effects for the investing firm, industry, or society because total investment increases, investments are reallocated in a way that contributes to renewing firms and society, or where ultimately profitable investments would not have been implemented, at least not at the time, had the correct outlay been known in advance. The results are summarized in Table 3.2.

Table 3.2 *Possible consequences of cost overrun, part II*

	Investing firm	Society
Mainly negative consequences		
Bankruptcy	Examples: Uddeholm; Northland Resources	Society had to financially support Uddeholm, and clean up after Northland Resources.
Impaired financial capacity	Examples: ABB; Alstom; ASSI; Lockheed; Rolls-Royce	Society had to financially support Alstom, ASSI, Lockheed, and Rolls-Royce.
Social consequences	Can affect a firm's organizational memory and the future of employees associated with the project responsible.	
Consequences of uncertain result		
Savings to reduce cost overrun	Postponements of and savings on investment often result in higher future investments and costs of operation. The saving potential depends on: – project divisibility – asset tradability – goal re-negotiability	
Mainly positive consequences		
Total investments	Might increase if major investment.	Might increase total investment.
Reallocation	Can contribute to renew firms.	Can contribute to renew society.
The implementation of profitable investments that would not have been implemented would the real cost have been known	Examples of such in investment are: – infrastructure projects opening up new markets for exploitation, – radical innovations creating business opportunities for exploitation, – new ventures opening up new product markets for exploitation, and – projects benefiting from changing value systems.	Uddeholm's paperboard machine became a profit generator in Billerud. The Rolls-Royce new high-bypass turbofan engine established Rolls-Royce on the world market.

Total investments.   Among the positive consequences of cost over-runs is the fact that, under some conditions, the total volume of invest-ment increases. This effect is probably mainly due to associated major investment projects and programmes in the private and public sectors. A firm's total investment budget is seldom reported as being exceeded. In fact, companies often overbudget so that they do not miss out on profit-able investments, knowing that some projects and parts of projects will probably be postponed. However, if additional capital is appropriated for investments, this can increase total investment and savings in both firms and society – which may be seen as a positive effect of cost overrun, but that depends on one's preference for consumption versus savings.

Reallocation.   Reallocation of investments is a considerably more com-mon and important effect of cost overrun and growth than increase in total investment. We know that cost overrun is more common in unique or rarely implemented projects, projects in new areas, complex projects, and projects that cannot be specified ex ante, such as R&D projects – all examples of projects that require the development of new knowledge. Cost overrun means that we end up investing more in these categories of project than planned, and less in the type of projects that are less likely to suffer cost overruns. It will reallocate funds from investments in maintain-ing and prolonging the life of existing product portfolios and production apparatus towards replacing these with new ones. It also counteracts firms' tendencies to overinvest in product variation and underinvest in product development and new knowledge, and might therefore contribute to renewing firms and industry. It might not be optimal for a single organiza-tion to reallocate resources in an unintended way, but on an aggregate level, this could be the most important positive consequence of cost overrun.

   This reallocation effect induced by cost overrun should not be confused with the renewal effect created by real estate bubbles. Such bubbles do not occur because of cost growth, but the result is similar. More money is invested in constructing new properties than otherwise would have been the case, and as buildings once erected are unlikely to be abandoned, new investors will step in and finish the building when the original investors fail. Real estate bubbles renew the city landscape and make it possible to build more extravagant architecture. At the same time, these bubbles withdraw capital from other kinds of investments. Whether this is good is open to debate, but it often gives our cities more optimistic and extra-vagant architecture than we might otherwise have had. Many architectu-rally highly acclaimed buildings and neighbourhoods would never have got the expensive design they now have if they had not been constructed during a real estate bubble.

4 A Model of Cost Overrun and Growth

Explaining Cost Overrun and Growth

Explanations for cost overrun and growth can be classified as either economic-technical or behavioural. In the former category, we include projects that are more prone to cost increases than others, projects where the decision to invest was made at such an early stage that reliable estimates could not be made or cost estimates were of poor quality for some other reason, projects where additional work or changes in the design were needed, and those where external or internal events caused delays and changes in the project which may have had knock-on effects for other parts of the project.

Behavioural explanations include examples where estimators and decision makers were overoptimistic and too self-confident, or did not reveal the true cost as it was in their self-interest to have the project implemented.[1]

The main difference between these two categories of explanations is that actors in the first case are assumed to evaluate information and make decisions based on rational reasoning, whereas decision making for actors in the latter is driven by emotions, or emotions at least have a decisive influence on decision making.

In this chapter, we will develop a model of cost overrun and growth based on economic-technical explanations and the literature review reported in Appendices A and B. In doing so, we will assume that cost estimators base their cost estimates on facts and reasoning using the information they have available, and that they re-evaluate their estimates in a logical way when better information becomes available. This is a variant of the rational economic man model, the hypothetical decision maker with perfect information who maximizes his own utility, which is used in many models in economics. However, we do not assume that decision makers have complete information covering all alternatives, only that new information is processed when it appears and that decisions are based on rational reasons.

Planning and implementing a project can be seen as a process of reducing uncertainty, where uncertainty about the final outcome of the project is gradually reduced as the estimator receives better information and greater knowledge of what is needed to realize the project. Deviations

59

in this process are a result of the characteristics of the technology involved and the way those involved reduce uncertainty and learn more about the project. When project planners launch an idea, they cannot specify in detail exactly what will have to be done to implement their idea. This is something they have to learn, which means that they might discover additional works that have to be done in order to complete the project, and/or have to make changes in the original design. The project can both increase in scope and change in design. The cost of making such changes increases with the amount of resources spent, as resources spent on earlier designs cannot be fully recovered. Design changes are not necessarily costly while the project is still in the planning process, but become increasingly expensive when the project is being implemented. The need for changes and unanticipated additional work drives costs upwards.

Assuming that actors behave in a rational manner might be seen as an unrealistic assumption, but nevertheless, as we will see, it is a powerful explanation.[2] We do not deny the role of emotions in decision making, nor that behavioural reasons may better explain actions made by individual actors. Most people are more confident in their own judgement than they have reason to be, and lean towards their own interests. Nor do we deny that people have different images of reality, interpret information differently, and can therefore act in a manner that is rational to themselves although not necessarily seen as rational by others. However, in our model we assume that such 'un-rational' interpretations of 'reality' and un-rational decisions will be de-biased as project planners learn more about the project, and project plans are reviewed and given negative feedback through internal control systems and external reviewers. The first estimate is always biased by emotions, often based more on hope than reality, but by the time the project is given its final approval, proper learning and a well-functioning control system should have been able to remove most of the influence of emotions and opportunistic behaviour on the cost estimate. Some projects and their cost estimates are of course more uncertain than others, but constant above-average cost overruns can be seen as a failure of the control system.

One question which has been discussed in the literature[3] is whether cost growth is due to optimistic bias on the part of the estimators or the result of a deliberate act to make a project look more appealing. Those estimating the cost might give an estimate that is too low because they are convinced of the merits of the investment but cannot prove it in a way that meets the financial manual of the company, or because the investment is in the interest of the planner.

Case studies from both the public[4] and private sectors[5] provide examples of projects where costs have been underestimated unintentionally, i.e. optimistic bias, and those that have been underestimated deliberately to ensure that they are explored and even approved. The Frövifors case is one such example, with a deliberately low initial estimate that promoted a feasibility study, and an unintentional underestimation of the time it would take to achieve the market goals of the project.

When the CEO of the ASSI group visited the company in Frövi to learn more about their still very vague plans to build a major new plant, the managing director of the company rented an air taxi to show the visitors the site of the new plant. While circling above:

[t]he CEO looked out and asked me [the company's MD] what it would cost. Three hundred million, I said. That figure came to guide the first investigation. (personal interview)

No cost estimates had yet been made. When the MD of the company was asked the cost, he made a very quick estimate in his head. He thought he had to present a figure, and SEK 300 million was what he estimated he might get considering the investment climate and the financial situation of the group at the time. Had he said SEK 500 million, which he actually thought was more probable, he would not have been given approval to conduct a feasibility study of the idea. But by picking SEK 300 million, he got approval to continue planning for a new plant and felt confident that, by the time group management got the appraisal and got used to the higher figure, they would realize that economies of scale made it better to build the bigger and more expensive plant.

In this case, the goal was to sell the project idea and make senior management so committed to the plan that they could not say no further down the line. The project proceeded as planned. The first estimate landed at the stated SEK 300 million for a 70,000 tonne per year machine, as it had to, after which top management were gradually per-suaded to go for a larger plant to exploit economies of scale. Several years later, when the board had decided to build the largest paper board machine in the world, the bill had grown to SEK 811 million excluding interest during construction. The cost had grown, but so had the size of the new plant, and inflation had by now reached double digits. 'You have to allow them to get used to large figures', as the MD of the company put it.

Requests for funding are frequently underestimates. Whether this is due to sheer optimism or deliberately to have a request approved is often very difficult to establish. However, there is no reason to believe that the proponents are trying to have investments approved that will not ulti-mately generate profits. The MD who chose SEK 300 million to ensure he would be allowed conduct a feasibility study believed that the project was the right move for his firm. He then had to provide an investment appraisal showing that his hopes for the project were correct and fulfilled the rate of return and payback period expected by the board. The figures can always be manipulated to show that is possible, but it does not mean that the manager was trying to fool the board, because he was convinced by then that the new plant would be profitable. The important thing to the company manager was to prevent a 'no' that would stop the project once and for all:

You have to be careful about making proposals which the group management or corporate board would say no to, because once the decision has been made, it's difficult to get round it. It has to be a project which looks attractive, is sufficiently vague in its contours to encourage further study. That's the decision you need when you produce your first draft. Then the door is open and you go back again. Later on things can develop in a completely different way. You have to give the board time to get used to the idea. (personal interview)

The board finds it difficult to assess investment proposals for expansion, and even more so to assess ventures in a new area, like this one. Therefore, from the proposer's perspective:

You have to go about things gradually so that you don't get a negative answer. It is a process of getting used to the idea. The technique is to give each other backing so that the board takes the initiative to study the project more closely; "Investigate this! We believe a 150,000 ton board machine is exactly what you need." Some time is needed to get used to the idea. Then you provide information and let them become acquainted with the new products and the new market, and preferably they should draw the conclusion: This is exactly what you need. (personal interview)

The Frövifors case also demonstrates unintentional underestimation, i.e. optimistic bias. The clearest example is that they underestimated the time and resources it would take to establish the product on the market:

Customer loyalty was stronger than we had imagined. It was difficult to win over customers from previous suppliers with quality. You had to offer a good price to be allowed to show that quality was better. . . . We realized, of course, that getting three thousand customers to buy carrier board was going to be hard work, but we didn't realize just how hard this was going to be. . . . We thought we had a good grasp of the situation, but it's like other situations in life, you can't really understand until you have experienced them. (personal interview)

Consultants had told them the new market was different from what they were used to and helped them form an intellectual understanding of the differences between the previous and the new markets, but they were not able to translate this intellectual awareness into action as they lacked practical experience and that took time to develop. Since they were not ex ante able to fully understand the implications of what they had learnt intellectually, they were not able to assess the barriers to entry correctly. That assessment was something that would be revised as they entered the new market:

It's like trying to learn to drive a car from a manual. You think you've got the hang of driving, but once you get behind the steering wheel, you realize that you are going to need quite a bit of driving practice before you really feel you're in control. (personal interview)

Selling the product was a learning process driven by practical experience and trial and error, and that is something the company could not develop until after they had introduced their new products to the market. This is not unusual. Theoretical knowledge and understanding can be gained ahead of time, but new practical knowledge can only be gained after implementation. This is why companies entering new markets recruit managers and buy smaller firms with experience of the market, and cooperate with firms in the new market.

The Control of Estimates and the Importance of Feedback for Learning

The Frövifors case gives us an example of both optimistic bias and a deliberate underestimation of costs in order to progress to a feasibility study. But these factors did not mean that the cost estimate finally approved by the board was unrealistic, because the board did not approve the project before all estimates had been thoroughly scrutinized. The control system is important, and we will therefore describe what it looked like in the Frövifors case.

Major private and public organizations have developed control systems to ensure that project cost estimates and proposals are evaluated appropriately and robustly. These control systems are vital if final estimates are to be reasonably correct and risks of later cost overrun minimized. Major cost overruns are thus not only a failure of the estimator, but, equally, a failure of the control system.

Organizations use a variety of means to control the outcome of investments. These are commonly categorized as representing[6] either social, bureaucratic, or market-based control.

Social control in organizations relies on the socialization of employees to make them share the same norms, values, and ideas about how and why things should be done. If employees behave in the same way as their CEO, additional control becomes unnecessary. An important means of social control is education. Professionals with a long formal education, such as physicians, engineers, teachers, and researchers, are socialized to the norms and values of their profession through their long education, and those norms can affect cost estimation practice.

Social control has gained renewed importance as production has become more knowledge- and service-intensive. Knowledge-intensive firms, and especially professional service firms, invest large sums in building a strong corporate culture. They have extensive employment procedures to select those they think will fit in, mandatory training programmes, job rotation and mentoring schemes, workshops, and informal meetings, all to socialize employees. They typically invest as much or more in training and socialization of their employees as capital-intensive groups in fixed investments.[7]

Bureaucratic control relies on formal organization and authority, written instructions, rules and policies, measurement and reporting systems, and career and reward systems. It works best when project activities can be specified and measured, and is an important means of control in both private and public organizations.

Market-based control is when business units and activities can be assessed as if they were players on a market. A key reason for the existence of major groups is that they create an internal market for capital, hence they can also assess business units in a similar way to companies on a stock market by evaluating their value creation. Observe that market-based control, in principle, only can be used for tradable assets such as a business unit.

Market-based control has gained importance in the public sector as public sector organizations have increasingly come to procure the services they offer from the private sector. It has also gained more importance in the private sector as innovation within telecommunications and computer software have made it possible to connect markets, sellers, and buyers globally. That has not only enlarged and made old markets more efficient, but has also created new markets. As a result, we have seen a wave of outsourcing in both the private and public sectors, and a marketization[8] of many value chains. Major companies have been broken up and come to focus on smaller and smaller parts of their value chains.

Resource allocation in divisionalized groups. The capital budgeting process in major divisionalized corporations[9] is well described by Joseph Bower.[10] Investment ideas usually originate from and are costed by engineers at the business level. However, to have the time and funding to investigate an investment idea, they first need to have approval from their business manager. When this leads to an investment outlay larger than the business manager has the authority to fund, the latter has to submit a request for funding to division level. To avoid having the request rejected, the manager will probably first have contacted a higher level to determine the chances of securing funding and whether changes in the proposal could enhance its probability of being funded. Having been assured that the proposal is suitable, the manager signs the request and forwards it upwards in the hierarchy. By signing the request, the manager becomes accountable for the figures presented in the request, and so by choosing a particular sum he becomes committed to this figure.

At the divisional level, the request is scrutinized and signed by marketing and technical staff, and then, if they do not have dispensation to approve the request, it is sent up to corporate level. As it is the business unit level that usually knows most about their machines and customers, the divisional level can seldom prove that they are wrong and stop the request. But they can ask questions and force the business level to provide a better case for their request, which forces the business unit to consider all aspects of their request carefully, learn more, and plan more thoroughly before they are given the go-ahead.

If the request is of such a size that it needs corporate- or even board-level approval, it will be scrutinized and signed by still more managers and staff asking questions and thereby contributing to the scrutiny of the proposal. Thus, a major investment in need of board-level support is scrutinized by several functions and employees with experience of similar, previous investments before it can be approved and implemented. The formal process and signing of the request transfers responsibility to those involved. The entire process creates the negative feedback loops necessary for learning. Some investments are initiated at higher levels, but in many groups the request still goes through the same process. This type of control precedes the decision to invest and is referred to as 'pre-approval control'.

After the formal decision to invest, the implementation of the project is evaluated against the approved budget, and sometimes the investment is followed up a year or two after implementation, when it is in full operation. However, top management considers the pre-approval control process to be of most importance and interest, as they can only influence the decision to invest and its direction before the final decision is taken. When the investment has been approved, it is much more difficult and costly to change anything.

The pre-approval control process allows top management to learn more about the way approved strategies are implemented, and the negative feedback that the project proponents receive during the process helps them to learn more about their project. To follow up the project after it has been implemented is more relevant to those learning about planning new projects than to top management. The importance of feedback from the control system for learning and improving cost estimates cannot be underestimated.

Balancing entrepreneurial and controlling forces. Organizations can be regarded as systems for dealing with large quantities of information. Of all the information which reaches a company and everything which happens in an organization, only an extremely small part reaches top management, and then often in the very compressed form of accounting data, memos, and presentations. The mechanisms for control we have described make it possible to reduce the information load on senior management. Its effectiveness in suppressing information and proposals that are not in accordance with the desires of top management is sometimes so strong that it becomes more or less impossible to gain approval for proposals to invest in new areas which do not fit in with the company's existing business idea.

The design of the control system raises many questions. An important one is the balance between championing and checking forces. If control is weak, unrealistic budgets and unprofitable projects might be approved. If control is too strong, profitable projects might be stopped, renewal cease, and capabilities wither. It is vital that the balance between these two forces is satisfying, for the supply of negative feedback for learning and for the evaluation and assessment of the project. How an imbalance between entrepreneurial and controlling forces can cause cost overruns can be illustrated by examining a real estate bubble and the rise and fall of Consafe Offshore AB.

When the Swedish capital market was deregulated in 1987 and real estate companies allowed to invest in foreign real estate, they found prices low compared with those in Sweden at the time. As a result, real estate companies invested €16 billion overseas between 1987 and 1992, mostly in England, Germany, Belgium, Holland, Denmark, and Norway, and most of it in the period 1988 to 1990.[11] This bubble ended in a crash that forced the Swedish government to interfere to save the Swedish banking system, and a financial crisis that at the time had no comparison abroad.

An imbalanced trinity of real estate investors, real estate valuation companies appraising the market value of properties, and newly deregulated credit institutions contributed to this bubble.[12] As real estate prices increased, property companies could pay a real estate valuation company to put a new and higher value on its property, take that paper to a credit institution, and borrow more money to buy more properties. And if the valuation company did not propose a high enough value, the property company could go to another. In this way, constant revaluations of the borrowing base created a spiral in which revaluations led to increased borrowing, which led to more capital chasing real estate for sale, which in turn increased real estate prices and cost estimates. The situation became a self-reinforcing spiral, creating a boom in real estate prices which sooner or later had to burst. This imbalance between entrepreneurial and controlling forces does not explain the boom entirely, but certainly contributed to it.

Another example of what such an imbalance can create is the rise and fall of Consafe Offshore AB. In the 1970s, when Swedish shipyards were fighting for their survival and oil companies were starting to exploit off-shore oil, Jan Christer Ericsson saw a business opportunity in the fact that oil rig workers lived under bad conditions. He rebuilt 21 oil rigs into residential platforms, and in 1977 he contracted with the Götaverkan Cityvarvet yard to build the world's first semi-submersible custom-built residential and service platform, a so-called floatel, for delivery in 1978.[13] Here, the imbalance was between a yard in urgent need of new business to survive, generous state credits to avoid mass unemployment in a city dependent on its shipyards, and a super entrepreneur, and the outcome was that Consafe became the largest in its industry, until the company crashed in 1985. The yard was obliged to take over 6 residential platforms that had not been paid for, 51 per cent of a drilling rig, and shares in 2 diving rigs, for which there was no longer a market. The yard was closed down and its rich patent portfolio on offshore rigs sold. All that remained were the loss-making rigs from the Consafe crash.

In both of these cases, estimates grew because the entrepreneurial forces were not balanced by controlling forces. Entrepreneurship is most promi-nent when organizations test new ideas, and is probably necessary to over-come the opposition that always exists towards something new. But the nature of new ideas means that information is fragmentary and ambiguous. How these fragments of information are interpreted is crucial, especially as the same information can probably be pieced together in different ways to produce both negative and positive visions of the future. Overoptimistic visions are a natural corollary of entrepreneurship, and lack of knowledge is an essential condition for renewal. The entrepreneur is often described as a person who is able to disregard problems and fire others with enthusiasm. Underestimates resulting from lack of knowledge and the optimism of the entrepreneur are, as shown in the previous chapter, sometimes more than balanced by the creativity which an organization has to demonstrate to realize its plans.

The importance of routines and practice becomes evident when com-panies face new kinds of projects for which these routines are insufficient. When making a reinvestment, the firm can normally base their cost estimate on data from their cost-accounting system, but an expansion investment also requires an estimate of the future market, which is more difficult. When estimates have to be made concerning new products and markets, existing routines and means of control become less important as they are based on experience of existing areas of operation and reliable estimates are replaced by emotions, more or less realistic hopes, and external knowledge.

Pre-approval control in the Frövifors case. Let us now return to the Frövifors case, this time to illustrate the important role of internal control systems in supplying feedback, the use of external sources to supply supplementary feedback when internal feedback is not sufficient, and the importance of ensuring that project management has not only the financial resources but also the competence to achieve the agreed goals.

The ASSI group had a pre-approval control system, i.e. a formal system stipulating the way investment requests were to be appraised and reviewed. Important in this particular example, group management and the board could give useful feedback to project management as they themselves had personal experience of major forestry sector projects. That is not always the case. In addition, information about the project was communicated and discussed through direct contacts between project management, top management and the board of the group. Direct communication channels such as this are often opened up when companies make major new investments.

For added confidence, the ASSI board asked the Boston Consulting Group to appraise the project. The consultants recommended an increase in capacity from 100,000 to 150,000 tonnes per year, and a narrower market mix implemented through aggressive pricing. They concluded: 'This is the only project in this industry in Europe that is commercially and economically justified' (personal interview). Their enthusiastic report created expectations, especially around the narrower market mix strategy, that those requesting the investment had to play down.

Jaakko Pöyry is a well-reputed consulting company in the forestry industry which, through their knowledge of numerous forestry projects, has access to topical cost data. Frövifors therefore assigned them to make an independent cost estimate for the project to further reduce uncertainty. As a part of this, the project was benchmarked against four previous similar projects. In some industries, companies cooperate on costing by supplying cost data to a trade association. This is not the case in the forestry sector, but data can be obtained through industry journals, Jaakko Pöyry, and other consultants.

However, having taken great care over establishing and approving an investment budget does not mean that the budget will necessarily be met. The approved budget is a commitment that has to be fulfilled and, as our Frövifors and Barsebäck examples in Chapter 2 showed, project management may have to make substantial changes in the project to meet their commitments. The management control system is important in the control of cost estimates and learning, but whatever budget is approved has to be met, and that does not happen by itself. Knowledgeable reviewers are needed to supply feedback, and competent project managers to plan and implement approved projects.

Achieving the budgetary goals is a process of constant problem solving, and as deviations will always appear, it is important that the project team has the competence needed to manage that process. Important steps in the Frövifors case were to recruit a new managing director, and subsequently a technical director who had an excellent reputation in the industry, considerable experience of project management, was close to retirement, and came from a competitor. His experience of the industry and major projects, and the chance to work with him and be involved in constructing the largest machine in the world, made it easy to attract other engineers. Additional recruitment and training programmes for operators and those that were to sell the new product were also important.

Major investments often require additional training in the new machinery, products, and markets. These are not outlays that can be deferred or written off as investments, but they are still a part of major investment decisions. Alternatives to training existing staff to implement strategies and major investments include acquiring other companies with the necessary technology or skill-sets, joint ventures or other forms of cooperation with other firms, purchasing licences and patents, hiring management and technical consultants, and recruiting managers with previous experience of similar investments or the new business.

Lessons from Studies of Groups of Projects

To be able to generalize about cost overruns and growth, a good start is to analyse a sample of projects to identify the factors that correlate with cost growth. There are plenty of such studies, and a review of a selection can be found in Appendices A and B. In this section, we will give a short account of the results of our review summarized in the form of ten conclusions and, based on these, formulate a model of cost overrun.

1. Cost overrun and growth is far more common than the opposite. It is difficult to find a study showing that, on average, projects become less expensive than anticipated. Cost overrun is the norm regardless of whether it is a construction, research and development, or computer software project.
2. Early cost estimates tend to be more biased towards cost overrun than later ones. Estimates tend to rise over time, and they tend to increase faster during the early phases of both the planning and implementation

processes. Furthermore, the variance in cost estimates decreases over time. Early estimates are not only lower than later ones, they also vary more and are less accurate than later ones.

3. The longer the period between approved budget and final cost, the larger the cost overrun tends to become. This relationship also holds when figures have been adjusted for inflation. One way of explaining this phenomenon is that the longer the time period is, the more changes are made in the project design, such as adjusting to market changes, incorporating newer technical solutions, and adapting to changing regulations. On top of this, prolonging construction time also increases accrued interest.

4. The larger the cost overrun, the larger the deviation for other project parameters such as estimated sales volume and price, product mix, planned capacity, and technical ambitions. Changes in funding, technical standards, and market demand necessitate changes in projects that drive costs, which is why there is a connection between deviations in market and financial plans and project costs. It also explains why there is a positive covariance between cost overrun and factors such as construction time, volumes of concrete and steel used, man hours, estimated sales volume and price, product mix, and planned capacity. External and internal changes drive costs. The final result will not be exactly the same project that was originally planned and approved. Dramatic changes in the original plans are sometimes necessary, but should be regarded as possible drivers of cost.

When it comes to changes, it is important to remember that the cost of making changes in the design increases sharply the closer the project is to completion. Making changes on the drawing board does not necessarily make a project more expensive, but when construction has started, changes becomes increasingly more expensive. What has been spent already before the changes cannot be fully recovered, and the changes may increase construction time and thus interest expenses.

5. For projects of the same type, the deviation in cost between approved budget and final cost calculated as a percentage of total cost varies more for smaller than for larger projects. However, this only applies to, or is at least more evident in, homogenous groups of projects – projects representing similar technology and implemented in the same organization. This phenomenon can be seen as a manifestation of the law of large numbers. Sub-projects and items in major projects can show large cost deviations but tend to cancel each other out.

6. The distribution of the deviation of cost for a group of projects is positively skewed for most types of projects. There are few examples

where it is not positively skewed. One simple explanation is that time and resources spent cannot be fully recovered when changes and additional works are added to the project. Also, as it is much more likely that changes and additional work will increase costs than decrease them, changes and additional works will create a positive skewness.

7. The greater the advance in technical knowledge needed, the larger the growth in cost. This conclusion initially derived from studies of new weapon systems,[14] but has since been proven to hold for civilian projects as well, and probably applies not only to technical knowledge but also to new knowledge in general.

Burton Klein[15] compared the building of a bridge with that of a military aircraft project. If the bridge is well designed, there is a very high probability that the bridge can be built without making changes in the original design during construction. This contrasts with military aircraft projects, which Klein found to be seldom implemented as originally planned. Regardless of how much attention had been given to the original design in the cases he studied, there were always surprises later on in the project. The project would start with one configuration, but the end result would involve another engine, different electronics, a modified airframe, or even a different tactical role for the aircraft. The essential difference between bridges and aircraft, Klein wrote, is that the construction of the former is a question of making best use of existing knowledge, while the latter requires quite a lot of learning. What Klein describes is the distinction between implementation and development projects: Projects which can be specified in advanced and projects where the goal is partly to specify something new.

Klein also tested whether these changes in the development projects he had studied could have been foreseen had project management allocated more resources ex ante to specifying the project and estimating its cost. The results were not conclusive, but they did show that surprises can appear late why spending more resources on planning ex ante not always help to make cost estimates more accurate. Surprises in projects where the aim is to develop new knowledge cannot be completely avoided by better planning ex ante.

8. The more complex the project is, the more cost tends to grow. Major projects can be split up into a number of sub-projects and activities which have to be completed in time so as not to delay other activities. The number of such dependencies, their interrelatedness, and their negotiability is by definition a measure of complexity,[16] and these dependencies can be due to both internal and external actors, processes, and events. Complexity is defined by the number of

dependencies and how little slack is allowed in time and trade-off between goals, rather than the size of a project, although large and high-tech projects tend to be more complex.

The problem is that the many separate tasks in a project are not independent.[17] Assume, for instance, a task that is estimated to take 100 hours to complete. If those performing the task know it well, they might be able to complete it in 80 hours, although this would be difficult. However, if they do not know exactly what to do or how to do it, the time to complete the task can easily slip to more than 120 hours, reaching 150, 200, or even more if they get stuck or make mistakes. There is a lower limit to how fast a task can be performed, but no upper limit – which also explains why the distribution of cost is almost always positively skewed. As tasks are not independent, a delay or change in one task can affect another, causing delays and additional costs, and hence projects with many dependencies are more prone to time and cost overrun.

High-tech projects are especially susceptible to cost growth due to delays and changes in interrelated activities, as high-performance products are more tightly optimized and, in general, also more dependent on external relations. Further, many very large projects, such as the nuclear waste programme, are of high complexity as they involve many activities and actors, and are implemented in a highly politicized environment. We should also remember that the more complex a project is the more likely it becomes that an event regarded as highly improbable, hence indeed unknown, in fact will impact on the endeavour. Possible solutions include modularization and standardization of components and interfaces, and systems to deal with dependences as soon as problems appear.

9. Cost overrun tends to be larger when those planning, estimating, and implementing the project do not have experience of similar projects. Unique, one-of-a-kind, or projects that are implemented infrequently, such as research facilities, town halls, and stadiums, show larger cost overruns than construction projects where there are many similar examples. Standardized items and work processes are easier to cost as data from earlier, similar projects can be used. Unique items do not offer the same possibility for updating and improving cost data. The project is new to those making the estimates, but not necessarily new to the world, or especially complex.

10. Cost overrun is more common in some organizations and contexts than in others. Some organizations are better at estimating costs, and some seem to be able to improve the accuracy of their cost estimates, while others do not. The organization and who is making the estimate

is without doubt a very important factor in determining the accuracy of cost estimates.

Where the project is located also matters. Several studies have shown that cost overrun is more common in certain countries and regions than in others. Projects in less developed countries have generally been assumed to shown larger cost overruns than similar projects in industrialized countries, but exceptions can easily be found. However, on average it seems that cost overrun is smaller in certain regions and countries than in others.

It might seem reasonable to assume that increased levels of education and research, better documentation, easier access to information, and experience gained from earlier investments would make cost overrun less common today than a few decades ago. However, whether that is the case is uncertain as studies have given conflicting results, and it is difficult to establish as estimation practices and contextual factors have evolved over time.

A Model of Uncertainty Resolution and Type of Project

We have seen that cost overrun is far more common than the opposite; cost tends to rise over time, and increase more at the beginning of the planning process than later on. Furthermore, cost estimates become less reliable the longer the time period between two estimates, and cost overrun is also associated with deviations in other measures of outcome, such as time overrun and changes in anticipated sales, price, product mix, and planned capacity.

These observations can all be explained by how we make estimates, acquire information, and form an increasingly clear image of all aspects of the final product as the planning and implementation process proceeds.[18] Cost estimates are based on an image visualized in drawings and calculations of the final product. As our plans become more detailed, and we acquire and form a better image of the final product and what is needed to have it implemented, additional work tends to become known, and changes in our plans necessary. These changes can be initiated by external factors, such as market demand, price changes, and new regulations, or internal factors, such as changes in the original design. Project development and costing is basically a learning process in which planners develop a more refined and better image of the final product while at the same time adapting this image to internal and external demands and changes as these become known. The outcome of the process depends on the preconditions, the prior knowledge and learning of those involved, and the way the process is organized.

We have also seen that cost overrun differs by product type and also in which organization and region a project is implemented. Technology and context matter, and we have identified three categories of projects in

Table 4.1 *Dynamic and static uncertainty and types of project prone to overrun*

Uncertainty		
Dynamic uncertainty will resolve during the planning period		*Static uncertainty will always be present*
Uncertainty can be resolved using existing knowledge	*Uncertainty can be resolved but requires the acquisition and development of new knowledge*	
Implementation projects	Development projects	Projects affected by exogenous static uncertainty
Complex projects which uncertainty will be resolved during the planning period		System innovations
Projects new to the actors implementing and costing them but which need not be new to the world or especially complex		

which cost is more likely to increase due to the need to develop knowledge new to the world (point 7, in the previous section), project complexity (point 8), and knowledge new to those making cost estimates (point 9). In Table 4.1, the last of these three categories is characterized by the need for those costing and implementing the project to acquire and develop new knowledge, the second to the existence of dependences, and the first allow us to distinguish between implementation and development projects. Implementation projects can be based on existing knowledge, while development projects require an advance in new knowledge.

To further elaborate our model, we need to differentiate between dynamic and static uncertainty.[19] Dynamic uncertainty can be resolved during the planning period, but static cannot. Static uncertainty derives from external factors[20] and will remain a source of unanticipated events that might necessitate changes in project plans throughout the whole planning and implementation process. One example of static uncertainty was the oil price shock in 1973. Even though there were warnings of radical price increases by OPEC, companies did not plan for an increase of 300–400 per cent. This was deemed a scenario too disruptive to be probable, and therefore an event that planning ex ante could not resolve.

This allows us to identify a fourth category of projects in which final cost have been affected by unforeseen events such as unanticipated price increases or inflation, war, strikes, flooding, etc., in Table 4.1 termed projects affected by exogenous static uncertainty. An example is two large hydroelectric power stations which the Swedish State Power Board designed and started to build before the oil price shock in 1973–74. The price shock led to an increase in the price of electricity, which meant the water that would flow through these two hydroelectric power stations became a more valuable resource. This led to redesign during construction to ensure the water was used as efficiently as possible. Adjusting to changing prices in this way led to a substantial cost growth that was not foreseeable ex ante. However, the changes might not have made the investment less profitable. They may even have improved profitability. Such cost growth due to exogenous static uncertainty cannot be avoided by careful planning and can hit any investor, even the most cautious.

Another category of projects in Table 4.1 which can be affected by static uncertainty is those termed 'system innovations'. An example is the development of electric vehicles. The success of electric vehicles is affected by both uncertainties exogenous to the new vehicle system, such as buyers' willingness to pay more for a more environmentally friendly vehicle; subsidies and advantages offered to owners and manufacturers of such vehicles; and endogenous uncertainties related to actors developing the infrastructure offering charging stations, service, and repair, and a cluster of firms developing components for such vehicles. Changes and decisions which one firm cannot control or foresee make system innovations complex and lengthy to implement.

When it comes to the resolution of uncertainty, it is important to recognize that what is resolvable uncertainty for one actor might not be so for another, and that the dissemination of new knowledge in an industry takes time. Studies of cost overrun in the construction of oil platforms in Britain[21] and Norway[22] showed that the first offshore platforms built by a company were subject to substantial time and cost overrun, and that it took several years to acquire and disseminate the knowledge that made the industry more efficient at costing and building these offshore platforms.

First movers in the offshore industry had to resolve the technical uncertainties associated with offshore drilling platforms; this is the cost of being a pioneer. Over time, the knowledge they gained disseminated to competitors, and certain technical solutions became standards in the industry. Late movers could resolve uncertainties faster by recruiting personnel from the first movers and applying the standards that they had already developed. It is much easier to acquire explicit knowledge and develop a theoretical understanding of the task of constructing something like an offshore platform than to develop the practical knowledge that is needed. It takes much longer to identify tacit knowledge and develop the new skills necessary to construct such a complex structure, and one might suspect that it is tacit knowledge and the development of skills that prolonged the dissemination process in this part of the offshore industry.

Cost Overrun and Growth as a Consequence of Static Uncertainty

Contrary to dynamic uncertainty, static uncertainty will not be resolved during the planning and implementation period. Static uncertainty can derive from external factors such as weather, war, accidents, changes in laws and regulations, and other events that are beyond the control of those planning and implementing a project. An important source of static uncertainty is political uncertainty or instability, i.e. uncertainty about the future course of a country, its inflation and currency rate, new laws and regulations, its growth rate, and enforcement of intellectual property laws. Cost increases related to such static uncertainty are not always regarded as cost overrun when the increases have not been anticipated. Whether or not that is the correct approach, it is still important to analyse whether static uncertainty can cause any systematic cost estimation bias, such as long-term changes in relative prices.

Most studies of cost overrun and growth use a consumer price index to deflate payments, while project cost estimators use a construction index. The former is a basket of consumer goods and services purchased by households, the latter a basket of input used in construction projects, i.e. labour and materials such as steel, lumber, and cement, each one estimated with the help of their own cost indices. Using a consumer price index to deflate payments, we can see if cost has developed faster or slower than households' purchasing power; using a construction index, we can see whether cost has increased relative to other construction projects.

An interesting issue is whether cost overrun and growth in some types of projects is a consequence of long-term costs in the construction index increasing faster than in the consumer price index, causing estimators to underestimate relative price increases. We know, for instance, that wages increase faster than the price of goods, a precondition for the standard of living to increase. This makes labour-intensive projects increase in cost relative to a consumer index. But while labour-intensive projects can become more expensive to implement over time, capital-intensive projects can become less expensive, and costs can decrease in areas where productivity can be increased by replacing manual work with machines, for example. The question is whether there is a bias due to estimators not correcting fully for such long-term relative price changes.

When the gross national product increases by 3 per cent in one year, this does not mean that consumers are allowed to decide freely how to spend that 3 per cent. Political parties and other stakeholders will try to affect the allocation of this surplus in a way that promotes their interests. Some of the increase will be tied up in increased standards, regulations, and legislation, often to make products more reliable and society safer for us to live in – standardizations which also can contribute to future growth. There may also be a drive towards acquiring more advanced products. When we can spend twice as much money, we buy a technically more advanced product, not two of the products which we would have bought if we only had half the amount of money to spend. The long-term effects of this drive towards greater safety and more advanced products might be underestimated for some types of projects, and add to a project's static uncertainty as they are taken for granted. We will demonstrate this effect in the development of costs for new nuclear power plants and weapon systems, but it is also present in many other areas, although not to the same extent.

Cost growth due to increased regulation in the nuclear power industry. The cost of new nuclear power plants increased dramatically in the 1970s[23] due to increasing regulation. Construction volume increased, the number of security systems increased from one to three, and more stringent requirements and controls on individual components were enforced. It has been said that if, in the early 1970s, a bolt was missing, it could usually be replaced by one of a similar quality steel, but ten years later work would be stopped until a bolt of the correct quality steel had arrived. Increased regulation meant more stringent technical requirements and less room for project management to improvise when drawings and specifications were inexact, and all changes had to be approved in advance by the regulating agencies. Additional safety systems and more stringent requirements made technical systems more tightly coupled and nuclear plants more complex, and also reduced the number of available suppliers, and, hence, competition. These factors contributed to making nuclear power projects more complex, increased component prices, and lengthened the construction period – all issues which we have learnt drive cost growth.

In addition, prices increased as manufacturers deliberately took losses on the first nuclear power plants in order to establish themselves in what was anticipated to be a growth market in the future. To counter the cost increases that followed, power companies ordered larger plants in the belief that economies of scale would balance out the increased security requirements, but that did not offset the increasing cost per megawatt production capacity of new plants.

The French nuclear power programme has been regarded by many as the most successful nuclear power programme. Today, it has 58 pressurized water reactors with a capacity of 66,000 megawatts, and accounts for about 80 per cent of France's electricity production.[24] The programme has had strong support from the state and enjoyed stable regulation, and all reactors have been constructed by a state-owned company. Under these circumstances, the preconditions should have been good for learning, standardization, and keeping costs down compared to countries such as the USA, where each power company has built far fewer reactors and support for nuclear power has been much more volatile.

Perhaps as a result of these more favourable preconditions, the average construction time in France has been 25 per cent shorter than in the USA.[25] Both countries have scaled-up constructions to reduce the cost of new capacity per megawatt. However, those potential economies of scale have not been realized, as evidenced by the fact that fixed cost per mega-watt of production capacity has not decreased. One explanation given[26] is that scaling up has led to increased system complexity. Each plant has become unique due to both its size and associated regulations, and the role in the production system that it plays, and this has reduced the transfer of learning from one plant to another. Nuclear power plants are composed of many different systems and parts, and as these systems are complex and tightly coupled and stringent standards and regulations delimit the opportunities for making changes in the design that can absorb the effects of new preconditions, costs tend to grow.

The French experience has subsequently been confirmed in a similar study[27] of US nuclear power plants, which have also been scaled-up in the hope that economies of scale would lower costs, but there is no evidence to suggest that this has been the case. As in France, there are no two reactors that are exactly the same, partly due to site-specific reasons, partly due to the fact that more recent reactors are more complex constructions, and partly due to the fact that larger and more complex reactors also take longer to construct.

Complexity coupled with a lack of standardization can explain why nuclear reactors exhibit a cost overrun of 117 per cent in Table 1.1, wind farms 8 per cent, and solar farms only 1 per cent. Solar and wind farms can be constructed from mass-produced units produced in long series, and it does not matter if one panel in a solar farm fails, hence one remedy which has been suggested[28] for nuclear power is to opt for smaller reactors built in long series.

Cost growth has, however, not yet made nuclear plants uneconomic to run once they have been constructed. Operating costs have remained fairly stable, and as the cost of operating a nuclear plant is relatively low once the plant is written off, it becomes economically justified to extend plant life, as has happened in many countries. When the first reactors were constructed, nobody knew exactly what their lifespan would be, which is why their economic life for the purpose of economic appraisals was set equal to that of coal plants.[29] With experience of operation, it has proved possible to extend that life much further, and we can expect many reactors to reach twice their original estimated life.

Cost growth when only the best will win – the armaments sector. In
the USA, researchers[30] started to study cost overruns for new military aircraft
and missile development projects in the 1950s. Since then, there have been
numerous studies of the causes but the problem has not gone away. The
development cost for each new generation of aircraft has continued to
increase, and the number of aircraft built has therefore constantly been
smaller than originally planned. This makes each aircraft more expensive,
as there are fewer aircraft manufactured to pay for the development costs,
and short production runs reduce opportunities for learning. While air forces
in the 1950s could maintain 1,000 aircraft, today that number is in the few
hundreds. The economy has grown, but the cost of new military aircraft has
grown faster than the economy. Similarly, the drive towards weapon systems
that can defeat those that already exist has led to cost growth exceeding
inflation and fewer and fewer of these superior weapons being produced.

A similar development is seen for naval ships both in the United
Kingdom[31] and the USA.[32] The cost of new naval ships has long been
increasing faster than the consumer price index and naval budgets. The
cost of wages, materials, and equipment has roughly followed inflation,
but improvements in labour productivity have been insignificant and each
new generation of ships is larger and more complex – and therefore more
expensive – than the previous generation. Fewer ships mean shorter
series, and fewer opportunities for cost reduction through standardization
and learning. It also means fewer producers and less competition among
shipyards and their suppliers.

It may seem strange that military planners do not correctly adjust down
the number of new weapons produced and up the cost of development
when they order a new generation of weapons that will ensure superiority
on the battlefield. As this trend for inbuilt cost growth can be traced in
naval ships back to the 19th century,[33] it should not come as a surprise.
Why the military system has not learnt to adjust for this bias is unclear.
We can speculate that one reason might be because military planning
does not take its point of departure as how to best use a fixed sum of
money and existing weapon systems, but rather what will be needed 30
years hence to counter and defeat perceived threats and opponents. Such
long-term plans are prone to cost increases as more becomes known of
their implications in the same way that advances in new knowledge tend
to increase project costs.

There are probably several other reasons for cost growth in the development of new military weapon systems. For example, cost overrun
becomes more important to avoid in peacetime than during war or an
arms race. When a new weapon system is urgently needed it becomes a
forced investment. Another is that military R&D projects[34] can have dual

purposes in that state support for military R&D is exempted from the restrictions imposed on state support for industry by international trade agreements. Support for military research has therefore become a means for some states to counteract the tendency of industry to underspend on fundamental research necessary to develop new technologies for commercialization. It might sometimes have made cost growth and the cost of new weapon systems of less importance. However, whatever the underlying reasons, the fact remains that the cost of new military weapon systems has risen faster than the consumer price index.

Other examples of long-term relative cost changes. Other examples of products for which costs have increased faster than the consumer price index include the price of passenger ships and health care. Advances in medical technology have made it possible to diagnose, mitigate the effects of, and cure diseases that were previously untreatable, but often at such increased cost that the new treatment cannot be offered to all patients. However, as the willingness to pay for having one's life extended is extremely high for those that are wealthy, the drive to develop more advanced and costly health care is similar to that for the development of superior weapon systems.

On the other hand, the cost of many consumer products has decreased relative to consumer price indices, making them affordable for an increasing number of people. Cars, refrigerators, telephones, radios, and cameras, once gadgets only for the rich, are today articles for everyday use for the great majority, not only in Western Europe and North America but with increasing speed all over the world. During the last 50 years, cost reduction has been particularly fast for electronic products, while at the same time product performance has increased dramatically. Cars have also become cheaper to buy and own, even if the cost reduction has been much slower. More important as far as cars are concerned is that modern vehicles have longer service-free life, are safer, and are more fuel efficient. In contrast, the euphoria for space travel in the 1950s and '60s came to a halt because the cost of lifting one tonne into space has remained roughly the same for the last 60 or 70 years.

For cars, refrigerators, telephones, radios, cameras, etc., producers have reduced manufacturing cost by learning how to produce these items faster and at lower costs. This process has encompassed both technical and operational learning, from performing a specific operation faster and more cheaply to coordinating logistics and the whole value chain better. The evolution has required production in long series, specialization of the work force and organization, standardization of inputs and the tasks that are performed, and sometimes relocation of activities. The result has been that prices have declined relative to consumer price indices.

Why do costs increase faster than inflation for some categories of project? For some products, such as new nuclear power plants, military weapon systems, and possibly also for some unique and rarely implemented projects such as arenas, cost has increased faster than the consumer price index. When it comes to nuclear energy, industry has countered this by constructing larger plants, but not even this has made it possible to lower cost per megawatt.

Why, then, does cost increase faster than inflation for these categories of project? There seem to be two roots to the problem. Firstly, the effects of increased regulation and standards on parameters such as noise, emissions, safety, and service might be underestimated. Such increased standards can sometimes dramatically increase project costs.

Secondly, we have the drive towards more high-tech products, and the desire to construct the largest and the best, which implies a greater number of unique solutions and more complex projects. We know from the innovation literature that each new generation of technology tends to combine an increasing number of technologies.[35] This is a driving force for firm specialization, increased external sourcing, and cooperation on developing new technologies. However, the internal and external complexity for a project increases as we combine an increasing number of technologies and involve more partners. It makes the project by definition more complex as well, as increasing the size of the project, which will increase the construction period and, as a result, the interest expenses during construction. Somebody has to develop these high-tech and unique projects. That means problem solving and a higher proportion of wages in the product budget, and we know that wages increase faster than materials. In addition, with increased specialization and fewer projects of this kind, the tendency is towards fewer contractors and fewer subcontractors, and hence less competition. This can drive up wages, and it is not unusual for major projects to create local inflation when they are implemented.

We have seen that the costs of nuclear power plants and military weapon systems have increased faster than inflation. The increased complexity of these projects has not been balanced by learning that reduces costs. One can speculate that the same phenomenon may have contributed to cost growth in other types of unique and rarely implemented projects for which there are no prototypes. Computerized design and 3D-printing may be able to reverse this trend.

One can also speculate whether this is making unique projects and unique solutions more and more costly relative to standardized solutions and projects in the long term. The cost of constructing standard buildings such as apartment blocks has decreased relative to both consumer price and construction indices in the long term. Unique architect-designed buildings have become less common in the urban environment and serve mainly as a luxury for the rich. The cost difference between standardized and unique projects has widened.

It seems that cost estimates for some types of projects have under-estimated the long-term cost increases inherited in the technology. It is difficult to know the causes, but systemic failure might be involved when it comes to military weapon systems, as the increase above inflation has been going on for centuries and those involved have learnt to adapt their estimates to this long-term trend.

A common means of reducing project complexity is to apply parallel development and make subsystems modular and less tightly coupled, principles[36] long applied in R&D and complex software projects. Furthermore, whenever possible it is best to settle for less advanced and less complex solutions, and to seek and adapt standardized solutions. This does not solve the problem of above-inflation cost growth, but it does lessen its impact.

Cost Growth as a Consequence of a Trade-off Between Expected Cost, Risk, and Return

Assuming that estimators receive better information as a project comes closer to completion and assess and act on information in a rational manner, we have identified three categories of projects more likely to be affected by cost overrun, and differentiated these with regard to whether uncertainty can be resolved or not. We have also identified long-term relative price changes that may drive costs in long-term projects. All of these factors can be mitigated through learning and uncertainty reduction.

Making the same assumptions about the decision maker, we can also identify cases in which cost growth becomes a consequence of a deliberate trade-off between anticipated return, risk, and the cost of resolving uncertainty. Thus, we have projects:

- for which it ought to be possible to make a more accurate estimate of the final cost ex ante, but for which expected return is deemed so high and dependent on early operation that waiting for uncertainty to be resolved is considered unnecessary.
- for which it should be possible to estimate the final cost ex ante, but where it would be too expensive to do so considering the expected return from the project.
- for which the investor is willing to pay an extra fee to avoid the perils of cost overrun.
- where cost increase is due to a move towards economies of scale and/or scope to increase the expected return.

A good and illustrative example of the first type of project is the Trans-Alaska Pipeline System project mentioned in Chapter 3 – a highly politicized project with large delays and cost overruns, but still a very profitable one. Its estimated cost rose from $863 million in 1968 to $9,300 million including interest payments[37] – i.e. the project became 12 times more expensive than originally estimated. The cost increases were so huge that the General Accounting Office (GAO)[38] deemed it necessary to determine why. Scrutinizing the appraisal on which the decision to invest had been taken, they found that a great number of things necessary to construct and ship oil in the pipeline were missing. Project planners:

- Greatly underestimated the number of miles of elevated pipeline required. It anticipated about 240 miles of elevated pipeline; about 422 miles were constructed in the more expensive above-ground mode.
- Did not anticipate the need to construct a highway bridge across the Yukon River.
- Did not anticipate the need to construct a 361-mile gravel-surface road from the Yukon River to the Prudhoe oil field.
- Assumed a system and design having a much lower level of environmental standards than was subsequently required.
- Gave no consideration to the magnitude of the support structure, such as camps and airstrips, that would be required.
- Made no provision for the vapour recovery facilities at the Valdez terminal and at pump station number 1, which were required for maintaining air-quality standards.
- Made no provision for the sophisticated ballast water treatment system required to meet water-quality standards.
- Did not anticipate the sophisticated elevated pipeline system needed, in part, to meet seismic and thermal stipulations, but, rather, contemplated an above-ground system consisting of pipeline mounted on wooden piles or raised gravel.[39]

In retrospect, it may seem inexplicable that those who carried out the study could have forgotten that roads were needed to transport building materials to the construction site, and how the board could have accepted such an appraisal. This examination led GAO to formulate five conclusions to be applied to similar future projects, of which all but the first have to do with the degree of specification:

The following lessons from the oil pipeline apply to similar future projects.

- First and subsequent cost estimates should be viewed with scepticism.
- As much site-specific data as is economically practicable should be obtained.
- Technical and geological uncertainties should be thoroughly investigated.

- Government approval should be contingent on detailed planning for management control, including budgetary controls.
- The Alaska natural gas pipeline project's expenditures should have an ongoing government audit to protect the public interest.[40]

The responses provided by the Alyeska Pipeline Service Company, which owns the pipeline, to the critique from GAO was that it would not have been 'economically practical' to undertake more detailed planning for this unique project before making the decision to go-ahead. The chairman of the board said that it was neither realistic nor economically justified to develop a detailed financial control system prior to start-up. The organization had to be allowed to evolve as the project developed, and the requirement for accurate decision information had to be weighed against what was 'economically practical', meaning that the cost of waiting for more accurate cost estimates was higher than the loss caused by delaying the production of oil.

The cost of the pipeline – $9,300 million – should be compared to an estimated profit of $44–100 billion during its lifetime.[41] In addition, the state allowed the company to deduct most of the cost overrun. It was more important to the company to have this revenue stream than to further investigate a project it felt sure was profitable and right, and that was also important to the US government. Due to OPEC price increases, the embargo, and declining US oil production, it was very important to pump oil from the oilfield at Prudhoe Bay as soon as possible. Possible cost increases had lower priority. Project cost was grossly underestimated as it seemed unimportant to know the correct cost in order to reach a decision to undertake the project.

The second category of projects were projects for which it should be possible to estimate the final cost ex ante but for which it would be too expensive to do so considering the expected return from the project. Repairing and renovating existing plants is a good example of such projects. It can be very difficult to know exactly which parts have to be replaced and how much work has to be done without disassembling the old facility. Attempting to determine the total cost of a repair and renovation project more accurately can therefore only increase the cost without increasing revenues. Also, many replacement investments have such a character as they often also presuppose repair, rebuilding, and extension of an existing unit of a plant. Neither is it necessary to allow time for better costing when a bridge has collapsed or there has been a fire in a transformer. Such investments become forced investments necessary to keep an existing system running.

The third category of projects were projects for which the investor has paid an extra fee to avoid the perils of cost overrun. It is not uncommon either in industry or the public sector to use fixed cost contracts without compensation clauses to avoid cost overruns. The risk of cost overrun can in this and various other ways be transferred from the investor to the firms implementing the project, or to an insurance company. This makes sense as risks should be carried by the party that has the best ability to do so, but it always comes at a cost. Those taking on the risk will charge an extra fee for doing so. Transferring the risk to the party performing the work will put a pressure on cost, but there are also projects where this may have increase the final cost of the project. One cannot therefore assume that fixed cost contracts or other ways of transferring risk will always reduce cost, as the investor has to pay a fee to offload the risk.

The fourth category of projects were projects which increase due to the use of economies of scale and scope to improve expected return. Major cost increases can be due to a deliberate effort to make an investment more profitable by increasing its scale or scope. A good example of the former is the new Frövifors paper board plant mentioned earlier, where costs increased from SEK 300 million to SEK 881 million prior to construction, and one of the main reasons for this was a planned increase in capacity from 70,000 to 160,000 tonnes per year because the board decided to aim for economies of scale and build a much larger machine.

In theory, one could also imagine instances where the initial estimate was radically reduced because a smaller plant was built than originally planned. It is uncommon, but the option exists if the investment is divisible so that it can be implemented in stages.

In industries where economies of scale are possible, estimated costs commonly increase prior to the decision to invest because the size of the plant is increased to achieve better economies of scale, for instance through a reduction in the average cost per unit produced, and this is found in both the private[42] and public sectors.[43] It is a little like buying a new car or house. You start looking in a specific price range but seeing what you can get if you go for a slightly higher budget tends to encourage you to go with the more expensive option.

Reasons, Emotions, and Cost Estimation

Our model assumes that decision makers evaluate all alternatives simultaneously, rank these and choose the alternative that best maximizes the decision maker's utility, and then constantly iterate the process as new information becomes available. It assumes decision makers have access to accurate information and process all information simultaneously in a logical way, and is a variation of the economic man model of human decision making. It is a model widely used in economics, although all economists know such human decision makers do not exist in reality, principally because we never have all the information required and our ability to process the information that we do have is limited. We are not computers, but it may be that those of us who act more like the rational economic man are more successful at the gambling table, on the stock market, and in business. There is much that points at that.[44] Notwithstanding its shortcomings, the model has proved very useful, for instance when predicting outcomes for a large sample of individuals or firms, or when researching how a change in input affects output.

'Economic man' has his root in rationalist philosophers such as René Descartes and Gottfried Wilhelm von Leibniz. They distinguished between the body and the intellect and argued that it is only through the latter that the truth can be established, that the world can be understood through logical reasoning. This signified a break away from religious dogma and superstition, and paved the way for modern science, the enlightenment, industrialization, mass production, consumerism, and the society we live in today. It was as much a change in mentality as in technology.

Influenced by the debate of his time, Adam Smith arrived at a slightly different position to that of Descartes and Leibniz. In his *The Theory of Moral Sentiments*, first published in 1759, Smith argued that the intellect cannot be separated from the body or what he termed 'passions', and by that he meant human needs such as food, sex, and security, and emotions such as fear and anger. Passions controlled behaviour, but people could overcome this bias by viewing themselves from the perspective of an 'impartial spectator', a rational reasoning individual who could correct emotionally driven bad decisions:

But these, as well as all the other passions of human nature, seem proper and approved of, when the heart of every impartial spectator entirely sympathizes with them, when every indifferent by-stander entirely enters into and goes along with them.[45]

It is from him only that we learn the real littleness of ourselves, and of whatever relates to ourselves, and the natural misrepresentation of self-love can be corrected only by the eye of this impartial spectator.[46]

Important to this view was that passions preceded reasoning. The 'impartial spectator' used logical reasoning to evaluate, assess, and correct thoughts created by our physical and emotional impulses and instincts. But according to Smith, our actions are based on how we perceive others to judge our actions and how we judge the actions of others, and this guides our formation of what constitutes a rational decision. It might be a rational decision to us but need not be perceived so by others, or be the best for others. Our inability to see ourselves through the eyes of an impartial spectator[47] is, according to Smith, a weakness of mankind that only can be alleviated through rules of moral conduct.[48]

Masanao Toda[49] has described emotion-driven decisions as part of a decision-making system that is not inferior to our cognitive-analytical system, but rather is a rational decision-making system developed earlier in our evolution and adapted to a very basic need to respond quickly to threats and opportunities. Although the analytical system is very prominent in humans, neuroscience studies show that both emotional and analytical systems are involved in human decision making.[50] Emotions affect our analytical thinking, and our analytical thinking affects our emotions.

With this in mind, we can postulate that cost estimates are based not only on reasons but also, to some extent, on expectations based on a mixture of facts, hopes, and, not least, emotions. To be able to argue well for a particular budget, to ourselves and to others, we have to believe in it. Three cost estimation situations can be identified in which emotions become more important the less hard data there is available.

Firstly, hopes and emotions are more important in earlier estimates than in later ones, as the closer you come to approval the more pressure there is to prove the figures.

Secondly, hopes and emotions become less important the better the information and the more knowledge the organization has about the investment in question. Thus, when a cost estimate can be based on accounting data, such as is the case for replacement investment and the closure of a plant, there is not much room for alternative interpretations if one accepts the norm of economic rationality. Investments for expansion in existing markets are more uncertain as they require an estimate of the future market. Still more uncertain are investments in new markets and technologies where the organization lacks previous data and experience. In such cases, estimates and the decision to go ahead are based more on hope and a vision of the future founded on a mixture of emotions and reasons. The less we know about the true cost, the more important becomes our belief that a given investment is the right thing to do.

Thirdly, emotions become more important relative to reasons when projects become politicized, as, for instance, was the case with the nuclear waste programme described in Chapter 2. Disagreements over the design of the project and the future energy system can be traced back to disagreements on goals, the best way to achieve common goals, and the way data and events should be interpreted. Reasoned arguments become more difficult to agree on and emotions more important when actors do not share the same basic assumptions or when the proponents and opponents draw different conclusions from exactly the same information. We will discuss this and the differences between the logics of economics and politics in the next chapter.

Emotions have given rise to a large number of cognitive biases, i.e. systematic deviations from what could be expected if decisions were based solely on reasoning. We shall touch on three of these, namely optimistic bias, self-serving bias, and anchoring. A more thorough review of behavioural causes of cost overrun is found in Appendix C.

Optimistic bias. People making estimates are generally overoptimistic. This optimistic bias can be defined as a tendency to overestimate the probability of a certain outcome, a tendency which is often accompanied by an inability to interpret and accept new, contradicting information and modify the original estimate accordingly. This observation is not new. Adam Smith in his *An Inquiry into The Nature and Causes of the Wealth of Nations* in 1776 observed that:

[t]he chance of gain is by every man more or less over-valued, and the chance of loss is by most men under-valued, and by scarce any man, who is in tolerable health and spirits, valued more than it is worth.[51]

He exemplified the tendency to undervalue losses with 'the very moderate profit of insurers'[52] and the tendency to overvalue gains by lottery:

That the chance of gain is naturally over-valued, we may learn from the universal success of lotteries. The world neither ever saw, nor ever will see, a perfectly fair lottery; or one in which the whole gain compensated for the whole loss; because the undertaker could make nothing by it.[53]

The last is of course correct, but such overoptimism has also been confirmed in a number of different types of decisions which we normally do not see as lotteries, such as economic forecasts, stock market estimates, starting a new firm, or investing in an existing company. There are numerous studies confirming decision makers as being overoptimistic,[54] be it investors,[55] CEOs,[56] consumers,[57] entrepreneurs,[58] or project managers.[59]

Decision makers tend to have more confidence in their own judgement than they have reason to, and there are also studies[60] showing that less knowledgeable people have more confidence in their own abilities than more knowledgeable people. Their incompetence seems to make them overoptimistic, or, as Charles Darwin put it, 'ignorance more frequently begets confidence than does knowledge'[61]. The importance of this overoptimism is uncertain, as there is evidence that management learns which individuals are overoptimistic and compensates for this when they assess investment requests.[62]

Research has also shown that entrepreneurs are more optimistic than managers, and Americans and Chinese more optimistic than Japanese. Optimistic bias differs by personality and culture, and is not specific to human beings: mammals and birds have also been found to be over-optimistic. Optimism has therefore been explained as a consequence of natural selection,[63] and as a prerequisite for the development of human civilization. Those that have underestimated future work, problems, and dangers have fared better than those who have held more realistic images of the future.

Self-serving bias. Another well-established bias which may contribute to cost overrun and growth is self-serving bias. In his *The Theory of Moral Sentiments*, Adam Smith writes:

So partial are the views of mankind with regard to the propriety of their own conduct, both at the time of action and after it; and so difficult is it for them to view it in the light in which any indifferent spectator would consider it. But if it was by a peculiar faculty, such as the moral sense is supposed to be, that they judged of their own conduct, if they were endued with a particular power of perception, which distinguished the beauty or deformity of passions and affections; as their own passions would be more immediately exposed to the view of this faculty, it would judge with more accuracy concerning them, than concerning those of other men, of which it had only a more distant prospect.

This self-deceit, this fatal weakness of mankind, is the source of half the disorders of human life. If we saw ourselves in the light in which others see us, or in which they would see us if they knew all, a reformation would generally be unavoidable. We could not otherwise endure the sight.[64]

This self-deceit is termed 'self-serving bias' in modern psychology. It can be defined as a distortion of the cognitive process in order to maintain and enhance self-esteem.[65] We absorb positive feedback and reject negative feedback, forget past failures and errors, and credit ourselves for the success and achievements of those we work and associate ourselves with, all to enhance our self-esteem.

Support for the concept of self-serving bias is very strong. A meta-analysis[66] based on 266 studies of self-serving bias found it to be high in Western and Chinese cultures, unnoticeable in Japanese culture, and moderate in Indian culture. People tend to attribute positive outcomes to themselves and negative outcomes to others or unforeseeable events. They also tend to have a positively distorted image of their own role and performance. This self-serving bias is associated with greater perceived happiness, lower incidence of depression, better problem solving, a stronger immune system, and lower mortality, and is more pronounced during childhood and after the age of 55.

Self-serving bias thrives in ambiguity as it is easier to maintain alternative views when there is room for alternative interpretations. The less we know about the true cost, the more important our belief that a given investment is the right thing to do becomes, which in turn increases the importance of our self-serving bias in justifying decisions made. Ventures in new areas are examples of projects more often based on beliefs in a vision than hard data.

Anchoring. The third bias we need to cover in this section is anchoring,[67] which is when later pieces of information are anchored in earlier information. Once an estimate has been presented, it then serves as a point of departure for future estimates, and individuals tend to not only attach more belief to this first estimate than they have reason to, but also to downplay new information that conflicts with it.

This phenomenon is well known from budgeting. Most budgets are just last year's budget updated with incremental changes. The same weather as last year, perhaps a little colder or warmer, but no perfect storm. Similarly, the level of the first offer in a negotiation affects the final level agreed on. The first offer affects the range of possible counteroffers, and where the deal will end. Property buyers decide how much they can pay based on prices paid previously for similar properties. Later project cost estimates are related to the first estimate, not least because estimators can be hesitant to deviate too much from earlier estimates made by themselves and others. Anchoring estimates on competitors' estimates or historical data are two strategies for a forecaster to avoid the risk of being criticized if the forecast turns out to be wrong.

Bounded rationality and the reduction of uncertainty. The model we developed in this chapter assumed that the problem and the solution was information. Our estimator and decision maker resolved dynamic economic-technical uncertainty as the project proceeded and new and better information became available. In an implementation project, most of the uncertainty could be resolved prior to the final decision to invest; for a development project, uncertainty would not be resolved until after the project had been implemented. The model dealt with how to move from the lower-right to the lower-left box in Figure 4.1. We also showed that cost overrun could be caused by uncertainty outside the control of the organization which could not be reduced: so-called static uncertainty.

	Economic-technical certainty	Economic-technical uncertainty
Bounded rationality	Problem: Limited information and cognitive ability to maximize shareholder value Solution: Evaluate and choose a satisfactory alternative	Problem: Lack of information and cognitive ability creates space for alternative interpretations Solution: Resolve uncertainty to a manageable level
Economic man	Problem: Maximize shareholder value Solution: Evaluate and choose the best alternative	Problem: Lack of information Solution: Re-evaluate the alternatives when better information becomes available

Figure 4.1 Economic man versus bounded rationality

In this last section of the chapter we relaxed the rationality assumption made in the model and assumed that estimators and decision makers have limited information, cognitive ability, and time to process information, and consider and choose between a limited number of alternatives that satisfy their goals. This is a much more realistic model of individual choice and is termed 'bounded rationality'. The problem becomes the limitations of the decision maker and the fact that the eventual solution depends on access to information and the ability to process information. High uncertainty, lack of information, and information that is open to multiple interpretations creates voids in which rationality becomes bounded. The differences between these models are illustrated in Figure 4.1.

Bounded rationality is attributed to Herbert Simon, the 1978 winner of the Sveriges Riksbank Prize in Economic Sciences in Memory of Alfred Nobel. It emerged from an effort to create a more realistic model of human decision-making behaviour and has gradually developed since Simon published his book *Administrative Behavior*[68] in 1947. Bounded rationality integrates economics and psychology, and today it is an integrated part of economics. Its influence was further recognized when psychologist Daniel Kahneman,[69] who has studied behavioural biases and introduced the notion of anchoring, in 2002 received the same prize in economic sciences.

We know that bounded rationality offers a much better description of the way humans behave. Most decision makers are overoptimistic and overconfident, mourn monetary losses more than they celebrate equally large gains, and have a higher preference for immediate return relative to future return than is rational. However, this does not alter the basic principles of uncertainty reduction, nor does it eliminate the risk of cost overrun.

5   The Logic of Economics Versus the Logic of Politics

Politics, Economics, and the Media

This chapter will deal with the difference between the logic of economics and the logic of politics, and how corporations and society control the accuracy and plausibility of cost estimates. Furthermore, we will add political uncertainty to our model from the previous chapter and analyse the way economic-technical and political uncertainty can be resolved. Starting with the differences between the logics of economics and politics, some of the more important aspects are summarized in Table 5.1.

Politics is a practice based on ideology.[1] An ideology can broadly be said to be a set of ideas of how society should be organized and should work, and the way to achieve this ideal society. It is a system of ideas about how things ought to be and are done, concerning the distribution and balance of power and resources, and the control of force. The execution of politics is a practice based on an ideology. It is not a science based on rational reasoning like natural sciences or economics, although it has sometimes been claimed that economics becomes an ideology when it is applied normatively.

The knowledge theory of economics is based on an assumption of rationality or bounded rationality, while politics deals more with emotions and especially with collective emotions.[2] Emotions are important to the formation of collective action because they help to overcome uncertainty and lack of shared meaning. Politicians have to convince others of their ideology to be elected, and they have to compromise and form coalitions to have their ideology and interests implemented. In principle it is not much different in meritocracies or for dictators, where those in power do not have to risk their office in general elections, but do have to maintain support to avoid opposition and unrest. To influence others in communicating images that evoke positive responses and emotions in the receiver becomes an important means of mobilizing support for decisions and collective action. It is not so important what the sender says, but rather how this is perceived by the receiver.

Economists and politicians play different roles. The economist is an expert in economic sciences; the politician is a representative who has

Table 5.1 *Key differences between the logics of economics and politics*

	Economics	Politics
Knowledge interest	Science	A practice based on an ideology
Knowledge theory	Rationality or bounded rationality	Emotions and reasons
Decision maker's role	Expert	Representatives are given authority to execute power
Core area of influence is where	Market exchange dominates	Redistribution dominates
Decision maker's goal	Economic efficiency	A resource allocation aligned to party ideology and the norms and values voters
Decision making means	Problem solving through information processing	Problem solving through conflict resolution and compromises

been given authority to execute power. Karl Polanyi identified three principle modes of exchange:[3] reciprocity, redistribution, and market exchange. Reciprocity stands for the exchange of goods and services between individuals that are hierarchically related to each other, and not conducted via the market – for instance, a gift that is reciprocated at a later date. Redistribution stands for a movement of resources, e.g. taxes and fees, towards a centre where somebody or some institution has the authority and power to reallocate those resources out from the centre. Economic forces rule where there is a market, and politics reigns where goods and services are financed by taxes and fees. This leads to a natural division of influence, although it is disputed as the political sphere wants to regulate the market and the market sometimes shows its power by forcing the political sphere to adapt economic measures dictated by the market. These principles of resource allocation are superimposed on each other, making the border between the logic of economics and that of politics blurred and drifting.

In 1936, Harold D. Lasswell published a book with the informative title *Politics: Who Gets What, When, How.*[4] Although politics once dealt mostly with power, relationships with other powers, handling disputes, and maintaining order, today politics, or at least many politicians, deal primarily with who gets what, when, and how, i.e. allocation of power and resource. It is easy to see in action – just measure how much time politicians devote to talking about how they want to allocate resources to various needs versus talking about creating resources to allocate. Creating resources has mainly been entrusted to private industry and entrepreneurs. Centrally planned economies have tried to take on that role but have not been able to meet consumers' wants, and industrial politics has often not achieved its stated goals. Politics tends to focus on allocating resources in a way that is perceived as fair and politicians tend to align allocation with their ideology.

Economics offers tools for the allocation of public resources in the form of, e.g. cost–benefit analysis, but its influence has been limited even when such appraisals have been mandatory, one reason being that the use of such economic tools can be seen as an intrusion into the political realm of influence. Economists use scientific methods to achieve their goals; politicians have to influence others, handle conflicting goals, and reach compromises to form the coalitions necessary to have some of their stated goals implemented. It is another kind of game.

Limited companies have to act in a rational manner to maintain their share price. To be elected, politicians have to consider not only economic aspects, but also the opinions and emotions of their voters. Voters legitimize their political representatives through elections and politicians have to legitimize their choices and actions by aligning these to the norms and values of their voters and society at large. These are thus two partly different logics: one which strives towards the norms of economic efficiency, and one where resource allocation has to be legitimized to the norms of voters, the party, and society. Some projects and some decisions affecting project cost estimates are governed by economic efficiency, others by ideology and perceived obvious needs, where legitimization and emotions play a vital role. The border between these two spheres of influence can sometimes be blurred and is constantly moving.

An example illustrating how this border can move is the widespread outsourcing of public services, which has been growing since the early 1980s. Many services previously performed by public sector employees are today purchased from private firms by the public sector or by those individuals who are served. An argument for this has been that the private sector can perform many services in a more economically efficient way, partly due to economies of scale, and partly due to the fact that private firms do not have to align their processes and functions with the norms that govern activities in the political sector in the same way that a public provider has to. In the hope of reducing costs, the political sector has handed over much of the influence on the way public sector service is performed. However, in some areas and parts of the world, the border has moved the other way. One example of this is public transport in Stockholm.

An underground metro line is more expensive to construct than a surface tram line, and a tram line more expensive than a bus route, but a metro can still be justified if there are enough passengers. Only half as many metro cars will be needed if it can travel underground twice as fast on average as a tram line above ground. The number of stops and their duration affect the average speed, which, together with the top load and passenger-packing density, determines the number of cars needed. Travel flows and their sizes at different times of the day, as well as expected future travel flows, and the effects of different pricing policies, can be estimated. There are also other factors to consider, but to determine if a bus, tram, or metro is needed, and where to draw lines and place stops, is an optimization problem that the logic of economics suggests can be solved with operational research and simulations, with rational reasoning.

But this is not the way the future public transport system in Stockholm is being developed today. Political parties have crossed the boundary and promised new tram and metro lines to match their ideology and win votes. If they form a strong enough coalition for their proposal, it then goes to planners to plan its implementation and estimate the cost, so what once was an issue for planners has become a political issue.

The political sector has advanced its position in many areas. One argument for this is the perceived need to have political decisions implemented faster, so as to counteract civil administrators who tend to do as they have always done regardless of who is in power. Public sector administrators are supposed to act according to their supposedly rational professional norms, and also to implement political decisions, while politicians are driven by an ideology and a vision of the future.

In small municipalities where bureaucrats and politicians work closely together, pragmatism often prevails and ideological differences are played down. Under these circumstances, an individual politician can become more important than the party and alliances can be formed between parties that would not cooperate at the national level. Ideology becomes much more important at the national level and in major cities. It moves the border delineating which decisions should be based on the bureaucrats' knowledge and experience and which should be based on the vision of the political majority.

The change to the logic of politics came early in the energy sector. Proposals for the Swedish energy sector had long been developed by energy experts and approved by parliament without much debate, but as environmental issues entered the political agenda in the late 1960s, and the 1970s oil crises caused oil and gasoline shortages and rationing, things began to change. Whether oil, gas, coal, nuclear, bio, sun, or geothermal energy should be supported became an issue governed by the logic of politics. To control the direction of investment according to this logic, taxes, fees, and subsidies were approved to such an extent that nobody today can tell what the market mix would look like without taxes and subsidies. What was once an issue for government bureaucrats and business managers has become an issue for politicians guided by their ideologies and the logic of politics. The border has been moved.

The Swedish nuclear waste programme described in Chapter 2 demonstrates this. The estimated cost of the nuclear waste programme increased from approximately SEK 89 billion SEK in 1982 to SEK 130 million in 2013 in constant money value as of January 2014, or by 46 per cent – an alarming cost growth. But if we look more closely at the figures, we can see that the total cost per tonne of spent uranium fuel has decreased by 15 per cent over the same period. The life of the reactors, and, consequently, how much fuel they will use, along with the new principles applied to calculate the costs, are political decisions. Most, if not all, of the cost increase can be explained by political decisions determining the input in these cost estimates. In this case, the logic of politics directly influences the way cost is estimated.

The political sphere can choose how to govern a state-owned energy company. It can limit political influence to the appointment of the board and allow the company to allocate funds the way it finds best, or it can, as is the case in some countries, approve major investments in the country's parliament. Even if Swedish state-owned companies have been run much like private firms, some political parties have wanted to force the state-owned energy company Vattenfall to invest in renewable energies such as wind and solar, despite company management deeming such investments unprofitable. Here, political interests are aiming to use public ownership to change society, demonstrating that the results of political elections and coalitions can move the border between the logics of economics and politics and make it unclear.

Communicating images that evoke positive responses and emotions in the receiver is an important way of influencing others and mobilizing support for decisions and collective action. This makes the media a key player in politics.

In the previous chapter, we concluded that decisions are based to a varying degree on a mixture of reasons and emotions. Important to politics is the way these reasons and emotions can be used to form collectively held images and emotions. Politicians reach their voters and communicate their message through the media, but in doing so, they have to adopt to the logic of the media. They have to show sensitivity to the views of voters and journalists, and also adapt their message to the current dominant agendas in the media. As emotions are powerful mediators of messages, especially on issues where the receiver lacks knowledge and information, this makes it of the utmost importance to be able to set the agenda and dominate the media debate. Unfortunately, this means emotions often become more important than reasons. How a message is perceived by the receiver becomes more important than what is said, and politics can become highly emotional. Some would claim that politics is emotions, or emotions and morality.

It is generally assumed that the media today is commercialized and the selection and presentation of news is governed by what sells newspapers and attracts viewers. However, media also drives politics. Politicians have to adjust their message to fit the rules of mass media, and, as a result, the political message is refined through an interaction between politicians and the media. This tighter connection between media and politics has led to politicians becoming more dependent on the media to get their message across to voters and has also given the media political influence. The media, through its influence when it comes to setting the agenda in the political debate and deciding the content of politicians' messages, has become a co-producer of politics. Some researchers[5] term this the 'mediatization' of politics.

Journalists ask party representatives what transport infrastructure they want to see constructed, and which type of energy they want to invest in, and then, by publishing the answers, can claim to be providing a service to voters who do not know which party they should vote for. However, these statements can easily be taken as election promises, especially when the media refer to them at the next election. The logic supposes that politicians first present their choices, whereafter voters cast their vote, and a government is formed that directs civil servants to implement the political promises of the winning party or coalition. But this seemingly democratic process can lead to less economically efficient decisions for the voters. It secures acceptance but not necessarily quality of decision making. That can be one of several reasons for privatization, i.e. moving an issue outside the sphere of politics.

It has become increasingly important for politicians and business leaders to know how to handle reporters and express themselves in front of microphones and cameras. CEOs are given media training and may be replaced if they cannot talk the language of financial analysts and give a good impression in front of a camera. For politicians, it is paramount to be good at communicating through the media. For example, when a disabled lady complained that a bus stop outside her home in Gothenburg had been moved, a local radio reporter asked the chairman of the board of the local public transport company, a leading politician, why he had moved it. The surprised politician promised to find out who was responsible for this, in a tone that implied some administrator had made a mistake. He probably did not have a clue about why this bus stop, completely unknown to him and one of several hundreds in the city, had been moved, but felt he could not say so as he was supposed to be in command.

The media market is changing. Today it comprises everything from newspapers and books, which allow their readers time to reflect on the message and therefore are better suited for communicating reasons, to television, music, film, and performances, where success relies on instant reactions, i.e. emotions, and blogs and social media such as Facebook and Twitter. One only needs to follow a few Twitter conversations to realize that the short messages that it allows are more often an expression of emotions than reasons.

Media is a heterogeneous industry. What sells is of course important, but there are also journals, television channels, and printed and Internet newspapers in which the content is determined by the norms and values of the owner, the journalists producing the content, or the users. This fragmentation has been accelerated by the new media that the Internet has created. There is now such a variety of media channels that politicians do not necessarily have to slavishly play the game that major mass media channels play to legitimize their actions. In the new media landscape, politicians of all kinds of ideologies can always find a channel through which to reach their supporters. The media, and thereby politics, have become personalized, but not more firmly based on reasons, only more fragmented as a result.

Resource Allocation in Major Companies Versus the Public Sector

In the previous chapter, we briefly described resource allocation and control systems in major corporations. Ideas for new investments usually originate at the business level as that is where the company meets the market. It is also at the business level that investment projects are developed and cost estimates are made. Top management decides the rules of the capital budgeting game and the volume and direction of investments, and can also drive strategic initiatives. Middle managers act as linking-pins between top management wants and business-level needs. Economic-technical choices are made at the business level while finance is handled on group level.

The same processes also exist in the public sector. Politicians and top civil servants decide the direction of investments and set the rules of the game. There is a process by which the technical and economic features of the investment are determined, and a process by which funding is requested and approved. Also, most public sector investments are initiated by a need; for instance, demographic studies might show that more schools are needed, a new road might be needed or an existing road repaired, a power plant or water treatment plant might have to be renovated or replaced. Investment ideas usually originate from below, but can also be the result of an electoral pledge, which might be behind a political party's support for investments in certain areas such as green technology, child care, or better social services, or new laws and standards for the services the public sector supplies. Politicians, interacting with top civil servants, decide the rules of the game, and public sector administrators coordinate the needs with the wants of politicians.

However similar, there is one important difference and that is that a larger proportion of investment ideas in the political sphere are initiated by external actors. Politicians, political parties, and stakeholder groups active in the political debate push for investments supporting their interests. This tends to generate investment projects that meet an urgent need, have backing from strong stakeholders, and can be legitimized as high priority.[6] Investments may also be initiated by new laws, regulations, and standards. A new service to be offered by the public sector automatically generates investments. So do, for instance, a recommendation to decrease the number of students in classes, better lighting or lower levels of noise in public spaces, and making public offices more accessible for disabled persons. A large part of all public investment made by local government is in fact initiated by political decisions at the national level, new laws and regulations, and changing standards. These forced investments tie up a substantial part of economic growth. Such decisions and local initiatives set the context of the local capital budgeting process.

A public project has to attract support from a political majority, which often means that it has to be modified to be legitimized. This also means that the defining and funding processes have to develop in interaction, and are an inevitable consequence not only of a democratic multiparty system, but also of the fact that the public sector has to cater for the needs of various groups in society. Unlike a company, the public sector cannot choose to focus on a specific, relatively homogeneous customer group and ignore those that do not like the services the company offers.

Nevertheless, there are similarities as well as differences between companies and the public sector, and some of the more important of these are summed up in Table 5.2.[7] The comparisons revolve around the types of investments made by major corporations and the public sector, the pre-approval control system, the transparency of internal processes to external stakeholders, and the allocation of responsibility, goals, and preconditions for learning. We will discuss them in due course.

Type of projects. Corporate boards and managers know that their company cannot do everything. To show a high return on investment, their company has to be one of the best at what they do. They have to

Table 5.2 *Differences between investments and investment processes in major companies and the public sector*

	Major companies	The public sector
Type of projects	Within approved strategies	All types of projects
Goals	One goal based on the logic of economics dominates	Multiple goals
Acceptance versus quality	Quality is emphasized by the logic of economics	The logic of politics does not put an emphasize on quality
Pre-approval control	Well developed	Less well developed
Transparency	Low transparency especially prior to the decision to invest	High transparency due to freedom of information acts and the political nature of projects
Accountability	Well developed	Less well developed
Project abandonment	Not all projects are implemented	Projects once started are seldom stopped
Preconditions for learning	Usually good when projects are within existing strategies	Low when prior experiences do not exist

focus their resources on a limited number of activities to be able to make money in the sectors where they compete. Investments, therefore, have to be not only demonstrably profitable, but also in line with approved strategies. Companies are very keen on sticking to their business strategy.

This means that companies generally only invest in areas where they have experience and therefore can assess proposed investments based on experience from past investments. The importance of this is seen when companies invest in new areas, new technologies, or new markets where they lack previous experience. When this is the case, it is not always certain that their management control system can supply adequate feedback to assess the investment correctly. Such investments are therefore sometimes taken outside the formal investment request process, and, although more resources often are spent on assessing such projects, time and cost overruns are generally larger than for projects in more familiar territory.

It is very different in the public sector. New projects are initiated and implemented to meet societal needs. The lack of experience in a particular area is not an argument to refrain from investing, and so the public sector regularly invests in projects for which they have little background knowledge. We should remember that cost overrun is generally small for public sector housing projects, because these are familiar and common. It is when the public sector builds a new town hall, sports complex, opera house, etc., that we see large overruns, because these are unique projects.

This diversity also makes it more difficult to accumulate experiences and create routines for reviewing new investments.

Companies invest in machines and production equipment, markets and marketing, personnel, and R&D. The public sector invests in both tangible investments such as roads and buildings, and intangible investments such as education and research. The share of investment in production has decreased over the last 50 years. Statistic Sweden estimates that, since the mid-1980s, Swedish industry has typically invested about one-third in each of production, markets, and R&D. The figures differ a lot between industries, but many industries invest more in new markets and marketing than they do in fixed investments, though the latter is the only type of investment that is treated as an investment in their accounting. Intangible investments dominate in many industries, and also in many parts of the public sector.

One obstacle with intangible investments is specifying the cost and outcome in financial terms. Funds for investments in markets and personnel are generally allocated as a budget frame. The departments of marketing and personnel are then free to allocate funds within their area and the limits of the budget. Investment appraisals and requests for individual investments are generally only made for investments in new production equipment which, if representing major investments, can include investments in marketing and personnel, and for acquisitions. So, when we talk about cost overrun, we usually talk about investment in tangible assets. This does not mean that cost overrun is more severe for tangible than intangible investments. On the contrary, cost overrun is probably more common for intangible investments as the costs and revenues are more difficult to measure. However, a marketing campaign, for instance, can be segmented and ended when funds have been used up, even though its goals – difficult to quantify at the best of times – might not have been achieved.

Goals. Joint stock companies have a clear goal against which investment proposals can be evaluated; investments should only be approved if they can be expected to improve the value of the firm, i.e. yield a positive net present value. Shareholder value maximization has been rightly criticized for focusing on the outcome and not what creates value. Likewise, it is true that a firm also has to satisfy stakeholders other than owners, and that investments have to be aligned with strategy and finance, and competent personnel have to be available, but it gives a point of reference against which investments and other activities can be evaluated.

It is very different in the public sector. Politicians and political parties represent different interests, which they are mandated to pursue through election. It is their role to promote and influence the design of public projects so as to bring them in line with the political ideas they represent and the interests of their voters. Public projects can have multiple goals because they need to satisfy a coalition of interests and stakeholders. Projects may have to be adjusted and redesigned to satisfy stakeholders who have a say in approval, which can itself drive cost, and can continue to drive cost after the decision to invest if negotiations continue and result in changes in the project. This constant negotiation and goal ambiguity is far less common in companies. There may be groups of owners and managers favouring different strategies and investments, but it is the vision and image of those in power that sets the scene. Joint stock companies are not democracies. In fact, reducing goal ambiguity can be one reason for privatizing public activities.

One way of creating agreement on a project or course of action is to redefine the goal as something that all can agree on, or find difficult to reject. It can be a project promoting social inclusion or a fossil-free city, saves lives or reduce the risk of accidents.

President Kennedy used much the same tactics when he responded to the Soviet lead in the space race in a speech to Congress in 1961, stating the goal to put a man on the Moon:

Finally, if we are to win the battle that is now going on around the world between freedom and tyranny, the dramatic achievements in space which occurred in recent weeks should have made clear to us all, as did the Sputnik in 1957, the impact of this adventure on the minds of men everywhere, who are attempting to make a determination of which road they should take. . . .

Now it is time to take longer strides – time for a great new American enterprise – time for this nation to take a clearly leading role in space achievement, which in many ways may hold the key to our future on Earth.

. . . I believe that this nation should commit itself to achieving the goal, before this decade is out, of landing a man on the Moon and returning him safely to the Earth. No single space project in this period will be more impressive to mankind, or more important in the long-range exploration of space; and none will be so difficult or expensive to accomplish.[8]

Creating a strong, shared vision makes it possible to overcome disagreements on such details as how to best achieve the vision. The ability to formulate and make others believe in their vision is a trademark of great leaders. They can sell a project and create action by painting a future people want, often glossing over negative consequences and the obstacles that have to be overcome to realize the vision. A characteristic trait in such grand political visions is that they create hope for a better life, or a greater meaning to life, by promising something that will leave an imprint long after we voters are dead. The project may strengthen the perception of a nation[9] or city, or renew and revitalize a region in decline.

Companies are not totally immune to this urge to attach hopes to vague visions. Entrepreneurs share the ability of great leaders to formulate and make others believe in a vision, ignoring the details and negative consequences of the same vision. We can see this[10] when a company's core business and future is threatened, because under these circumstances there is a tendency to accept badly thought-out suggestions promising a great future from entrepreneurs who had previously gone unheard.

This lack of clarity about goals can even sometimes lead to increasing cost being perceived as something positive, as a sign that a project has been successful. The Swedish National Audit Office[11] found several examples of this in a review of 13 public reforms. Some of these reforms had experienced major cost growth. One of them was state support provided to promote publication of smaller daily newspapers, to enable more voices to be heard and encourage competition in the daily newspaper market. In 1971, this reform was estimated to cost SEK 35 million a year; 10 years later, SEK 288 million was paid out yearly to support newspapers. The Audit Office concluded:

A rapid increase in cost may indeed suggest that a reform is inefficient, over-administrated, etc. . . . But it is also possible that the rapid cost growth is inextricably linked with the positive purposes of the reform. It becomes a manifestation of the fact that the reform has been successful. . . .

If the answer to the question as to why the cost has been high and why these reforms have become more expensive than originally anticipated is to be summarized in conclusions, the first must be: The reforms have been costly because great efforts have been made to achieve important societal goals. . . .

The fact that the cost of the reform has been high is thus in many cases directly linked to the fact that a growing number of individuals and companies – albeit in a manner unforeseen – benefitted from various types of social benefits, with corresponding benefits to recipients.[12] [author's translation]

Political reforms often have multiple goals, or goals which are difficult to measure. This makes it easier for them to attract the broad support that is needed if they are to be implemented, but it also makes it more difficult to evaluate to what extent they have achieved their goals.

When the political sector formulates economic policy, there is more likely to be a set of goals than a single goal, such as full employment, price stability, a satisfactory rate of economic growth, free trade, fair distribution of income, efficient allocation of resources, etc. – goals that are all well worth pursuing, but which are partly contradictory. For instance, an extreme redistribution of income can have a negative effect on economic growth, and full employment can impact price stability. Political parties thus have to make trade-offs between such goals. They generally agree on the overarching goal of improving the welfare of all voters, but they often have very different views of how that might be achieved. Take, for instance, the energy sector, where all parties agree on the need for society to have access to cheap and clean energy, but very different views on which sources of energy – oil, coal, nuclear, wind, or sun – will best serve these goals. The disagreement is often more about consequences than goals when environmental issues are involved. There are many different roads heading towards the same final destination.

Acceptance versus quality. All projects have to attract funding. A good idea is not enough. But to gain the necessary support, projects often have to be modified. The proposer of the project has to adjust the idea he or she is selling to get the project approved, which means that the processes of definition and funding are intertwined, constantly present, and develop through interaction and iteration. The funding process is not confined to the formal investment request process, and support for the project and commitments must be built up gradually from the start of the definition process.

Norman Maier[13] drew our attention to the fact that effective decisions have to have both quality and acceptance. By quality, he meant that the decision has to be based on facts and logical reasoning. Acceptance has to do with how those executing the decision feel about it, and that is based on emotions. Effective decisions have to satisfy both reasons and emotions.

It is not enough to have developed an excellent project proposal based on reasons; the project also has to gain acceptance. This is generally less of a problem in the private than in the public sector. The former has, as pointed out earlier, a goal built on the logic of economics against which investments can be evaluated. It is very different in the public sector, where politicians and political parties are supposed to represent different interests. They often agree on general goals such as economic growth, better health care, and lower environmental pollution, but often disagree on the best way to achieve these goals. They are in fact supposed to disagree, as they represent different interests and ideologies, but they still have to reach a decision, and that is done by forming proposals that can gain sufficient support from a majority to reach a decision. Formulating goals that will gain acceptance becomes very important in the political decision-making process. The nuclear waste programme presented in Chapter 2 constitutes a good example.

Decision processes in companies that operate in multiple product sectors can also be politicized. There are often competing views of what is best in major companies, but companies are no democracies. Top management decides. That makes it possible to act faster. It takes longer to come to a decision in the public sector when conflicting interests have to come to an agreement.

Public sector projects have to handle multiple logics competing for influence. One way of reducing possible conflicts that might delay the process is to decouple problematic issues and pursue these in parallel. In a study of the location of a new power plant in Stockholm, Bengt Jacobsson[14] identified three such processes. One process was driven by engineers in the energy company in which technical and economic consequences were analysed. Another process was around energy policy, and was driven by actors from government departments, company top management, and councillors. A third process, environmental policy, was driven by politicians and managers.

This ambiguity can in fact be an asset when forming a coalition to get a decision accepted. A foolproof way to fail in a negotiating process is to present a finished proposal to which other parties can only say yes or no. The other party must be able to show they obtained something by supporting a deal, and this is recognized through a change in the project proposal. Therefore, the proposal needs to be vague, not too detailed and open to alternative interpretations. To reduce all economic-technical uncertainty prior to the formation of a coalition would not only be costly, but would also make it more difficult, perhaps even impossible, to develop a project that will be acceptable to the political majority. Ambiguity is an asset in political negotiations.

Pre-approval control. Management accountants distinguish between pre-approval control, i.e. the control of investment prior to a final decision to invest, monitoring of approved investments, and following up of investments that have been implemented, sometimes a year or two after the new investment has come into full operation. It is the pre-approval control that is of special interest when comparing major corporations with the public sector.

Major companies have well-developed pre-approval control systems. They have, as described earlier, written rules for authorization and control of capital expenditure and, where the volume of investments is substantial, an investment manual as a part of their financial manual specifying the design of the capital expenditure process, the way investments should be appraised and reviewed, as well as who is responsible for what.

Organizations such as publicly owned power companies also have written capital budgeting manuals and well-developed pre-approval control systems, so essentially there is no difference between a privately or publicly owned power company. However, for society generally, there is no comparable equivalent to pre-approval control. There are no authorities that scrutinize requests for public investments in the same way as in companies. As there are no major differences between private and public companies in the same business, one can assume the lack of pre-approval scrutiny has to do with the context – of more diverse investments, goals, and actors. There is of course a comptroller general, who may conduct excellent reviews of projects that have been implemented, and of planning and control procedures, but there is no function that conducts pre-approval control of individual investment proposals.

Many public authorities have carried out cost–benefit analyses[15] to evaluate and rank their investment requests since the 1960s, and in 1981 President Ronald Reagan signed an Administration and Executive Order making cost–benefit analysis mandatory in federal agencies for projects exceeding $100 million a year, with some exceptions. This action might have contributed to a better allocation of resources, but it has not stopped cost overrun or growth; one reason for this may be that the requirement to supply such an analysis is not accompanied by a proper pre-approval review system that can supply feedback based on accumulated knowledge from earlier projects and reviews. It is probably easier to agree on conducting an analysis than to ensure that it is thoroughly scrutinized by an independent control system, as that would move the investment decision from the logic of politics to economics and thereby threaten to stop many desired projects.

The review system specifies who is responsible for what in the review and implementation processes. This ensures that no major investments are implemented before they have been so thoroughly examined that those who approve funding can feel reasonably certain that the investment is right. This forces the business level to prove that they have done their homework before they are given the go-ahead. Importantly, the feedback they receive enhances the learning of all involved. It forces those advocating the project to learn more about the investment, and those at higher levels to learn more about what is going on in the business. It also creates commitment to achieve what is promised.

One should also observe that a pre-approval control system works best with routine investments (decisions about types of investments of which the organization has previous experience). For non-routine decisions, multiple goals and goal ambiguity make formal pre-approval control less reliable. Non-routine decisions are more difficult to give proper feedback on, and multiple and ambiguous and contested goals need to be reviewed relative to each goal. Pre-approval control is, however, no less important for investments in new areas, but more difficult to perform for the diverse kinds of investments with multiple goals that are implemented in the public sector.

Transparency. Politics (as we use the term in this chapter) is the art of government. It involves influencing others to ensure that decisions are approved and implemented, and staying in power long enough to be able to do so. The control of political power rests on a constitution and trust. An important means of control to create this trust between the public and politicians is transparency. Most countries have some form of 'Freedom of Information' legislation which gives the public access to certain administrative documents and information, and thus a chance to assess the work of their politicians and their administration. Transparency offers the media and voters an opportunity to control their political leaders and the public sector, but it is not a means without shortcomings.[16]

Firstly, plans, cost estimates, and budgets will be made available for those putting in tenders. They can adjust the level of their offer to what the procurer is willing to pay. Moreover, the fact that earlier plans and estimates are public and the procurement process follows a strict protocol makes it difficult for the buyer to lower the price by acting quickly on opportunities that appear. The buyer's budget frame is known and the buyer has little chance to act, which undermines the procurer's position relative to those tendering offers. This can place public procurer and politicians in a more difficult procurement situation than private firms, and is one reason why the public sector has placed certain services in publicly own companies. Issues are moved away from transparency and to a setting where the logic of economics has more influence.

Secondly, since the media sees its role as monitoring and uncovering the wrongdoings of politicians and public servants, they report much more often on project cost overrun and failures than on less problematic projects. A positive side effect for the media is that wrongdoings inspire headlines and stories that attract attention and sell newspapers. However, as the media need to maximize sales and as most readers do not have experience of project planning and cost estimation, the media simplifies the message, does not report on changes in the project, and tends to compare figures and other details that are not strictly comparable.

Media coverage can become very black and white, and focus on finding a scapegoat.

Compare what happened to the Frövifors and Sävenäs plants. Cost estimates for the Frövifors plant increased from SEK 300 to SEK 811 million, mainly due to inflation and the decision to construct a larger plant, prior to the board's decision to invest. That was not a problem as group management and the board had experience of the kind of investment they were making. It was not even considered as a cost overrun as long as the final decision to invest had not been made. However, the fact that cost estimates for the Sävenäs plant had increased from SEK18 to SEK 65 million became a major argument for not implementing the project. The fact that there were no prototypes and that the very first estimate had been made on a table napkin in an autobahn restaurant was not a valid argument for the media and voters. It should not have come as a surprise to anybody with experience of developing a new technology that costs would grow, but neither the public nor politicians had such experience. Thankfully, the environmental movement and its ideas had gained a foothold in public opinion after Rachel Carson[17] raised awareness about the unknown effects of chemicals in her book *Silent Spring*, published in 1962. This saved the plant from becoming a political scandal.

A project such as the Sävenäs waste incineration plant can easily become an electoral pledge without having been investigated. A politician might express a vision to prevent waste from being dumped, or for the construction of a new sport or leisure facility, and then find it difficult to back down when better information about the real cost of his or her vision becomes available. The vision always precedes the appraisal. It is tempting to make such pledges in the press and media. It is tempting to do so as a politician, because it is often more important to be associated with what voters feel are the right ideas at the time, rather than to be right oneself. This is not illogical from a politician's point of view, because they need to be elected to be able to realize their political programme.

Thirdly, as always in communication, there is a risk that the sender says what he thinks the receiver wants to hear or what he thinks he is expected to say, instead of what he perceives as truthful or accurate. The scope for doing so is limited when communicating with knowledgeable receivers, as is the case for companies investing in known markets and technologies. Unfortunately, opportunities for self-serving behaviour increase with higher levels of ambiguity and less informed receivers, i.e. information asymmetry, and simplified black-and-white information becomes open to alternative interpretations. This is problematic, since we know that self-serving bias is not uncommon in high positions. The need to adapt arguments and information about new investments to satisfy media and voters can create incentives to communicate only information that is expected to be received positively and withhold information that might be perceived as negative.

Sweden has had a Freedom of Information act since 1766, known as the Principle of Public Access,[18] which is part of the Swedish constitution. It is an important act, but it has led to measures to avoid transparency, such as important meetings and agreements not being documented, and written materials supporting government decisions not being filed. This may solve the problems of transparency, but it makes it difficult for researchers to establish ex post what has actually happened, who was involved, and who was responsible. It also degrades the value of what is written down. Transparency can cause its own problems.

Accountability. In *The Secret Agent*, a novel by Josef Conrad first published in 1907, Chief Inspector Heat is assigned to investigate a bomb explosion at Greenwich in London. The incident had political importance due to a pending visit by a Russian delegation, knowledge of Russian anarchists, and the symbolic importance of the Greenwich Observatory. The Inspector regularly informs his superior, the Assistant Commissioner, about his findings, who in turn uses this information for his own gains. In chapter 7, the Assistant Commissioner passes this information to the Secretary of State, Sir Ethelred, who is distracted by other issues. When the Commissioner wants to explain that things might not be how they appear, Sir Ethelred interrupts him with, 'Spare me the details'.[19]

This story illustrates two aspects of accountability. Firstly, the fact that actors on different levels live in their own shells. They have different motives and priorities, interpret information differently, and pursue different goals.

Secondly, the story illuminates the problem of transferring responsibility. One reason Sir Ethelred does not want to be informed about the details is that if he doesn't know, he can't be accused of being responsible. This is a common strategy in companies, as well as in politics. You cannot be made accountable as long as others cannot prove you were informed, and hence somebody else has to take the blame if things go wrong. This is a wise strategy for issues where you cannot influence the outcome even though you might be formally regarded as responsible. Thus, it is not surprising that those who stick their necks out and become identified with a decision often have to take the blame even if they themselves are not the ones behind the idea or the ones promoting or enforcing the decision.

Accountability is more clearly specified in firms than in politics,[20] but does vary in firms nonetheless. Market-based control usually makes those in charge clearly accountable, while bureaucratic and social control can be both individual and collective, and more or less clearly specified.[21]

Project managers may be replaced when costs grow, managers may be obliged to resign because of cost overruns or when projects and strategies fail, but has a politician ever had to resign because of cost overrun? Accountability for estimates and public sector investment decisions is low, and voters' memories are short.

A general problem in publicly financed projects is that groups representing certain interests can initiate the creation of large public projects and influence their design and implementation without having to bear the risks and the financial implications of the project or the decisions they want politicians to make. We have special interest groups driving their own agendas, political parties and politicians seeking election or re-election, private industry that sees an opportunity to make money, and anonymous taxpayers paying for the venture, but often no individual or department that can be held accountable. This can cause a spiral of excessive risk-taking.

The decision process for major public investment can be very complex. Major projects are often based on political compromises and include several interwoven decision processes in parallel. Politicians do not need to be aware of the decisions that ultimately lead to cost growth, but the lack of clarity over who is really in charge also makes them ultimately responsible for discrepancies between plan and outcome.

Furthermore, major public projects often take decades from idea to operation. This means that it is often not the same person or people who made the decision to implement the project who have to take responsibility for the financial consequences of that same decision. Those that initiated and promoted the project may no longer be in the organization or may have moved to a new position. This reduces the risk for decision makers in approving a popular project. It is also a problem in long-term private projects, but more evident in the public sector as public memory is short. Being associated with a once-popular project can in fact boost a politician's career, making a decision on long-term investments essentially risk-free.

In addition, lending money to a public authority is almost risk-free. Although a project may be hit by huge cost overruns, lenders almost never have to take losses, hence they do not really take any risk. As a relatively risk-free borrower, the public sector can borrow at lower rates. These conditions do not incentivise lenders to scrutinize the profitability of public projects, because although it makes capital cheaper, lenders are only interested in getting their money back and they can expect to be repaid where government guarantees exist. Therefore, there are always new lenders willing to lend additional funds when the cost of a public project increases.

One must also remember that, despite the increasing professionalization of politics and ample media training, politicians are laymen in most of the areas where they exert influence. They cannot be expected to have the knowledge to make accurate cost estimates, design, or assess all the projects implemented by a public authority. They lack the knowledge and skills to be able to assess the risk of most, if not all, the projects they formally approve. The media love to trace outcomes back to the politicians' supposed decisions and promises, but that is to paint a decision process that does not exist. The process is, just like in major groups, much more of a muddle-through, bottom-up process.

Instead, politicians have to act as a board in a company and rely on influencing values and assigning the right people to do the work. They must find and appoint knowledgeable people who can and will ensure that there is a control system that checks proposals thoroughly, and delegates risks and accountability appropriately. It is by forming the organization that they can influence the outcome, and in that respect their job is not much different to that of a company board.

Project abandonment. As stated in Chapter 1, the term 'cost overrun' has different meanings within firms and in studies of public sector projects. In the firm, a cost overrun is a budget overrun. Until the final investment decision is made, there cannot be a cost overrun, just differing earlier cost estimates.

In the public sector, the final cost is often compared with estimates made during the planning process, sometimes against the very first estimate, and the cost growth termed 'cost overrun'.

This is why some studies of public sector projects show such large cost overruns. Cost tends to increase more between the very first estimate and the final approved project budget than during implementation, but the outcome is still compared with the first known estimate. It is not entirely illogical, as public sector investments are less likely to be stopped due to growing costs once the project has caught momentum than investment proposals in industry. There are several reasons for this, which have to do with differences in type of project, decision making, and transparency.

Firstly, the public sector continues to invest in new weapon systems even though the cost of developing such systems is constantly growing. Public organizations find it difficult to refrain from also implementing many other types of project that are necessary due to public need or new laws and regulations just because cost is increasing or the investment cannot be proven profitable to the organization making the investment. Many public sector investments are thus forced investments.

Secondly, an investment proposal in the public sector has to gain support from a political majority. This means negotiating a proposal that can give all parties in the majority something, which means concessions and compromises. As all parties must gain something in a negotiation, such negotiated agreements can necessitate changes in the project, and for various reasons also changes in the project during implementation and during operation. This is not uncommon, and such changes can, not surprisingly, make costs grow. The risk for changes after agreement has been reached is smaller if the coalition is based on long-term relations and shared values, but can never be fully reduced. It is not necessary to share the values of those one reaches an agreement with, but the risk of later disagreements that cause changes in the project becomes bigger. The situation is very different in a company. There might be different ideas about which investments should be made, but there is agreement that all investments have to deliver a good return. Projects have to gain executive commitment and support, are developed, requested, approved, or rejected. Those approving funding seldom interfere and make changes in projects apart from making cuts in the budget. This makes goals more stable.

Just as it can be difficult to reach a majority for an investment, there are also reasons for playing down known and future anticipated problems and costs so as not to risk an agreement. For the same reason, it can also become more important to defend a political agreement than to keep costs down or abandon a failing project. In a study[22] of ten municipalities, none of those interviewed could recall an investment decision that had been stopped, despite costs typically increasing. Approved investment projects were completed even though in some cases the decision to invest was made based on the very first cost estimate included in the long-term investment plan. Cost growth has seldom stopped a public sector project once it has gained the support of a political majority.

And thirdly, the transparency surrounding public sector projects makes it more costly to make radical changes in what has been promised. Changes would not only break an agreement with other parties supporting the project, but also with voters, and thus would raise questions of trustworthiness. Therefore, transparency and the need to compromise to form an agreement with actors whose goals are different create a stronger path dependence to early commitments.

Preconditions for learning. Maynard Hufschmidt and Jacques Gerin[23] studied the cost development for 346 water resource and hydroelectric power projects in three utilities. The sample ranged from projects initiated in the early 1930s as part of President Roosevelt's New Deal to those started in the late 1950s. The Corps of Engineers and the Bureau of Reclamation showed cost overruns of 10 to 25 per cent, which was significantly better than at the beginning of the period. Tennessee Valley Authority (TVA) had been notably superior at estimating cost throughout the period compared to the other two companies, an advantage that remained into the 1960s and 1970s when TVA was better at estimating the cost and keeping to the timetable of their new nuclear power plants than other US utilities.[24]

The Bureau of Reclamation and Corps of Engineers were substantially larger organizations than the TVA. The Corps was divided into 11 divisions and 37 districts which appraised their own investments, requested funding and made the estimates needed for their investment requests. The ability to make good estimates varied between the divisions of the Corps. With regard to size and geographical area covered, TVA could be compared with one of the divisions in Corps. The sheer size of the Corps did not help them produce more reliable cost estimates than the smaller TVA.

Closer scrutiny of these three organizations showed that the cost of investments in the Bureau of Reclamation and the Corps were calculated in a decentralized capital budgeting system. Not so in the TVA, where all project planning, design, construction, and estimates were made by staff at the head office. The group was small but proud of their achievements and had very low staff turnover. Their accumulated experience from earlier projects gave them access to better cost data and created favourable preconditions for future estimates. The preconditions were not as favourable in the decentralized organizations, where estimates were made by employees who were not regularly involved in planning and estimating projects. These observations made Hufschmidt and Gerin conclude that organizational factors are more important determinants of the accuracy of cost estimates than technical factors.

Hufschmidt and Gerin's observations illustrate the weakness of decentralized capital budgeting systems. Decentralization has many advantages, but when it comes to making accurate cost estimates those who do this on a full-time basis are generally better at doing so. This is one reason why most companies with decentralized capital budgeting systems require the figures to be checked and approved by particular staff before an investment request can be approved. Some large companies have elaborate systems of control, but Hufschmidt and Gerin do not mention the existence of a pre-approval control system in the Corps of Engineers or the Bureau of Reclamation. It does not mean that such control did not exist, but it was perhaps not well developed.

The TVA case exemplifies how major publicly owned power companies can be as good at managing and appraising their investments as private companies. It is not a matter of ownership but a matter of specialization and creating good preconditions for learning. However, municipalities and cities are unrelated conglomerates and that makes it more difficult for them to accumulate experience and supply relevant feedback; also, this is not facilitated by the fact that politicians are rarely experts in the kind of investments they approve. This makes it important to have an adequate cost accounting and pre-approval control system to ensure reliable cost estimates.

Private industry has been using standard costing to estimate product cost for one hundred years. Product costing became an urgent problem with the emergence of the mass production of complex products in the late nineteenth century.[25] The solution advanced by the efficiency movement was standard costing, which means that the firm has one department for estimating the cost of new products and assignments ex ante, and one for analysing the actual cost of production ex post, issuing standard costs to be used in future cost estimates. The innovation was not the use of pre-determined costs, which had long been used, but the formation of a unit that delivered up-to-date cost data based on analyses of actual product cost. Most municipalities are perhaps too small to develop such a cost-accounting system, but could have much to win on cooperating with other municipalities on costing. However, it presupposes that cooperating municipalities first standardize their cost accounting in order for the figures delivered to the analysing cost unit to be compared.

Such product costing practice can also be applied to projects as a whole. When private companies want to invest in something for which their accounts do not have up-to-date cost data, they try to compare their cost estimates with recent similar investments made by other firms. Such data can be available through trade organizations, industry journals, and major consulting firms, and this is not a new practice: as early as 200 years ago a Swedish iron industry journal published a review[26] of investment in new blast furnace which gave the actual cost of various parts of the investment. Today, however, industry turns to major consultancy firms. In the Frövifors and Uddeholm cases, a Finnish consultancy, the Jaakko Pöyry Group, were called in to determine the accuracy of cost estimates. Jaakko Pöyry is often hired in the forestry industry because it has access to up-to-date cost data and a model to calculate costs. Using its services provides both cost estimates of individual budget items and their relative size as compared to total cost in recent comparable projects.

Despite private industry having used such reference costs for a very long time, the public sector has only recently followed suit. The Association for the Advancement of Cost Engineering has recommended that cost estimates should be reviewed from different perspectives by benchmarking or validating them against past internal and/or external estimates and experiences of similar projects.[27] And, in 2005, the American Planning Organization issued[28] a similar recommendation through the use of so-called reference class forecasting[29] for public sector projects. Such validation of public sector project estimates, as well as external reviews, has been used since then: e.g. in Australia[30], Norway[31], and the United Kingdom.[32] Thus, it looks like the public sectors in some countries have started to develop something that can mimic the pre-approval review systems found in major corporations.

Studying project costing in Swedish municipalities 30 years ago, it was amazing to find that they did not cooperate.[33] They visited each other to find inspiration for the design of their own buildings and other construction, but they did not exchange cost data. Today, some smaller municipalities cooperate on costing and procurement. Others use independent consultants or consultant firms to cost and procure building projects. Some also transfer the risk for cost overrun through procuring to a fixed cost. However, transferring risk usually means paying an insurance fee, and outsourcing does not automatically solve the problems of cost growth. The procurer has to have the competence needed in-house to procure the services needed, which leads us back to the problem of politicians as laymen.

There are also positive conditions for learning in the public sector. With the types of long-term investment involved, the public sector has more time to study and learn about the investment before it is implemented. For private industry, strong competition and fast-changing markets often force organizations to act quickly, and sometimes before they have had time to make proper studies. In addition, the market sometimes changes so fast that adjustments in projects have to be made during implementation. The demand for public sector service can be prognosticated, changes are slower, and the public sector can to some extent influence the market. The market risk is low compared to the private sector. Thus, conditions for estimating project costs should generally be better.

Preconditions for cost estimation. We have identified seven differences in preconditions for making cost estimates, and have seen that the main divide is not between private and public companies, but between whether organizations are dominated by the logic of economics or the logic of politics. Three main themes emerge: type of project, goals, and control. Let us start with type of project.

The type of project is important because when private sector companies invest, they invest in areas and projects where they believe they have the capabilities necessary for success. They focus their resources on becoming one of the best in their sector of industry at achieving return on capital. This enables them to accumulate knowledge and skills in the areas in which they invest. It makes it easier to evaluate new investments, and also gives the organization learning opportunities to improve the skills of those making estimates and appraisals. Organizations which repeatedly implement similar projects tend to develop pre-approval control systems that manage investments within their business well. The importance of such feedback systems can be seen when companies invest in areas where previous experience is of less use. Cost overruns and failures are much more common in these instances.

The preconditions are not different in public sector organizations that repeatedly implement projects of a similar type. However, the public sector is a conglomerate. Projects are not initiated by a need to stay competitive relative to other organizations, but by social needs that the private sector does not cover. In addition, some public investments are in goods and services whereby use cannot be separated from those that pay, such as streetlights, and which therefore are paid for by taxpayers instead of users as it is impossible to charge those who use the lights. Other similar areas are defence, and law and order, although private defence and police forces exist. Historically, the public sector has financed major infrastructure projects, gas networks, major railway lines, roads, dams, etc., which the private sector has not been able to finance. Society also offers many services, such as social welfare programmes.

We know that projects which are new to the organization implementing them are more prone to overrun their budget and that the public sector implements such projects much more often than the private sector. The public sector also implements investments that the private sector considers too risky. Private industry tends to invest too much in product variation and too little in basic research, and basic research is therefore mostly financed by taxpayers' money. The same with education. Private industry requires employees who have the knowledge and skills they need, while the public sector historically supplies the knowledge that students will find of use during their lifetime. By having a shorter time horizon and avoiding high-risk investments, the private sector is less prone to cost overruns.

It has been argued that there is no reason to add a risk premium to the discount rate for public projects, since society as a whole has so many projects that it can pool these risks.[34] It is interesting to note that this argument rests on an assumption that cost overruns are as common as cost underruns, something we know is not true. Implementing riskier projects means taking on larger cost overruns. Outcomes do not cancel each other out. This phenomenon increases the need for funding and displaces other investments.

The second theme incorporated goals and acceptance versus quality. Private firms have a clear goal against which projects can be designed and evaluated. The public sector has to consider multiple goals. Political reforms often have multiple goals, and projects are often designed to satisfy a diverse coalition of interests and stakeholders. A consequence of this is that economic efficiency is not necessarily the right measure when evaluating all public projects. It may be more useful to evaluate the extent to which the project has achieved the individual goals of the different stakeholders.[35]

Private firms can argue for solutions that are economically efficient. The logic of politics requires that solutions are aligned with the norms and values of voters, the party, and society. Decisions have to be legitimized. To implement economically efficient solutions is not the only objective. Such solutions have to gain acceptance, which can require lengthy negotiations and alterations in the original plans. Acceptance is also important in private firms so that those working with and being affected by the project are fully engaged, but companies are not run by parties which openly oppose each other.

Our third theme was control. Cost overrun is hardly something that can wreck a political career. Accountability for major public projects is too difficult to specify, politicians do not have the knowledge to be responsible for cost estimates, and voters' memories are short. These conditions do not foster accountability and learning.

Another important difference is transparency, which in the public sector makes early, often very rough, estimates public. The project may become more expensive due to natural causes such as inflation and because the size of the project has been increased to reduce unit cost, but such changes can be difficult to communicate through the media to an audience that is unfamiliar with project planning and cost estimation. As a consequence, the proposer of the investment may find it necessary to conceal some of the facts to avoid jeopardizing the project. Transparency can also put the public procurer at a disadvantage as it gives those putting in tenders access to information that can help them negotiate better prices and terms. Public authorities place certain activities in public companies to get round these problems, because that way it becomes possible to perform public services under conditions more similar to private industry.

It is not uncommon to blame cost overruns in the public sector on incompetence, but that is far too simplistic an explanation. Private companies also encounter problems and cost overruns when they implement projects in areas where they lack previous experience. We have given several examples of this. However, unlike private companies, the public sector cannot refrain from implementing projects that have a high risk of cost growth.

On the other hand, competition forces private companies to take more market risks. The public sector does not face such market risks – there will always be a market for a service if the service is free. But this creates other problems. Free and under-priced services create overconsumption. In addition, the planning process is often more difficult due to the many stakeholders that are involved, the requirement for transparency, and because the right amount of leadership flair is needed to address the logics of politics and the media.

However, decisions to implement projects in the public sector are less likely to be made under time pressure. There is time to learn, to try to foresee what might happen, and to make estimates that are as good as possible before implementation. Considering the large number of projects implemented in the public sector, many types of project would not be unique to those implementing them if experiences from previous, similar projects in the sector were accumulated in a more systematic way. Much could be gained by cooperating on systematically collecting and making cost data from earlier public projects available to project planners.

Resolving Economic-Technical and Political Uncertainty

In Chapter 4 we showed how cost overruns in certain types of projects could be understood as a consequence of efforts by estimators to resolve economic-technical uncertainty based on the information they have at the time. Their estimates become more reliable as projects come closer to completion and they gradually receive more accurate information. Although people are not rational decision makers, the model still illustrates decision making in companies when there is an agreement on what the goal of the project is.

In this chapter we have introduced political uncertainty. It is different to economic-technical uncertainty because actors disagree on issues such as how information should be interpreted, the problem the project is supposed to solve, and the best way to solve the problem. Disagreement can derive from different ideologies, interpretations, lack of knowledge, or simply personal interests and benefits. Such political uncertainty will have to be resolved to form a decision that will gain acceptance. Political uncertainty affects public sector projects directly, and economic-technical decisions indirectly, through laws, regulations, economic policy, and the political climate, and this political uncertainty usually has to be reduced before the economic-technical uncertainty can be resolved.

Figure 5.1 shows the different problems and solutions that characterize the two types of uncertainty – political and economic-technical. In the upper-left box we have the situation that the project, i.e. the solution to a problem, might be certain, but there are disagreements over the correct description of the problem and the solution. It might be necessary to modify the project and the solution, but in the best case that will not be necessary to get the project accepted, if, for instance, the problem is

Political uncertainty	Problem: Disagreement Solution: Create acceptance for one solution	Problem: Lack of knowledge, shared mental images, and agreement make the outcome of the process unpredictable Solution: Move the issue if possible to the left before approving a solution, or isolate the issue
Political certainty	Problem: Maximize shareholder value Solution: Evaluate and choose the best alternative	Problem: Lack of information Solution: Re-evaluate the alternatives when better information becomes available
	Economic-technical certainty	*Economic-technical uncertainty*

Figure 5.1 Resolving economic-technical versus political uncertainty

perceived as urgent. In a business setting, company management can avoid a situation where limited information and abilities create space for alternative interpretations. The political sector cannot do so. They may also have to reach a decision as depicted in the upper-right box, where the information is vague and lacking, and therefore open to alternative interpretations.

We referred earlier to Norman Maier, who described how effective decisions require both quality and acceptance. Quality referred to how well the decision is backed up by objective facts, and acceptance with how those executing the decision feel about the decision. Effective decisions have to satisfy both reasons and emotions. Maier analysed alternative routes to achieving effective decisions and argued that '[a]iming at both objectives achieves neither'.[36] Aiming at quality makes acceptance of secondary importance, and aiming at acceptance risks quality becoming of secondary importance.

Maier's distinction between quality and acceptance, and the principles of problem-solving, can be applied to our problem of how to best resolve uncertainty over the risk of cost growth. This gives us four alternatives. One can resolve economic-technical uncertainty first, political uncertainty first, economic-technical and political uncertainty simultaneously, or a decision can be taken without having resolved either of these uncertainties.

Resolve economic-technical uncertainty first. This is normal practice in companies, and when political uncertainty is low and does not risk to initiate costly changes, additions, and delays.

Engineers at the business level suggest investments that will solve production problems. They investigate alternatives and resolve economic-technical uncertainty around one of the alternatives, sometimes involving variations of this alternative. When this is done, acceptance is sought higher up in the hierarchy by requesting funding. Important in the comparison with the public sector is that the project is developed by people close to production and reviewed in a pre-approval control system by people knowledgeable about needs, plans, technology, and markets. Furthermore, companies distinguish between strategic and operative investments. There is a business process by which the strategy for the group and its units are developed, and a process in which operative investments are assessed and approved against previously approved strategies. Companies first approve a strategy, which can include major investments and investment programmes, then they approve operative investments as part of the implementation of the approved strategies. This is the ideal, although new needs can sometimes make it necessary to approve urgent emerging needs and modify approved strategies.

In the public sector, this practice has its equivalence in administrators planning and developing new project proposals approved by the political body. This was much more the case in the 1930s to the 1960s than it is today. It gave politicians little influence over identifying and defining future projects. This and inflated long-term growth plans that were based more on visions than facts gave this model of public management a bad reputation.

One could assume that the political body dealt purely with strategic decisions and projects, and that operative projects were delegated to bureaucrats, but that is not the case, at least not in more recent times. The public sector does not make the same clear distinction between strategic and operative decisions. What is a strategically important project to one politician and political party might not be so important to another, meaning that all projects can become disputed. It is not difficult to find examples of minor issues which have been debated much more than major strategic issues. Nor are public sector projects always reviewed in a pre-approval control system that considers the quality of the estimates made. Public companies can have such systems, but not the public sector as a whole. This creates opportunities for marketing bold visions.

Resolve political uncertainty first. This means that the project gains acceptance before cost estimates have become reasonably reliable. One can interpret it as having been more important to form an agreement than to know the real cost of the agreement. Project cost becomes of less importance relative to acceptance, and the risk of cost growth therefore higher. The question becomes whether it is important to know the cost at all.

This decision strategy might be applied simply because it is easier to agree on the approval than to define the project. Solving the easiest problem first can be a good strategy, but it can also be a consequence of early commitments and what we have termed the logic of politics. Major public infrastructure projects are often the result of political negotiations and an agreement between several political parties and stakeholders. The agreement comes first, and only when that is secured can a detailed project plan be developed and its costs estimated. An example is the way decisions on new expansions of local transport in the Greater Stockholm area are reached today. First, political parties agree on an expansion, then planners develop and cost the proposal. The same planning philosophy has been applied to most contemporary major road and infrastructure projects. They are all the results of political negotiations and agreements.

The result is that the cost estimate upon which the agreement is based is both uncertain and out of date, the latter as it often takes several years to reach an agreement. And when planners further develop the project, additional needs might be discovered, the agreement might need to be re-negotiated, and inflation might make the approved budget worth less – all of these contribute to cost increases. Alterations and additions may have been necessary to achieve a political majority to support the project. Every stakeholder needs to gain something from a deal. The media will later compare the very first estimate (made perhaps ten years earlier) with the new estimate and trumpet that they have revealed yet another scandal – almost inevitably without going into the details of why cost has increased.

One can find similarities between this decision strategy and the way industry allocates funding to intangible investments. Funds for personnel, marketing, and also often research are allocated by a budget frame within which the department is allowed to choose how to allocate the funding. This does not need to lead to a situation where the financial framework is insufficient as intangible investments are usually divisible. Thus, cost does not need to increase as ambitions can be lowered to meet the budget.

This decision strategy also exists in industry in the sense that decisions on strategy and strategic initiatives initiate operative investments. However, strategic investments are usually also reviewed in a pre-approval control system, and companies now and then make specific reviews of strategies and strategic initiatives.

In a similar way, political decisions on new laws and regulations, public services, and expenses generate investments in departments, municipalities, and public and private organizations. Most local government investments are in fact generated by political decisions at the national level. What the cost of a new law, increased regulation, or a new or improved public service will be has only been very schematically estimated, if at all, when these decisions are made. Often the costs the reform will cause are totally unknown. There is no system to systematically review the effects of such decisions apart from those reviews that the national audit office conducts occasionally, and those made in organizations that are affected by these decisions.

Resolve economic-technical and political uncertainty simultaneously. Project planning is to some extent always an iteration between reducing economic-technical uncertainty and forming the commitment necessary for approval and funding. Strategies and strategic initiatives require investment, and project planners must secure funding. It is often a good decision strategy to iterate between problem and solution because that can reveal issues that have not yet been considered. This should not be a problem unless the existence of political uncertainty means that the preconditions for the project change. If the project has to be modified in an uneconomic way to gain acceptance, then this will increase cost, and the worst case is if such changes become necessary during implementation. The risk will remain as long as uncertainty has not been resolved.

The Swedish nuclear waste programme is one example of a project where this decision strategy has been chosen. The focus has not been on constructing a deep repository, but on developing and proving that such a solution will work. The programme is supervised by industry, government authorities, and independent environmental groups financed by the industry. The actors get to know each other as they communicate and meet quite frequently, partly due to the limited amount of expertise in a small country. They have not yet come to an agreement, but the more you get to know each other the more difficult it can become to disagree. In the USA, there is more distance between performing and controlling agencies, perhaps partly due to a greater pool of people knowledgeable in the field, and partly due to a different tradition when it comes to industry–government relationships.

Avoid resolving uncertainty. This means that decisions are made without first reducing either economic-technical or political uncertainty. Business leaders, and sometimes political leaders, may have to make decisions based on vague information because of urgency, the need to seize a window of opportunity, or some other reason, without securing acceptance for the decision. It is a risky political decision strategy when it comes to the possibility of cost overrun, and as the decision does not have firm support from a majority, the decision can come to be reversed if the political situation changes.

A positive consequence of the ambiguity that lack of information creates is that stakeholders can inject their vision and wishes into the potential outcome of a given project more easily. Facts can be replaced by hopes as nobody knows exactly what the facts are. It can make it easier to reach an agreement, and that can sometimes be the reason why a project is approved before good cost estimates exist. It is a possible way forward, but also risky because disagreements over what has been agreed can appear later and necessitate changes that increase costs. The agreement might even have to be re-negotiated as more becomes known about the consequences of the project and the decision, or even abandoned altogether.

A safer alternative when neither economic-technical or political risk uncertainty can be reduced is to decouple and isolate the issue. This can be done by postponing the decision, by moving the issue from the daily political agenda by appointing a commission to study it, or by moving the issue to a specific organization whereby administrators or business are allowed to take it over. This can be an organization especially created to handle the issue, such as moving a service from a public department to a publicly owned company, or it can mean outsourcing to a private company. The issue is at least temporarily transferred from the political agenda to a politically controlled commission or organization, or to an environment where the logic of economics prevails and the political uncertainty is instantly reduced.

6 Explaining Cost Overrun, Summary, and Conclusions

When Cost Becomes of Secondary Importance

Bounded rationality stood for the proposition that decision makers have limited information, cognitive ability, and time to process information. It gives a much better description of the way individual decision makers make decisions than the economic man model, but the research approach used to analyse is the same for both models. The existence and effects of cognitive biases and information asymmetry are analysed as deviations in the rational model using rational reasoning. Economists and experimental psychologists testing behavioural biases use the same type of methods. This makes it easy to integrate the two models.[1] However, having done so, to an observer there are still many kinds of seemingly non-rational actions that are not dealt with within bounded rationality modelling that can explain cost growth. We will give some examples of such actions in this section and propose an explanation. It is about instances in which cost seems to be of secondary importance to the decision maker relative to the decision makers' urge to satisfy their biological instincts. A non-rational behaviour to the observer, covered by Smith's concept of 'passions', which is not merely a cognitive bias, rather an instinct that develops and is given space to do so in interaction with the social context in which the individual decision maker acts.

Descartes and Leibniz distinguished between the body and intellect. Their contention that truth could only be established through logical reasoning made it possible to break away from religious dogma and superstition. It laid the foundation for the revolution in the natural sciences, and the society we know today. Nevertheless, the division between body and intellect remains, and is reflected in many projects ridden by cost growth.

Take architecture, for instance. Relying on intellect, the development of new construction methods, increased standardization, and the division of labour it became possible to offer more and more people larger homes and higher quality housing. However rational this is, it did not end the construction of uneconomical buildings. The erection of many well-known, tall, richly decorated, and impressive buildings can simply not be justified by economic reasons. That was the case, for example, for medieval church builders who competed in constructing ever larger and taller cathedrals. Some, such as the builders of the Saint-Pierre de Beauvais cathedral in Beauvais, France, went too far, with the 153-metre-tall tower of their building collapsing in 1284, only 12 years after completion. Nonetheless, later church builders still tried to exceed their predecessors. Constructing high towers could be interpreted as getting closer to the almighty one, but the race for taller buildings is not confined to the religious sphere. Gustave Eiffel constructed the 324-metre-tall Eiffel Tower, which does not offer any office or living space, just restaurants and a view of Paris from above that people suffering from vertigo cannot enjoy. Moreover, it is built from wrought iron which needs to be cleaned and repainted every seven years to keep the rust in check. This in itself is not a rational way of allocating scarce resources, but the Tower is an iconic symbol of Paris and a top tourist attraction, perhaps even because of its irrationality. It is obvious that these construction projects fill important needs that are not dealt with in construction firms' cost estimates or the public sector's cost–benefit analyses.

Some additional examples of projects difficult to motivate on economic reasons. The Romans knew how to build high-rise buildings in concrete. There were shops at street level with wealthy people residing directly above. The poorer people had to climb farther up the stairs to their abodes. The development of steam-driven (and later electrical) elevators reversed the order. It made it possible to lift the rich to the top floor and build even taller buildings in city centres, where the cost of land was highest.

Cheaper steel, due to the exploitation of the Bessemer process and the development of steel frames for structures, made it cheaper to construct taller buildings. The Empire State Building broke the record with its 381-metre-high (443 metres, with its antenna spire) structure when it was completed in 1931 – a record it would keep for 40 years until the World Trade Centre, at 526 metres, overtook it in 1972. It can be noted that the first building was designed before the stock crash in 1929, and the second before the stock market decline of the 1970s. Tall building projects tend to cluster in time, which has led some stock analysts to view these projects as an indicator of market sentiment.

However true this may be, when industrialization and wealth have spread to new areas of the world, high-profile building projects and the arrangement of major international events have followed suit. Several Asian countries have entered the race and built even taller buildings on land far less expensive than that of Lower Manhattan, with Burj Khalifa in Dubai reaching 830 metres. The construction of such tall buildings cannot be validated by purely rational reasons. It is simply not economically justifiable to construct buildings taller than 300 metres, not even where property prices are at their highest levels, as the elevators will take up too much space. Cost seems to have been of less importance to these buildings' owners; there must be other reasons for constructing them than pure economic. Really tall buildings are not only seen far away, they become symbols for the cities they watch over in relation to wealth, success, capabilities, and power, as was so painfully illustrated by the 9/11 attack. Economic centres compete on symbolic power visually conveyed through architecture, art, and media.

Cities have long been competing on architecture. Italian city states did so, and Budapest, Prague, and Vienna did too within the Austrian–Hungarian Empire. Modern cities also compete along the same lines. The Soviet Union and the USA started a space race. Moreover, large cities and would-be upcomers compete on holding the Olympic Games, world championships, world exhibitions, and other high-profile events. Many of these projects have been economic disasters. Not rarely has cost grown beyond all expectations, but that does not seem to matter. New advantages have been invented and the events have often been popular among taxpayers who essentially have had to pay the bill. Such advantages relate to tourist attractions and increased local property prices. The final cost seems to have been of far less importance than if it had been an ordinary project based on economic rational reasons.

The fact that dictators and authoritarian regimes tend to construct gigantic buildings and monuments that are difficult to justify by purely economic reasoning illustrates how power can diminish the importance of cost. Pharaohs and other ancient emperors, as well as Hitler, Stalin, Mao, and Ceausescu in modern times, all started many gigantic projects wherein cost, and rationality is difficult to comprehend. Among the more remarkable is the Romanian president Nicolae Ceausescu, who quite recently in Europe, in a country with relatively small economic resources, constructed a building – the Palace of the Parliament – which, with a floor area of 360,000 square metres, is the world's second largest administrative building (the Pentagon being the largest). It covers an area of 240 x 270 metres, and reaches 86 metres above ground and 92 below. With 1,100 rooms, it is an impressive building, and a clear expression of power. What is difficult to explain is not that people seize the opportunities that power presents to them, because that is what all entrepreneurs do, but why their subjects often associate themselves with the grandeur their rulers express, or, as Adam Smith put it:

Upon this disposition of mankind, to go along with all the passions of the rich and powerful, is founded in the distinction of ranks, and the order of society. Our obsequiousness to our superiors more frequently arises from our admiration for the advantages of their situation, than from any private expectation of benefit from their good-will. Their benefits can extend but to a few; but their fortunes interest almost everybody. We are eager to assist them in completing a system of happiness that approaches so near to perfection; and we desire to serve them for their own sake, without any other recompense but the vanity or the honour of obliging them.[2]

People associate themselves with their rulers, and today, in our media-driven world, with actors, rock, and sport stars, as well as personalities from television and the Internet. The general public participates in the joy and sorrows of those they admire, and ascribes them virtues and knowledge they do not possess. Essentially, this also applies to the business world. Employees tend to ascribe their top managers' abilities, probity, and trust that is not reflected in their actions, and to an extent that would probably surprise many top managers.

These exaggerated constructions are usually not only big, they are typically richly decorated, tall, pompous, and boastful constructions, designed to impress and express grandeur. They become not only monuments and symbols for the ruler, but a certificate of what the nation and its culture can achieve. It is difficult to know whether cost estimates were really made, but cost seems often to have been of secondary (or even no) importance. Yet still, such constructions can often come to be celebrated artefacts.

Ancient advanced cultures in Egypt, Mesopotamia, Pakistan, China, Mexico, and Peru are admired for their achievements in science and their huge constructions, such as the pyramids and the Great Wall of China. August Wittfogel[3] termed these early advanced civilizations 'hydraulic civilizations' as they all, due to regular flooding, relied on flood control and irrigation which required a well-functioning bureaucracy to coordinate work. The geography and climate of Europe did not require the development of such centrally controlled societies. Seldom is it mentioned that most of its inhabitants were unfree in these very hierarchal societies and were ruled by a small elite carrying the knowledge needed to manage these societies. The knowledge and constructions that remain are perceived as an expression of what the society was able to achieve and a hallmark of an advanced one.

The use of symbols of power is not confined to the public sector. Large companies are important symbols for many nations. Not long ago, it seemed as though all self-respecting countries had to have their own airlines, and many still do, even though competition is tough and a large amount of smaller national airlines are making losses. In many countries, the same has applied to steel works and petrochemical plants. Is it because such plants have symbolized industrialization? In a mercantilist spirit, oil-producing countries have constructed refineries to export petrol, although it is more economical to export crude oil and have it refined closer to its market. The high-tech industry is another area many countries like to boost with tax-payers' money. It expresses the pride, aspirations, and hopes of the nation and its people. Countries are competing not only on economic power, but also on symbols of economic power. That is, in industrialized countries industrial achievements have symbolic values which can make the cost of new investments, and their future costs and revenues, of lesser importance than rational reasoning would assume.

In the 1950s, the slogan 'Kilroy was here' was still scribbled on walls. Nobody knew what it meant or where it came from. It was first long after that I learnt that during the war Kilroy had been an American shipyard inspector at the Fore River yard in Massachusetts who had signed the steel plates he had inspected with his tag. US troops observed the strange notation, spread it, and started an avalanche. Graffiti is not a new phenomenon. There are inscriptions marking places that were visited by Romans, Vikings, Pilgrims, and so on. People seem to have an urge to leave a mark for posterity, and this is also true in the business world.

Decision makers might have hidden motives. I once visited a company that was about to implement a major investment. The company produced electricity and district heating, and some of their boilers burning coal, pellets, and waste had long past their assumed technical life. Their life had been extended, but they required constant maintenance, so there was no question that they had to be replaced, and studies had been going on for 20 years regarding how best to extend their life and replace them. The other part of the plant was much younger and an analysis had estimated its remaining technical life to be 15–20 years. There was no urgent need to replace this part of the plant. However, something happened: the former boiler replacement project was transformed into a much bigger one in which the whole production plant of the company was to be replaced with a new integrated facility partly using new, unproved technology.

The greatest worry was finance and the risk of cost overrun. The implementation of this twice as large project would become a substantial financial burden for its owner during the next decade. As the investment could be made in two steps I asked the MD of the utility: 'Why don't you ease the financial burden by waiting fifteen to twenty years to implement the new part of the project?' He hesitated for a while and then said: 'That's impossible. By then I would be retired.' The director had been initiating both studies and it became clear to me that he wanted to see the problems of the company solved for the foreseeable future so that he could leave a clean table when he retired.

This was far from the first time when talking to project managers, directors, and politicians that I have sensed that there must be strong personal emotions behind the alternatives chosen that I have not been able to fully comprehend by logical reasoning. Among those were two managing directors, one in a mining company and the other in a manufacturing company. They had both, after a long career in major companies, taken these jobs in the municipalities where they were born, partly as they wanted to do something for their respective hometowns before retirement. Both managing directors pushed through major investments that would secure the future of their companies, yet may not have been the wisest way to spend shareholders' money, and engaged in supporting local entrepreneurs – the latter to the extent that the mining group fired the company manager, claiming that he spent too much on issues of little interest to the company.

Another example was the university rector that pressed through the decision to construct a larger and costlier university building than needed to be inaugurated before he retired, paid for by his successors' cuts. Moreover, the manager who left a secure and well-paid job for the uncertain job of building up a new company based on a new untested business idea is another example. These were all decisions made by managers closely identifying themselves with their work. The problem for research is that decision makers very rarely admit that these, and other decisions which are difficult to understand by an external observer, are not based solely on economic reasoning. However, whatever the reasons may be, the impression remains that their strong engagement in such projects can only be understood as an instinct, to set a footprint for posterity. This is what their actions all share: not an urge to impress their contemporaries, but to impress future generations. Adam Smith saw this as a universal instinct:

Men have voluntarily thrown away life to acquire after death a renown which they could no longer enjoy. Their imagination, in the meantime, anticipated that fame which was in the future times to be bestowed upon them. Those applauses they were never to hear rung in their ears; the thoughts of that admiration, whose effect they were never to feel, played about their hearts, banished from their breasts the strongest of all natural fears, and transported them to perform actions which seems almost beyond reach of human nature.[4]

The denial of death, and terror management theory. The examples of seemingly non-rational reasoning given in this section – the propensity of nations, companies, and individuals to compete on symbols and craving to leave footprints to be read after death – have been interpreted and theorized by Ernest Becker[5] in his posthumously published Pulitzer Prize winning book, *The Denial of Death*. Building on psychology and mythico-religious perspectives from Søren Kierkegaard to Sigmund Freud, and especially Freud's follower Otto Rank, Ernest Becker argues that we as humans are, more than by anything else, haunted by our awareness of our inescapable death, and that this drives us to commit heroic feats to deny death necessary to maintain self-esteem, self-worth, and a meaning of life. The roots of human achievements and culture lay in our reflex to defy the terror of death by acts that will outlive our own existence.

We control the anxiety that our knowledge of our destiny creates by trying to achieve symbolic immortality through children carrying our genes and culture, and through religious belief in the resurrection, or a soul that lives on after death. Herein, creating works of art and science, businesses, buildings, and other artefacts of civilization, as well as collecting valuables and building fortunes, are ways to achieve such symbolic immorality. It can also explain why many emperors have erased traces of their precursors and hired historians to glorify their own achievements. Every society, be it based on religion, science, or consumerism, offers what Becker terms a 'hero-system' based on myths which provides those who live their lives according to these myths meaning and value. Constructing cathedrals, skyscrapers, and iconic buildings, forming families and having children, creating art and advancing science and technology creates meaning based on a hope and a belief that what outlives us will outshine death and bring meaning and value to our lives.

Becker offers an explanation as to why certain decisions on the national level and in organizations go against stated goals and therefore cannot always be understood as a result of economic reasons. It can, e.g. be decisions to spend resources on projects that cannot be motivated solely by economic rational reasons, as well as that the justification of their cost growth can be explained by an urge to defeat death. When projects are mainly or partly driven by actors' need to gain self-esteem and a heroic self-image in face of death, cost overrun and cost growth may become less important. It becomes a struggle between the need to deny our mortality through our myth of the meaning of life and the norm of rationality.

This is not to deny the ability of iconic buildings, museums, historical artefacts, well-known games, and cultural activities to attract tourists, competence, and capital. Some of these artefacts and activities have probably, through the image they convey, become very profitable investments for the society and their investors – but far from all.

Becker's theory has formed the basis for terror-management theory,[6] in which the drive for meaning and self-esteem are seen as a way to handle the awareness of one's mortality and avoid existential anxiety. In terror management theory, self-esteem is built on the perceived validity of, and living according to, the standards of one's cultural worldview, acting as a buffer to handle the terror of death. Researchers have tested this so-called mortality salience hypothesis in experimental situations and found support for a heightened thought-related awareness of one's mortality which increases our efforts to strengthen our cultural worldviews and self-esteem. The hypothesis has been tested in a great number of studies. A meta-analysis[7] of 277 experiments reported in 164 articles found that 221 of these experiments, or 80 per cent, were both positive and statistically significant in support of the mortality salience hypothesis.

The connection between the way we live our lives, our achievements, and immortality is not new. Becker merely synthesizes old wisdom and Freudian psychology into a coherent theory. Nevertheless, the support for humans striving to achieve symbolic immortality is strong, and can explain why cost and cost growth in some situations become of less importance than rational economic reasoning would suggest. It can explain seemingly non-rational behaviour such as: building higher buildings than economically justifiable; arranging Olympic Games and world championships that require huge investments that cannot be economically warranted; engaging in prestigious projects expressing the immortality of one's cultural worldview, not to mention the use of force to impose one's worldview on others; and also the ignoring of cost overrun and why cost grow. All of these can be of secondary importance to actors driven by such motives.

The Logic of Economics and Explanations to Cost Overrun

We started by analysing results of cost overrun studies for samples of projects, referred to in Appendices A and B. These results were then used in Chapter 4 to identify categories of projects that are more prone to overrun, before formulating a model. In Appendix C, we review other types of cost overrun studies. The great majority of explanations used in these could be related to behavioural biases, information asymmetry, or path dependency. The advantage of these kinds of explanations is that they can all be tested, and that is probably one reason why they are so frequently advanced in the literature.

Such logics are also suitable explanations for the reason that we, in today's society, like to see ourselves as rational. Our economic decisions are not driven by subconscious instincts, emotions, or faith. Others might be, but we understand the chaotic world we live in, and base our decisions on objective facts and logical reasoning – or at least that is the image of ourselves we want others to have, although research contradicts us. We are all susceptible to a range of behavioural biases, such as optimistic and self-serving biases, which may make us underestimate time, cost, and resources needed.

However, as the previous section has illustrated, there is no shortage of project observations and cost overruns which cannot be explained entirely by economic reasoning and behavioural biases. It is in this context that Ernest Becker and terror-management theory fills a gap by offering a theory capable of explaining from the logic of economics point of view seemingly irrational behaviour causing cost overrun and cost growth. It shows that actors and investment projects need not be motivated and driven entirely by economic reasons and emotions that lend themselves to being modelled as behavioural biases. Also, more or less subconscious instincts can initiate and drive support for projects.

Furthermore, the logic of politics, defined and discussed in Chapter 5, can also generate cost overrun and cost growth as the result of, for example, the need to win elections, forming decisions that have strong enough support to be implemented, and maintaining support for a coalition. Both this and Becker's causes are given less space when the logic of economics is the norm, as is the case in profit-maximizing firms. The context does not offer actors the same scope to pursue self-interests which depart from that norm. The risk of cost overrun generated by the practice of politics and individual actors' drive to be remembered after death should therefore be higher in the public sector.

Observe, however, that not only seemingly irrational acts can lead to unwanted outcomes. There is a long tradition[8] of analysing unintended consequences of economic and political decisions, showing that decisions can have both unintended negative and positive outcomes. It can be that a purposeful action by an individual has unintended consequences on a project, organization, other individual, or society. A well-known example of negative consequences described by Garret Hardin[9] is the problem of avoiding the overuse of natural resources, such as the commons, when these are free to use by individuals maximizing their own benefits from using the resource in question. Hardin termed the dilemma 'the tragedy of the commons', but it also applies, for example, to public sector projects in general when influential stakeholders manage to have taxpayers pay for projects implemented to cater for their own needs – a situation that can drive cost growth. An example of a positive unintended outcome is given by Adam Smith's 'invisible hand': 'By pursuing his own interest he frequently promotes that of the society more effectively than when he really intends to promote it.'[10]

Unintended consequences of purposeful action become more probable and difficult to foresee when the complexity and ambiguity of the decision situation increases. This has partly to do with our limited cognitive abilities, and partly with the fact that an event of low probability, hence regarded as improbable, increases when the number of variables rises.[11] It also becomes more difficult to foresee unintended outcomes when ambiguity increases due to the motive for action being found in the logic of politics or our unavoidable death. It might be a rational decision to the actor, but it can be difficult to prove as such motives often are hidden, partly as actors want to be seen as acting according to the logic of economics. What we can do is to create and enforce good control systems, and to strengthen the norms associated with the logic of economics in areas where such behaviour is wanted.

The importance of a well-functioning pre-approval control system to lessen the risk of cost overrun was highlighted earlier. Major companies have well-developed pre-approval control systems, forcing those requesting funding to specify what they want to do and what it will cost before they are given what is needed to implement their project. Projects are monitored during implementation and implemented projects reviewed; companies also have control systems which set targets and evaluate the outcome of business units. Such control systems also exist in public sector companies which mimic the private sector, but for the public sector at large, such control systems are much weaker, and for many parts are virtually none-existent.

Still, we must remember that investment cost estimating and appraisal are basically means used to control and direct investment ideas. They are control processes. The calculated return of the investment is only one of several reasons for the decision to invest. More reliable cost estimates lessen the risk of cost overrun and unintended allocation of resources, and also help us to select proposals and align these to the logic of economics.

Turning to the public sector, cost–benefit analyses and similar forms of control systems aim to make decisions more in line with the logic of economics, and that is why the political sector often has an ambiguous attitude towards such control. Control systems are not politically neutral in that they affect the allocation of public spending, thereby restricting the freedom of pursuing non-economic goals in politics, formulating problems and setting the political agenda, the preconditions for forming political decisions, and whose project ideas are implemented. This has often created a reluctance to hand over decisions to the logic of economics and measures to put such control systems under political control. We need to ask ourselves where the border between the logic of economics and politics should be drawn, and what kind of control system is needed and is politically acceptable in the political sphere when it comes to costly projects? And, do we want to live in a society where resource allocation is determined solely by economic rationality? It would be an unexciting and predictive society to be in.

Resource Irreversibility, Project Divisibility, and Goal Re-negotiability

All investments and projects are more or less irreversible, i.e. resources spent cannot be recovered should the investment be abandoned. Tradable assets might be sold, but rarely for the same price they cost to develop. Assets that are not sold might find other uses in the organization, and the knowledge gained might benefit other projects, but resources spent cannot be entirely recovered. Without this irreversibility, cost over-runs could be avoided simply by going back to the point in the project where the deviation appeared, but that is not possible. Time is not reversible.

All fixed investments are more or less indivisible. This, coupled with the drive to achieve better economies of scale, creates increasingly larger indivisible projects, and associated financial risks when such projects are implemented. The Frövifors machine is a good example of this. After having researched installing a smaller machine, the company decided to construct the largest machine in the world to better exploit economies of scale.

Our Frövifors, Sydgas, and Kvarnsveden cases all exemplified how project divisibility made it easier to meet the budget. If a project is divisible, then the budget can always be met by postponing parts of the project to a later date. Some of these postponed elements might never be implemented; others might be implemented when the market and finance exist. Alternatively, external finance can be sought for parts of the invest-ment, which are then leased back. It requires that the asset that is sold is tradable. Divisibility makes it possible to meet the budget, but postponed investments usually become future investments, and leasing and lower ambitions usually result in higher operating costs in the future.

Projects are not specified in detail when the investment decision is made. Market estimates can change, new and better technical solutions are developed, and new safety and environmental regulations can be enforced after the decision to invest. Changes will inevitably be necessary, especially in projects that take a long time to implement. However, making such changes and adjustments is only possible if project goals and requirements can be re-negotiated, and this is not always the case. Nuclear power plants offer a good example of this. Strict enforcement of safety requirements and special local arrangements make it difficult for project management to renegotiate and solve the unanticipated problems that always appear during construction. The restrictions also lead to longer construction times, which also contribute to cost overruns. The nuclear energy sector has tried to counteract cost overrun by constructing larger plants, but economies of scale have not been achieved because each new plant requires different solutions to comply with increased safety requirements and adapt to the specific location. Solar and wind parks, on the other hand, demonstrate small cost overruns. One explanation is that these technologies can achieve economies of scale, since each new park consists of a large number of identical, mass-produced solar panels or turbines.

It is interesting to compare nuclear energy with coal-fired energy. The latter is not regulated to the same extent as nuclear energy, but serves the same role in an energy system and therefore is considered as an alternative when considering replacing decommissioned nuclear energy plants. Several studies claim that radiation from nuclear energy kills far fewer people than emissions from coal mining, burning mines, and coal-fired power plants, and that the use of coal contributes to global warming. However, while nuclear energy safety is regulated, monitored, and constantly updated following each new nuclear reactor incident in a worldwide cooperative network, no such global network exists for fossil fuel. Some countries require coal-fired electricity plants to have effective scrubbers, while other countries have few or no regulations regarding cleaning emissions. Coal-fired power is considered by many to be a bigger risk to health and global warming. but it is not burdened by the same levels of regulatory and safety costs that the nuclear sector faces. If the use of coal had been regulated to the same extent as nuclear energy, the cost of coal-fired power would be much higher.

Regulations and design traditions vary by technology, but the difference in regulation between nuclear and coal energy is perhaps unique. Organizations have been created specifically for monitoring and regulating nuclear power, but no such organization exists to control the use of coal technologies. One explanation might be that coal is an old technology, another that it is more difficult to measure the long-term negative effects of burning coal, while radioactivity can be measured easily and its long-term effects more easily calculated.

The problem of cost overrun in investment planning is associated with economies of scale and the appearance of large indivisible investments in what can be termed the industrial era. Early textile and metal industries were not very capital-intensive. The costs of labour, raw material, stocks, and transporting the product to the customer were usually much larger than the cost of constructing a new plant. Thus, capital investments were not a major concern – until the development of the very capital-intensive railway technology. During the peak of the British railway boom in 1846–8, the railway industry accounted for more than 50 per cent of total investment in the United Kingdom and employed a quarter of a million construction workers.[12] The huge investments needed contributed to the creation of the British Joint Stock Company Act in 1844, and initiated a process that led to the regulation of depreciation regimes and financial accounting, and the development of the discounted cash flow technique for both the appraisal and design of capital investments.

Economies of scale became important in the steel, electro-mechanical, and chemical industries, which started a second wave of industrialization in the late nineteenth century and led to the development of the assembly line. This gave us cheap products and a mass-consumption society, but economies of scale also gave us larger plants and firms, and investments in large indivisible plants and production units.

Since the 1970s, intangible investments, such as R&D, markets, software, and personnel, have come to make up a larger share of total investments. Stocks and warehouses have been replaced by just-in-time production, and more emphasis has been put on flexibility and the ability to respond to changes. Large indivisible capital investments are still made in the process industry and other industries to achieve economies of scale, but intangible investments are usually divisible and written off the year they are made. Thus, it is safe to assume that indivisible investments make up a smaller share of total investments today than, say, 50 years ago, and that the twentieth century constituted the heyday of indivisible fixed investments in industry.

The same shift in the composition of investments is not so evident in the public sector, which still implements many large-scale infrastructure investments due to its societal role. Some of these investments might be indivisible, such as bridges, but many could probably be conducted in stages. The public sector invests in areas where it is not efficient to allocate resources on a free market basis – so-called market failures. There are many such situations, such as when a private investor cannot appropriate the necessary economic return from an investment, or where there is a risk of abuse of a natural monopoly. We have therefore seen public investments in hydroelectric power, mainlines connecting private railways, roads and streets, canals, airports, street lightning, military forces, police and law enforcement, schools, social and medical care, and services – all to a certain degree indivisible and governed by non-negotiable requirements, factors which make cost overrun more probable.

The Problem of Measuring Cost Overrun

A key difficulty when interpreting results from studies of cost overrun and growth is the almost total lack of information on what is included in the figures that are being compared. This is a major weakness, as it is paramount to make sure that we do in fact compare apples with apples, and not with oranges. The four examples discussed in Chapter 2 illustrated this and showed that to estimate the real cost overrun we need to make sure that we know:

- which costs should be included in the investment amount,
- whether the estimates represent the most probable outcome,
- whether we should view cost from the perspective of the project or the company,
- whether we should consider changes in the project, and
- whether estimates and payments have been adjusted for price changes and inflation.

Determining what should be included in the investment is not a trivial task. The press section example in Chapter 2 illustrated how difficult it is to decide the size of an investment, and what is included in its budget. Should such things as training of operators, production losses, and increase in working capital be included?

Our second problem was that the estimates we compare do not necessarily represent the most probable outcome. We know that experienced project leaders might try to make things easier by having some slack approved in their budget, and we know that company managers can prefer to approve a tight budget, well aware that additional funding might be needed, or, as in the Kvarnsveden case in Chapter 3, approve a generous budget so as not to have to admit to big cost overruns on yet another major project. We also recognize that the dramatic cost increase in the Swedish nuclear waste programme can be explained by political decisions around reactor lifespan and the way risk should be considered when estimating and calculating cost.

Our third problem was whether we should look at project cost in isolation, or in terms of the total cost of the project to the company. Projects often use in-house resources, and how these resources are priced affects the cost of a project. The real cost of these in-house resources can be difficult to calculate and can also be manipulated to meet the project budget. Furthermore, finance and taxes are usually handled outside the project and can become more or less costly than anticipated. Have all costs borne by the company due to the project been correctly credited to the project in both the budget and the later review?

Our fourth problem was to make estimates comparable despite changes in the project. We need to sort out to what extent cost has been affected by work that was not anticipated in the budget, savings, and changes in the project. It is not unusual for project planners to discover new works that are necessary to complete the project during the course of planning. The

Trans-Alaska Pipeline example showed how even the roads necessary to transport building material to the construction site had been forgotten. On top of project-related changes, there may also be changes if the budget becomes difficult to meet – for instance, postponing part of the project, outsourcing and leasing back other parts, and choosing parts and solutions of lower quality. These are all examples of measures that will increase future cost of operation and investments. The project may even have been redesigned or redirected to adjust to changing market demand – the goals and requirements of the project may have shifted or changed. An example of this is the two hydroelectric power stations that were redesigned due to the oil price shock in the 1970s increasing electricity prices. When projects encounter substantial cost overrun, there have usually been changes during implementation, with the original budget being based on one design and the follow up reviewing a modified design.

Finally, we have to transform the estimates we want to compare to the same price level to make them comparable. This is not a trivial task as we need to have knowledge of price clauses and terms of payment, which are seldom available to external observers.

Cost overrun is a topical subject. Newspapers and trade journals tell us about projects that have become 50, 100, or even 200 per cent more expensive than intended. We must remain sceptical about such figures. The increase in cost can be caused by expanded scope, changes in the project, or inflation, and we usually do not know the extent of these effects. A proper project review must consider additional items and savings, changes in scope and goals, in-house resources and price changes, what was expected, and what was achieved. Superficial cost data is a major flaw in much of the research on cost overrun. In the best of worlds, one would hope that possible biases will level out in studies with large enough samples.

A Model of Cost Overrun and Growth as a Result of Uncertainty Resolution

In Chapter 4 we formulated a model of cost overrun based on studies of groups of projects reviewed in Appendix B. In this model we distinguished between static and dynamic uncertainty (see Table 6.1). Static uncertainties originate from external factors such as changes in politics, currency rates, laws, regulations, weather, and natural disasters. It is a form of uncertainty that will always be present, and will not disappear as the project is completed. Dynamic uncertainty, in contrast, resolves as the project comes closer to completion and more reliable information regarding what the completed project will look like and what is needed to implement it becomes available.

Table 6.1 *Dynamic and static uncertainty and types of project prone to overrun*

Uncertainty		
Dynamic uncertainty will resolve during the planning period		*Static uncertainty will always be present*
Uncertainty can be resolved using existing knowledge	*Uncertainty can be resolved but requires the acquisition and development of new knowledge*	
Implementation projects	Development projects	Projects affected by exogenous static uncertainty
Complex projects which uncertainty will be resolved during the planning period		System innovations
Projects new to the actors implementing and costing them but which need not be new to the world or especially complex		

We assumed that estimates are made by a decision maker who bases his or her estimates on increasingly reliable information as the project progresses and uncertainty about the final state of the project is resolved. It is not the ideal economic man making the final decision at one point in time, but a variant of this in which the decision maker has access to increasingly better information. This model makes it possible to explain well-known conclusions from studies of groups of projects. Examples of such conclusions are: that estimated costs increase over time, and that cost overrun correlates with the length of the time period between two estimates, with changes in other measures of output, with advances in new knowledge, with project complexity, and depending on the familiarity of such projects to those planning and implementing it.

In this model, we distinguished between implementation and development projects. Implementation projects were projects that could be specified in detail reasonably well before the formal decision to invest and before they were implemented, if enough resources were spent on planning ex ante. Examples included bridges, standard housing and boats, and other types of projects that can draw on existing knowledge. However, when a project requires the development of new knowledge, detailed specifications cannot be delivered before the decision to invest, as is the case with projects like this book. It did not start out with a clear idea of what the last chapter would look like or even the final structure of the book; this evolved as the author created a better image of the final product. This is generally the case in development projects that include research. The goal is to arrive at a specification, rather than implementing a specification.

A second cause of cost overrun was project complexity. Projects consist of many interrelated tasks and actors, and the more dependencies there are between tasks and actors in a project, the higher the risk of cost increases. If a delay in one task cannot be covered by slack time or by re-negotiating plans and requirements, it will propagate delay in other parts of the project and increase the final cost. The problem is that if something goes wrong a task can take twice as long time to perform as planned, but it will never be possible to perform a task in no time at all. The outcome is not symmetrical and this also offers an explanation for the positive skewness observed in studies of groups of projects.

Our last category of projects was those that were unique and therefore implemented rarely, at least by the entity implementing them. We cannot generalize as to whether they are implementation or development projects, as that depends on the knowledge of the entity responsible for planning and implementation. What might be a routine project for one organization can be an entirely new type of project for another. Regardless of project, for those in charge, this category of project requires the acquisition and development of new knowledge.

To illustrate the effects of exogenous static uncertainty, we used two hydroelectric power stations in which cost overruns could be partly explained by the need for redesign during implementation because the value of electricity increased when the OPEC tripled the price of oil. A hydroelectric power station can be designed ex ante, but this radical change in energy prices was not foreseen. Static uncertainty can also drive cost when the success of a new complex system is dependent on several independent actors succeeding in their part of the development work. We termed this 'system innovations'. To the individual firm developing a component in such a new system, uncertainty about other actors' intentions and development work can become static uncertainty.

A related issue is whether estimators tend to over- or underestimate long-term price increases in any systematic way. Our examples from the nuclear energy and military weapon sectors indicated that this can be the case. The cost of implementing yet another nuclear power plant or developing a new weapon system can be decreased by standardization and transfer of learning from earlier projects. However, in these two cases, it seems that these cost-reducing factors have been overestimated, while cost-increasing factors, such as greater complexity and the development of unique or state-of-the-art solutions, have been underestimated.

Based on our model, we also identified four situations in which cost might have increased as a result of a rational decision to improve expected return and reduce project risk. These included projects:

- for which it ought to be possible to make a more accurate estimate of the final cost ex ante, but for which expected return is deemed so high and dependent on early operation that waiting for uncertainty to be resolved is considered unnecessary.
- for which it should be possible to estimate the final cost ex ante but where it would be too expensive to do so considering the expected return from the project.
- for which the investor is willing to pay an extra fee to avoid the perils of cost overrun.
- where cost increase is due to a move towards economies of scale and/or scope to increase the expected return.

The third category might need a comment. The risk of cost increases can be reduced by, e.g. procuring a completed project at a fixed price, or, as in the Swedish nuclear waste example, by increasing the risk premium included in the estimate. This does not guarantee that resources are put to best use, but it helps to avoid cost overrun, and can explain why some seemingly risky projects are implemented to an approved budget.

The Logic of Politics Versus the Logic of Economics

In Chapter 5 we discussed differences in preconditions for making cost estimates when the logic of economics versus the logic of politics dominates, and therein identified three main distinguishing factors: type of project; goals; and control.

Companies invest in projects that they can implement successfully; the public sector invests in social needs which the private sector does not cover. This makes it easier for companies to accumulate knowledge and skills in the areas in which they invest and to evaluate the types of investments they wish to make. The role of the public sector forces it to invest much more frequently in projects that are unique to the organization, and also in projects that the private sector would consider as too risky to undertake.

Private firms also have a clearer goal against which projects can be designed and evaluated, while the public sector has to consider multiple goals and multiple stakeholders. Good decisions always have to be of high quality in an economic-technical sense, and gain acceptance, but as political parties represent different interests, forming a decision that will gain acceptance becomes more important than for firms. Political agreements in which all parties have to gain something makes accountability diffuse and opens up the possibility of alternative interpretations of the outcome, as well as the possibility that individual stakeholders might initiate changes later on in the project that drive costs up.

Our third factor was control. The public sector is forced to implement all kinds of investment projects and satisfy multiple goals under full transparency, which makes it more difficult to avoid cost growth. The diversity of projects makes it more difficult to supply internal feedback to proposers of future projects. Transparency can put the public procurer at a disadvantage, as those putting in tenders have knowledge that can help them when negotiating prices and terms. And, when freedom of information acts make early plans and estimates public, this can force actors to make early commitments which will prove difficult to abandon later.

Perhaps even more important is that politicians and administrators might focus on how their image is received by media and voters, and adjust what they say to match what they think the receiver wants to hear. Whatever the case, the public sector seldom demonstrates the same planning urgency as the private sector: the financial risk is low, and the market risk is low since the public sector does not risk finding that there is no use for a service since the service can be provided free of charge. The problem is, rather, that free and under-priced services create overconsumption.

Economic-technical uncertainty derives from lack of information. Political uncertainty is different because political parties represent different world views and interests. Their role is to pursue these interests, which means that they have to disagree on goals and negotiate consent or a compromise in order to gain their 'win'. Those involved can disagree on a variety of issues, such as how information should be interpreted, the problem the project is supposed to solve, or the best way to solve the problem. Disagreement can derive from different ideologies, interpretations and mental images, lack of information and knowledge, or simply personal interests and benefits. Such political uncertainty affects public sector projects directly, and economic-technical decisions indirectly, through laws, regulations, economic policy, and the political climate.

An economic-technical solution to a problem exists in the upper-left quadrant of Figure 6.1, but the actors disagree over the correct description of the problem and the solution. To gain acceptance for a solution, it might be necessary to modify the project, but not necessarily if the project is perceived to be urgent and is backed by influential stakeholders strong enough to enforce their will on other stakeholders. Companies can avoid investing when there is a lack of knowledge and agreement on possible outcomes, but politicians cannot always do so, and may find themselves in the position indicated in the upper-right quadrant.

Political uncertainty	Problem: Disagreement	Problem: Lack of knowledge, shared mental images and agreement makes the outcome of the process unpredictable
	Solution: Create acceptance for one solution	Solution: Move the issue if possible to the left before approving a solution or isolate the issue
Political certainty	Problem: Maximize shareholder value	Problem: Lack of information
	Solution: Evaluate and choose the best alternative	Solution: Re-evaluate the alternatives when better information becomes available
	Economic-technical certainty	Economic-technical uncertainty

Figure 6.1 Resolving economic-technical versus political uncertainty

Finally, we have static uncertainty. This type of uncertainty can be reduced through economic and political stability – a stable business climate with a stable and transparent legal system. When we have static uncertainty, we have a situation where society is fragmented, with a range of different perceived problems and solutions and a risk of anarchy creating new coalitions and disruptive events if politics fail.

We have four alternatives for resolving dynamic uncertainty. We can resolve economic-technical uncertainty first, political uncertainty first, economic-technical and political uncertainty simultaneously, or make a decision without having resolved either.

Resolve economic-technical uncertainty first. This is a common alternative in companies, which distinguish between strategic and operative investments. There is a business process by which the strategy for the group and its units are developed, and a process in which operative investments are assessed and approved against previously approved strategies. Companies first approve a strategy, which can include major investments and investment programmes, then they approve operative investments as part of the implementation of the approved strategies. This is the ideal, although new needs can sometimes make it necessary to approve urgent emerging needs and modify approved strategies.

The public sector does not make the same clear distinction between strategic and operative decisions. What is a strategically important project to one politician and political party might not be equally important to another, meaning that all projects can become disputed.

Resolve political uncertainty first. This decision strategy might be applied simply because it is easier to agree on the goal than to define the project leading to goal fulfilment – for instance, it is easier to agree on the principle of lowering emissions or traffic congestion than on how to achieve these goals.

Major public infrastructure projects are often the result of political negotiations and an agreement between several political parties and stakeholders. The agreement comes first. Only then can a detailed project plan be developed and its costs estimated, and, as it can take several years to negotiate a political deal, the cost estimate upon which the agreement is based is often both uncertain and out of date. When planners develop the project further later on, changes in the project may be needed and additional requirements discovered, and, by this time, inflation may have made the original budget worth less. All of these contribute to an increase in estimated costs.

Resolve economic-technical and political uncertainty simultaneously. Project planning is to some extent always an iteration between reducing economic-technical uncertainty and gaining the commitment necessary for approval and funding. Strategies and top management's strategic initiatives generate investment requests, and project planners must sell their proposals to secure funding.

It is often a good strategy to iterate between problem and solution because this helps to surface ideas and issues that need to be addressed. This process does not necessarily drive cost, unless political uncertainty means that the preconditions for the project could change. If the project has to be modified in an uneconomic way to gain acceptance, then this will increase cost, and the worst case is if such changes become necessary during implementation. The risk will remain as long as all uncertainty has not been resolved.

Decide without resolving uncertainty. Both business leaders and political leaders may have to make decisions based on vague information, due to urgency, the need to seize a window of opportunity, or some other reason, without securing acceptance for the decision or knowing the cost. This is a risky strategy for the politician when it comes to the possibility of cost overrun, and as the decision does not have firm support from a majority, the decision may be overturned if the political situation changes.

A positive consequence of the ambiguity that lack of information creates is that stakeholders can project their vision and wishes into the potential outcome of a given project more easily. Facts can be replaced by hopes, as nobody knows exactly what the facts are. This situation can make it easier to reach an agreement, and can sometimes be the reason why a project is approved before accurate cost estimates have been obtained. It is a possible way forward, but also risky because there is always the possibility of later discord about what was agreed, which in turn can drive the costs of the project upwards. The agreement might have to be re-negotiated when more becomes known about the consequences of the project and the decision, or if the political situation changes. It may even prove to have been a non-decision, the project outdated, and the agreement forgotten.

A safer alternative when neither economic-technical or political uncertainty can be reduced is to isolate the issue. This can be done by postponing the decision, by moving the issue from the daily political agenda by appointing a commission to study the issue, or by moving the issue to a specific organization where administrators or business interests are allowed to take it over. An organization can be created especially to handle the issue, or a service can be moved from a public department to a publicly owned company or outsourced to a private company. The issue is at least temporarily transferred from the political agenda to another scene that is either politically controlled or where the logic of economics prevails and the political uncertainty is instantly reduced.

Project Profitability and the Effects of Cost Overrun on Resource Allocation

It has been claimed that cost overruns make investment projects unprofitable. In situations where the investment might not have been made had the full costs been known, that might sound intuitively like the correct conclusion, but, as we have shown in Chapter 3, it is not always true. The way investment appraisals are made, who pays and who can appropriate the return from the investment are all reasons why we need to dig a little deeper into this issue.

Many investments never achieve the return originally promised. This is easy to conclude. Just compare the return to firms ex post with the return promised in investment requests ex ante. The hurdle rate for investments is usually higher than ex post returns from the unit making the investment. One explanation for this phenomenon is that unprofitable businesses are not stopped in time; another is that the return on new investments is systematically overestimated – and one reason for this overestimation could be that the investment outlay was underestimated. Whether that is the case or not, however, is difficult to establish, and we will examine three factors that make generalizations difficult.

Firstly, we have the measurement problem described in Chapter 2. We need to know more about the project than is reported in the media to know if and why the cost has increased.

Secondly, the investment outlay for many technologies constitutes a rather small part of the total cost of the investment during its lifetime, and this varies a lot from technology to technology. The total lifetime cost of a power line placed in the ground is almost equal to the original investment outlay, while the cost of investing in a new tram car is split into thirds: investment, maintenance, and electricity, excluding the cost of drivers. Still, tramways are a capital-intensive technology. Refineries are also capital-intensive, but although it is very expensive to construct a new refinery, the value of the products processed during one year is often higher than the investment outlay. Thus, only a percentage increase in the price of inputs relative to output will have a significant effect on profitability. The investment outlay can be very large but still constitute only a minor part of the total cost of the system during its life.

Thirdly, we have the problem of dependencies. It is difficult to separate the cash flow of one investment from other contemporary and future investments. The profitability of an investment is dependent on earlier investments, and also affects the profitability of other investments in the organization, and sometimes also the profitability of investments in other firms and society at large. The distinction between basic and later additional investments exemplifies the problem.

The Frövifors cartonboard and liquid packaging board machine produced 160,000 tonnes per year when it was commissioned into service. Today, it produces 400,000 tonnes, and in August 2014 its owner, BillerudKorsnäs, decided on an investment programme that will increase production to 550,000 tonnes per year.[13] That is an increase in production of 244 per cent over the original production figure, and such an increase is not unique for paper machines. Production can often be radically increased through additional investments in this and many other process industries.

In the vehicle industry, manufacturers develop a platform which can be used as the basis for several models. The platform in itself is seldom profitable if it cannot be used in this way. The same applies in the computer software industry, where companies develop a software platform that can be used in a large number of customer projects. A platform is developed to establish a presence in a market, or to create a technology that will pay for itself in the future by making it possible to take advantage of several profitable business opportunities. Another important factor in the profitability of such projects is knowledge creation. Development projects, and sometimes also ordinary investments, can generate new knowledge that can be used in future investments. There is an interdependence between present and future investments.

In appraising a basic investment or platform correctly, we need to consider the cash flow from all future payments. It can be additional investments or customer contracts, but most of these future options are unknown; those that are known are described as future possible options, but are seldom valued because they are uncertain and difficult to value. The basic investment is often not profitable without the later additional investments, but has to be proven profitable without these difficult-to-prove future investments. Thus, in practice, the investment appraisal when requesting a basic investment is more of an evaluation of financial risk than of profitability. Can the firm manage the financial burden during the first few years? If so, it creates a platform for exploiting future profitable business opportunities if and when these appear.

A return on smaller additional investments of 30 per cent is not unusual, as such investments do not have to pay for using the resources provided by previous investments. Evaluating investments as such leads to a situation where the profitability of the basic investment tends to be:

- underestimated, as the economic life of the investment is set at 5 to 20 years when in reality the project often has a far longer economic life and sometimes a payback period not much shorter than this planning horizon;
- underestimated, as investment appraisals often disregard the profit received from future profitable additional investments that increase the capacity, productivity, or product quality of the basic investment; and
- overestimated, as investment appraisals often disregard expenditures for future additional investments necessary to adjust the basic investment to changing market conditions.

Investment appraisals are biased. One could claim that all investment appraisals, or at least most, are only partial as they do not consider all future payments during the life of the investment.

These examples illustrate that the profitability of an investment depends on past and future investments. There is also an interdependence with investments outside the firm, as one firm's investment may make it possible for other firms to make profitable investments, and the new knowledge that is created will sooner or later be disseminated in the industry. However, the fact that other firms can profit due to one firm's investment does not matter as it will not increase the profit of the initial investment. The correct question for the firm is to what extent it can appropriate return[14] and knowledge from its investment.

If, for instance, a firm invests in educating its employees, there is a risk that competitors will reap the benefits if the firm cannot retain those employees, a fact that reduces employers' willingness to invest in education programmes. Knowledge spillover also affects software development strategies and other areas where intellectual property rights are weak. Computer software programs and code can easily be copied and reproduced, which results in firms developing software in smaller steps than they otherwise would have done. Such positive spillovers might make certain investments profitable for society and industry but not for the firm making the investment.

We have shown that the cost of investments that generate new knowledge, or have high complexity, is often underestimated. These are types of investment that tend to generate spillovers. It is difficult to generalize about the extent of such spillovers. What we do know is that R&D has a considerable spillover effect because research results can be disseminated easily, allowing all firms in an industry to benefit sooner or later from the productivity gains of all other firms' R&D in the industry. R&D is a considerably more profitable operation for an industry, and for society as a whole, than for the firm performing the R&D.[15] Society's return on R&D differs by industry[16] but usually exceeds private return.

Investments and projects can have positive effects for the firm implementing them apart from profit from the investment in question. Firstly, implementation can generate knowledge that, together with the firm's previous knowledge, becomes a source for discovering and exploiting new and profitable investment opportunities. Secondly, the implementation of a bold high-tech project, or a project in cooperation with a highly regarded high-tech firm, can enhance the image employees and customers have of the firm. However, as always, it is difficult to estimate the value of new knowledge and improved image.

In Chapter 3, we identified both negative and positive consequences of cost overrun. In the worst cases, cost overrun can cause bankruptcy. This can be a disaster for investors, but does not need to be so for society if the project finds another owner. It can also affect careers and settle as negative sediment in a firm's collective memory. However, the greatest negative consequence at the firm level of underestimating the true cost is that it will impair the financial capacity of the firm. It will reduce the firm's financial flexibility and ability to take advantage of future profitable investments opportunities, acquisitions, and business deals when these appear. This will hamper future growth and profitability, and may very well be the most important consequence of large cost overruns on major investments and projects.

A positive consequence of cost overrun is that it can be assumed to increase savings and the total volume of investment. To what extent this occurs is, however, difficult to know, partly as cost overrun also induces savings and postpones activities, and partly as it typically means that some of the investment planned for the year can no longer be implemented.

A more important positive consequence is that underestimating cost reallocates investments from types of investments that seldom increase in cost to types of investments that do so more often. This is important as investments where cost is more prone to increase are typically also riskier investments, such as investments in R&D and the development of new technical knowledge and markets – the type of investments that contribute to renewing the product portfolio of firms, industry, and society. Cost overrun can thus have a positive effect as firms have a tendency to overinvest in product variation relative to more long-term development of new products, technologies, and markets. It counteracts the short-termism that haunts firms. While it might not be optimal for a single organization to reallocate resources in an unintended way, on an aggregate level it ought to be a positive consequence of cost overrun.

A specific kind of investment is that which is profitable ex post but would not have been made if the real cost and resources needed to implement it were known ex ante. We have given several examples of this and identified four categories of investments for which there is a tendency to underinvest if the estimated investment outlay was correct, due to the tendency to underestimate the contribution from future profitable additional investments. These examples were:

- infrastructure projects opening up new markets for exploitation;
- radical innovations creating business opportunities for exploitation;
- new ventures opening up new product markets for exploitation; and
- projects benefiting from changing value systems.

However, when talking about the consequences of cost overrun on resource allocation in firms and society, one must remember that we consider the effects on tangible investments and R&D. Tangible investments make up a decreasing amount of total investments. For industry as a whole, tangible investments account not for more than a third of total investment; for knowledge-intensive firms the figure is lower.

Studies of cost overrun and growth deal mainly with fixed investments. The reason is obvious – the result can be quantified and measured. However, the problems of poor estimates are probably no less when it comes to intangible types of investment. It is probably a larger problem as such investments are more difficult to measure.

Intangible investments are both more difficult to define and their result more difficult to measure. How many marketing campaigns reach their goal? How many investments in education give those that are educated the knowledge expected? Compared to this, it is very easy to establish the size of a cost overrun of a new building, machine, or plant.

Appendix A   How Common Is Cost Overrun and Cost Growth?

Case Studies of Cost Overrun

There are plenty of case studies of cost overrun and cost growth in scientific journals and daily newspapers. One project that reached iconic recognition due not only to its architecture but also to its cost overrun is the Sydney Opera House. The project started in 1956 with the announcement of an international architectural competition for a multipurpose opera, concert, and theatre building. The competition received 233 entries and in 1957 an international committee selected an innovative proposal from the Danish architect Jørn Utzon, which the assessors deemed had the potential to put Sydney on the world map.[1]

Construction started two years later, with estimated completion in 1963. By then the estimated cost had risen from $A 7.2 million to $A 9.76 million and the well-known London based engineering firm Ove Arup and Partners had been chosen to construct the building.

Contracts were signed before Utzon's innovative proposal had been transferred into drawings that could be implemented with existing building techniques.[2] The proposal did not have room for enough seats, and new building technics had to be developed as the design could not be built using pre-stressed concrete. This led to conflicts between the architect's vision and user requirements, and Utzon left the project in 1966, at a time when there still was no complete architectural drawing of the interior of the building, and the project was delayed as a result. The Sydney Opera House was completed in 1974 at a cost of $A 103 million – 14 times more than the original estimate made 16 years earlier. Costly, yes, but all cost increases since 1959 were covered by popular lotteries.

The Sydney Opera House exhibits many traits in common with other projects where estimated costs have increased dramatically in that the investment decision was based on (a) poor or non-existing cost estimates, (b) a partly unspecified design with unsolved technical problems, leading to subsequent development through trial and error with substantial re-work and modification throughout the construction process, (c) iterations between the wishes of users, architects, and construction firms, and (d) a long construction time which inevitably makes estimates outdated and increases cost due to inflation, all factors which we see recurring in projects with large cost overruns.

From a project planning point of view, the project was a failure, but its promoters wanted a building that would put Sydney on the map, and that they got. It is one of the most popular tourist attractions in Australia, visited by more than seven million people each year. In 2003, Jørn Utzon received the prestigious Pritzker Prize[3] for his design of the Sydney Opera House, and in 2007 UNESCO made the building a World Heritage Site. It was yet further recognition that the initiators of the project had indeed achieved their dream of a world-renowned iconic building that would become a symbol of Sydney.

One might wonder if those involved would have dared to choose Utzon's innovative sketch had they imagined all the technical problems that had to be overcome. However, had they settled for a traditional building, for which there was a prototype, the Sydney Opera House would not have appeared on the World Heritage list, and might not have fulfilled its purpose of putting Sydney on the map. And by the time the building was finished, financed by lotteries, its large cost overrun contributed to rather than marred its iconic status.

There are many books and articles written about problem-ridden projects with large cost overruns like the Sydney Opera House, usually about public projects as freedom of information acts give the public access to documentation on such projects. The question is whether experiences from these well-known projects are project-specific or if one can draw any general conclusions from their stories. Do any aspects of these projects show common traits or have common denominators? Let us try to paint a brief picture.

Such case studies often deal with projects that have been at the centre of attention in the political debate and in the media, which also probably explains why they have been dealt with in the literature. The aim of the projects has often been rather diffuse and partly political in nature. Some presuppose sophisticated technical solutions and the development of new technology, which has been put forward as an argument for implementing the project.

The decision to go ahead has often been taken at a very early stage, when the design was not yet finalized and reliable estimates were difficult to make. These early decisions were often a result of the political decision-making process which presupposes a political decision upon which the administration can act.

The market risk has been low as the future owners, due to their market monopoly, have been assured provision for costs by increasing tariffs or taxes. Financing has usually not been problematic as public projects can be financed by governments, and public organizations are regarded by lenders as reliable borrowers. In the end, it has been taxpayers and consumers who have had to pay for the implementation and cost overruns of these projects through fees and taxes.[4]

It is doubtful if a private company with liability for payment would have taken the risks such public projects represented, which raises the question of how similar these well-known and often very politicized public projects are to private sector projects, and also to public projects that generate less political and national attention.

One can of course look for similarities in private industrial projects. More thorough follow-ups are sometimes made for major private sector investments with large budget overruns, as well as for strategies when management feels targets may not have been achieved. We can learn quite a lot from such reviews, but in most cases it is difficult to generalize as the reasons suggested for the problems are case-specific. Reviews can find that cost overrun was due to, for example: it taking longer than planned to make the plant control equipment work; supplies not being received in time; suppliers having financial problems; unanticipated price increases; a lack of skilled labour causing local inflation; poor cost control; or problems of seasonality, i.e. an unusually cold winter. Such explanations can be correct and relevant for the project in question, but many are difficult to generalize to other projects. However, three overarching explanations repeatedly turn up when going through reviews of a number of large projects, namely:

- Changes in design
- Increase in scope
- Inflation and price increases

These three causes interact. Changes in design can be partly due to inflation and price increases, and lead to an increase in scope. When a project shows a large cost overrun, it is almost always not exactly the same project as was originally costed because the original design has been revised and the project re-costed. Some project managers might object by claiming that the final cost of the project should not be compared with the budget, as the changes mean that we now have a much better building, plant, or machine than what was originally approved. That might be correct, but, nevertheless, if the final cost is higher than the approved budget, then we have a cost overrun.

In the next three sections of Appendix A, we shall review what studies of groups of similar projects have to show us about the occurrence of cost overrun and growth. Building mainly on these studies, in Appendix B we will generate some general conclusions on cost overrun and growth, which we will use in Chapter 4 to build a model of cost overrun.

Construction Projects

To be able to generalize about cost overrun, we either need a theory that helps us to understand our observations of cost overrun, or data on a large enough number of projects to identify statistically significant differences between projects of different types. In the former case, we rely on theories applied earlier to other areas of social science, and explanations at the individual and organizational levels, to explain cost overrun in case studies of individual projects; in the latter, we rely on descriptive explanations based on the similarities and dissimilarities identified in the dataset.

We will draw on both kinds of research, and we will start by reviewing statistical studies of deviations in cost estimates for groups of projects, as such studies provide a good point of departure for theorizing about cost overrun. First, we explore studies of construction projects, then research and development projects, and, finally, software development projects. Some of the studies of cost overruns in construction projects are listed in Table A.1. Figures on average cost overruns in parentheses are in constant money value. It is difficult to find a study showing that construction projects taken as a group become on average less expensive than anticipated; cost overrun is the norm.

Although the number of studies and projects is high, we still have to be careful about drawing overconfident conclusions from them as the quality of the data analysed is sometimes questionable, and this makes it difficult to compare data from one study with another. Admittedly, investigators have considered inflation in several of the studies, but the way this has been done is not always described, and in many of the studies project cost data is compiled from different sources, estimators, organizations, and decades. Considering how common and unwanted cost overrun is, there are relatively few studies of cost overrun of sufficient size and quality that they allow us to draw statistically significant conclusions about cost overruns. We are forced to assume that the errors in project cost data balance each other out when we pool projects in groups of similar projects. Moreover, most of the studies in the social science literature concern major public sector projects. Studies of private sector projects are far less common, and to what extent ownership influences project outcome is poorly researched.

Product Development Projects

Studies of groups of product development projects show great similarities to construction projects. Not only is cost overrun the norm, but also the

Table A.1 *Cost overrun in construction projects*

Year of study	Type of project	Number of projects	Average cost overrun in %
1970[5]	US water resource projects in three utilities		
	Bureau of Reclamation		
	Projects implemented before 1955	103	177
	Projects 1935–60	128	72
	Projects 1946–60	54	9.4
	Corps of Engineers		
	Projects implemented before 1951	182	124.1
	Projects 1933–65	184	36.1
	Projects 1954–60	68	−0.2
	Tennessee Valley Authority	34	−5.3
1973[6]	US public infrastructure and mostly non-US rapid transit projects		
	Water resource projects	49	38
	Highway projects	49	26
	Building projects	59	63
	Rapid Transit projects	17	54
	Ad Hoc projects	15	114
	All Merewitz' projects	189	59
1980[7]	British offshore projects		179 (146)
	Norwegian offshore projects		178 (148)
1983[8]	US public sector military and civilian projects	444	122
	Whereof military projects	244	127
	Whereof civilian projects	200	92
1985[9]	Turkish public sector construction projects	394	44
	Data from public agencies	126	111
	Data from private contractor	258	11
1986[10]	Major investments in plants in Sweden	35	10
1986[11]	Investments made by Vattenfall		
	Power line projects	37	4.6 (1.5)
	Transformer projects	67	5.1 (−0.1)
	Hydroelectric power projects	11	82.5 (21.6)
1990[12]	Indian public sector projects	133	82
1994[13]	Swedish highway projects	8	86 / 9.8
	Swedish railway projects	7	17 / −8.3
2002[14]	Transportation infrastructure projects		
	Railway projects	58	(44.7)
	Bridge and tunnel projects	33	(33.8)
	Road projects	167	(20.4)
	All projects	258	(27.6)
	European projects	181	(25.7)
	North American projects	61	(23.6)
	Other geographical areas	16	(64.6)
2004[15]	Norwegian road projects 1992–95	620	7.9
2008[16]	International mining and smelting projects	63	25 (14)

Table A.1 *(cont.)*

Year of study	Type of project	Number of projects	Average cost overrun in %
2008[17]	Korean road projects	138	28.6 (10.7)
	Korean rail projects	16	81.0 (47.6)
2011[18]	Swedish road projects	102	(11.1)
	Swedish rail projects	65	(21.1)
2014[19]	Norwegian road projects	434	10.06
	Norwegian road projects 1997–2003	323	11.14
	Norwegian road projects 2004–07	288	8.79
2014[20]	Power plant and electricity transmission projects		
	Nuclear reactors	180	(117)
	Hydroelectric dams	61	(71)
	Thermal power plants	36	(13)
	Wind farms	35	(8)
	Electricity transmission projects	50	(8)
	Solar farms	39	(1)
2014[21]	Major oil and gas projects		
	Upstream gas and oil projects	163	70
	Liquefied natural gas projects	50	41
	Pipeline projects	46	69
	Refinery projects	106	53
	Major oil and gas projects	205 of 365	59
	The same 205 projects divided on:		
	Africa	–	51
	Asia-Pacific	–	57
	Europe	–	57
	Latin America	–	102
	Middle East	–	68
	North America	–	51

Note: Figures on average cost overrun in parentheses are in constant money value. Observe, however, that the way the authors have transformed nominal to constant money value is not always stated and might differ.

causes of cost overrun are very similar to those found in construction projects.

Military product development projects tend to demonstrate cost growth. The US authorities commissioned the RAND Corporation, a policy think tank, to study the causes of cost overrun in weapon development programmes in the 1950s. Two of these early studies are listed in Table A.2. Figures in parentheses are adjusted for inflation. The first study was conducted by Andrew W. Marshall and William H. Meckling in 1962[22] and the second one by Robert Summers in 1967.[23] They both used regression analyses to study 68 estimates in various phases of 22

Table A.2 *Cost overrun in R&D projects*

Year of study	Type of R&D project	Number of projects	Deviation in cost in %	Deviation in time in %
1962[24], 1967[25]	US military aircraft and missile projects	22	226 (79)	50
1971[26]	US pharmaceutical firms			
	New chemical entities	17	125	89
	Compounded products	29	70	60
	Alternative dosage forms	29	51	33
	All projects in company A	75	78	61
	Product improvement	33	41	164
	New products	36	175	224
	All projects in company B	69	111	195
1990[27]	Swedish engineering firms			
	Engineering company A	15	120	60
	Engineering company B	20	30	40
	Survey of 54 engineering companies	91	80	60

Note: Figures on average cost overrun within parentheses are in constant money value.

military aircraft and missile programmes undertaken between 1945 and 1958 in the USA. In doing so, they corrected their figures for inflation and the number of airplanes produced.

One major reason for cost overrun in military aircraft projects has been that the estimated system cost has been based on the assumption that the cost of development would be paid for by a larger number of aircraft being built than were actually constructed. In this context, one must also mention Merton J. Peck and Frederic M. Scherer's study[28] of the weapon acquisition process. Since these studies, there has been a constant flow of analyses of cost growth in US military and other public sector projects, but none of the studies have solved the problem.

Building on this earlier work at RAND, Edwin Mansfield[29] led a research team that analysed product development in two US pharmaceutical companies. They had data from 75 projects in one of the companies and 49 from the other, all carried out between 1950 and 1967. The data from these two different companies is not directly comparable, but the researchers did correct their data for inflation. Their study showed, among other things, that one of the companies was better at estimating costs, and had improved its cost estimates, but not the other. Organizational factors matter.

A later study of development projects in Swedish engineering firms shows similar figures. As is evident from Table A.2, one of the companies

Table A.3 *Yearly cost growth for new military weapon systems*

Year of study	Number of weapon systems	Number of projects	Yearly above inflation cost increase in %	Average yearly above inflation cost increase in %
2008[30]	7	116	2.1–7.3	4.1
2011[31]	10	39	0.7–7.6	4.5
2012[32]	7	39	2.6–5.9	4.3

showed cost growth four times as large as the other, or 120 per cent. Project cost not only grew more in one of the companies, but also the outcome varied more. The standard deviation was twice as large. Three causes of cost overrun were stressed. The most important was that the level of ambition had increased, i.e. the final product had more functionality than originally planned; the other two were uncertainty and lack of resources due to development resources being shifted to competing products.

As can be seen by comparing Tables A.1 and A.2, cost overrun is, in general, somewhat larger for product development projects than for construction projects, as demonstrated, for instance, by the American study from 1983 of 244 military and 200 civilian projects. In fact, one of the most important conclusions from studies of cost overrun in product development projects is that the larger the advance in new knowledge that is made, the larger the cost overrun tends to be. This connection, which was formulated by Marshall and Meckling in 1962, has been confirmed in many later studies, and has also been advanced as one of the reasons behind military projects being more prone to cost growth than civilian ones.

Cost growth in weapon development projects continues to be scrutinized. Studies at RAND[33], in the UK,[34] Norway,[35] and Sweden[36] have focused on how the cost per unit produced for each new generation of weapon system increases faster than can be explained by the rate of inflation alone. This type of cost growth is called intergenerational cost growth, as opposed to intragenerational cost growth. The latter can decrease as cost per unit may lower due to the learning curve that exists in all repetitive operations.

The cost of naval ships and aircraft has increased faster than the rate of inflation for a very long time, and, because of that, the number of fighting ships and aircraft a country can afford to acquire and maintain has gradually decreased. Three such studies are summarized in Table A.3, and show that the unit cost of a specific piece of military equipment in constant monetary value has increased by 0.7 to 7.6 per cent per year, or more than 4 per cent on average. Unit cost has increased faster for high-tech weapon systems produced in low quantities than for more standardized weapon systems. With each new technology generation, navies can acquire increasingly fewer ships, air forces fewer aircraft, and armies fewer tanks.

Computer Software Projects

Another type of project that is often affected by cost overrun is computer software projects. A study that aroused a lot of public attention is the Standish Group's CHAOS Report, published in 1995.[37] This report was based on a survey answered by 365 IT managers representing 8,380 projects. Thirty-one percent of the projects had been discontinued, and the average cost overrun for these, and the other 52.7 per cent in which costs had increased, was 189 per cent. Schedule overrun was even larger, or 222 per cent; only 61 per cent of the 52.7 per cent of projects with cost overruns had achieved the specifications originally set out. See Table A.4.

The CHAOS Report has been criticized[38] on the grounds that the results of the study do not correspond with other American, Canadian, and Dutch studies showing an average cost overrun of 33 to 50 per cent. One factor that can distort the figure is whether discontinued projects are

Table A.4 *Cost overrun in computer software projects*

Year of study	Type of software project	Number of projects	Deviation in cost in %	Deviation in time in %
1984[39]	American projects	72	34	22
1988[40]	American projects	191	33	–
1992[41]	Canadian projects	89	33	–
1992[42]	Projects in 598 Dutch organizations	–	50	50
1995[43]	Standish Group's CHAOS Report	–	–	–
	Successful projects 16.2%	–	–	–
	Projects with cost overrun 52,7%	–	189	222
	Discontinued projects 31.1%			
1997[44]	Projects implemented to budget	91	18	22
	Projects with cost overrun	243	158	133
2006[45]	Projects in one US firm	121	100	–
2008[46]	Dutch organization X	713	<0	–
	Dutch organization Y	125	0	–
	Dutch organization Z	253	0	–

Note: All figures in running money value.

included or not. Many Software and R&D projects are abandoned as they do not meet their targets. This separates software and R&D projects from construction projects. It is unusual to start but not finish the construction of a house, bridge, road, or industrial plant. This is the difference between what can be termed implementation projects and development projects, i.e. projects that can be implemented based on existing knowledge, and projects that require the development of new knowledge to be completed.

Software projects and many other development projects have high complexity because they are made up of many sub-activities that have to be delivered on time for the next phase to begin. In the case of software, there are also external dependencies as customers often cannot specify exactly what they want the programme to be able to do. Project requirements are vague, which is why it often becomes necessary to change them during the course of the project.

The pioneer in the field of software cost estimation, Barry W. Boehm,[47] estimated the cost of making a change in the design phase to be 5 times higher than in the requirement phase, 10 times higher in coding, and 50 in testing. Later studies[48] have arrived at even higher costs in later phases. The cost of making changes increases dramatically the nearer the project is to completion. Computer software firms try to reduce the risk of costly late changes by involving customers in all phases of the project.[49] The anchoring process becomes very important and one can speculate whether the fact that many software projects are abandoned, some are finished close to target, and some exhibit large cost overruns is in part a reflection of the outcome of this anchoring process.

More recently, a Dutch study[50] showed that the organizations examined had on average no cost overrun on their software projects. The cost of some projects increased and some decreased, but on average organizations Y and Z had no cost overrun. In organization X, many projects did not use up what was budgeted. The reason was that estimators aimed at the maximum cost, while appropriation allocators made cuts and seldom approved additional funding. In a study of software development in one American firm,[51] the main causes of cost overrun were identified as underestimation, changes, and a corporate culture seeing estimates as targets and giving priority to customer satisfaction.

Cost overruns vary by organization, cost estimating, appropriation, and control practice. Results are conflicting and one reason can be that, unlike, say, a bridge, software programs can become operational even when all specifications have not been met. This makes it possible to meet the budget despite not meeting goals and specifications.

Appendix B   Explanations Based on Studies of Groups of Projects

Uncertainty Decreases over Time but Cost Tends to Increase

Projects can become less expensive than anticipated, but the opposite is far more common. Peter Morris and George Hugh[1] reviewed 35 studies of groups of major projects and did not find a single study in which the projects studied had become less expensive on average than anticipated. In fact, only three studies listed in Tables A.1–A.3 showed cost underrun, and then only for a specific type of investment project in a single firm. Cost overrun is the norm regardless of whether it is a construction, research and development, or computer software project.

The estimate on which the budget or the decision to invest is based is often preceded by at least one earlier cost estimate. Three or more estimates and appraisals are not uncommon in major capital investments before the board feels certain enough to give the investment its final approval. As well as a tendency for costs to rise after the decision to invest, there is also a tendency for costs to rise between the very first estimate and the one on which the decision is based. The largest increases tend to occur between the first and the second estimates. This tendency for costs to rise over time has been observed in US military aircraft,[2] all types of US defence projects,[3] and pharmaceutical ventures,[4] as well as in smaller projects.[5] Early estimates tend to be more biased towards cost increase than later ones, and there are several possible reasons[6] for this.

Firstly, many estimators do not want to put their name on pure guess work. Therefore, when there is great uncertainty about whether an item or work is really needed, it is often omitted. Estimators want to avoid the risk of being wrong, but as the omission of uncertain future cost is not balanced by some equally large omitted revenue stream, this is a bias that tends to drive costs up when the uncertainty surrounding the omitted items has been resolved.

Secondly, there is a tendency for project planners to choose simple and cheap solutions in the hope that they will work, although they might not.

160

By doing so, they hope to keep cost down and avoid the uncertainty associated with more advanced solutions. Although a means of uncertainty avoidance, this will drive cost up if more expensive solutions prove necessary later on.

Thirdly, there are instances in which the initial estimate has been deliberately set too low, in order to allow a study of the proposed idea to go ahead, or to help the external contractors to gain a contract. The former does not necessarily mean that the estimator wants to deceive; in most cases the estimator is probably fully convinced of the merits of the idea but unable to prove it.

Fourthly, costing is a learning process. We can only cost those items we are aware of, and, as uncertainty is resolved and our knowledge of the final product becomes more detailed and realistic, we will discover that additional items and works are needed to achieve what we intend to do.

And finally, early in this learning process expectations and estimates are based more on emotions than in later phases, when the control system forces project proponents to prove that the investment is the right thing to do. Also, investments in new areas and technologies are based more on hope than investments in existing areas and technologies. Emotions get more space to influence expectations when cost data is lacking and control systems weak.

Thus, the first estimate tends to be an underestimation, and the minimum cost always more reliable than the maximum if such a cost span is given. And as long as we only consider the cost side, there is no way to balance these tendencies out by increasing revenues. Moreover, starting the process by omitting uncertain future cost, choosing solutions based on hope, or setting the budget to a level that allows the project idea to be studied can make the initial budget unrealistically low.

However, early estimates are not only lower than later ones, they also vary more and are less accurate than later ones. The variance in cost estimates decreases over time.[7] Estimates become better as the uncertainties in the project design are resolved, but more reliable information comes only at a certain cost. Donald S. Remer and Harry R. Buchanan[8] estimate that it costs 1 per cent of the investment outlay to achieve an accuracy of −5 to +15 percent; more in smaller projects, and less so in larger projects. In practice this seems like a rather low figure for major investments, as they are often preceded by several appraisals of different design alternatives, and evidence from case studies of such major projects suggests otherwise; Om Prakash Kharbanda and Ernest A. Stallworthy[9] conclude that some 3–5 per cent of total investment is needed to develop a realistic estimate.

In a study by the author[10] of 13 major ventures in new areas, the companies that implemented these successfully spent about 10 per cent of total investment before the board felt certain enough to give the venture its final approval. These were major investments in new areas in the order of almost $500 million in today's money value. When making such an investment in a market and a technology new to the firm, it is not surprising that the firm first spends a tenth of the budget gaining expertise in the new technology and market, e.g. by studying the market and technology, recruiting managers with experience of the new business, acquiring smaller companies in the new business, test-selling the new product, and signing contracts for parts of the production. If the investment had failed, it could have forced some of these firms into bankruptcy. To spend 10 per cent of the investment outlay on reducing that risk is not a high cost considering that these projects were all ventures into new areas where the parent company lacked previous experience, and that most of the pre-investment could be recovered if the new venture succeeded. This is the cost of learning a new technology and market – the ticket to the industry. For major industrial projects in general, the 3–5 per cent Kharbanda and Stallworthy recommended might very well suffice.

An interesting observation from this study of 13 new ventures was that there seemed to be a relationship between success and the amount of funds spent prior to the decision by the board to invest. Those ventures that had been successful had all been carefully evaluated and planned before the board finally approved the venture, while commitment had preceded careful investigations in many of the ventures that had failed. Strong early commitment to implement the venture is a trait shared by many project failures[11] in both the private and public sectors. Positive but critical feedback from a well-developed pre-approval control system forcing project proponents to try to foresee what might lie ahead before they are allowed to implement their idea seems to be a good form of insurance.

Cost growth can be explained as the outcome of a learning process which is not totally predictable. To make a cost estimate, estimators need a design to cost. A cost estimate takes its point of departure in an image of a design and path to realize a design, and as we learn more about the design we often tend to discover that additional work and changes in the design are necessary, making earlier estimates outdated and increasing the final cost. This bias towards cost growth is compounded by the fact that estimators tend to exclude items and work which they are unsure will be necessary. As uncertainty is resolved, changes in the design become smaller and additional costs appear more infrequently. When the design is fixed, work becomes more foreseeable and cost estimates more reliable. Thus, later estimates might be higher, but they are also more reliable. The variance in estimates decreases as more is learnt about the project that is to be implemented.

But this increased precision comes at a cost. The situation then requires a decision as to how accurate the estimate needs to be to approve a budget and give the decision to go ahead. This also means that the size of a cost overrun depends on what we compare it with: an estimate in the idea phase, or in the planning and design phase, or a preliminary budget when approval to ask for tenders are given, or when tenders exist and the final budget is approved. Many studies of cost overrun do not state what the final cost is being compared against.

Decision makers have to have an estimate upon which they can justify their decision to appropriate funds to further investigate a project idea. They cannot allocate funds to unspecified projects. Formal procedures prohibit that. Experienced managers know that these early estimates are uncertain and probably too low. This is generally not a problem in companies, but it can create problems in the public sector as early estimates and commitments become public and estimates can be interpreted as a correct figure. Such a misconception can later make it difficult to explain why project cost has increased due to inflation and changes in the proposed project.

Small Projects Vary More than Large Ones

Calculated as a percentage of total cost, the deviation in cost between approved budget and final cost varies more for smaller than for larger projects, i.e. smaller projects are more often hit by large cost overruns, and also large cost underruns. This tendency for smaller projects to vary more has been observed in power generating,[12] infrastructure,[13] road,[14] and pharmaceutical development projects.[15] For projects of the same type of technology, smaller projects account for both the largest underruns and the largest overruns; larger projects are usually found closer to the average. However, it should be said that this applies to, or is at least more evident in, homogenous groups of projects – projects representing similar technologies and implemented in the same organization.

This proposition is illustrated by Figures B.1 and B.2, which show the deviation in cost as a function of project size for 67 electrical transformers and 37 power lines.[16] The figures derive from a study of the 115 investments reported to the board of the Swedish State Power Board: 11 hydroelectric power stations, 37 power lines, and 67 transformers. On the vertical axis we have approved project budget and on the horizontal axis deviation per month. Deviation in per cent per month was the measure preferred by the Power Board. Exchanging this measure with total deviation during implementation makes the smallest projects vary less but does

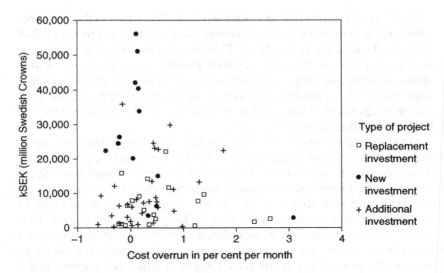

Figure B.1 The size and frequency of cost overrun in 67 transformer projects

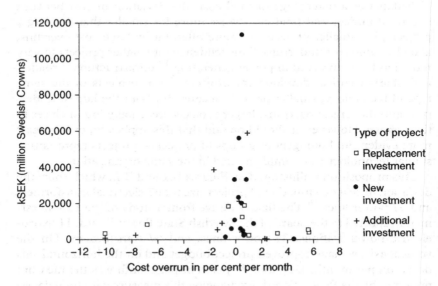

Figure B.2 The size and frequency of cost overrun in 37 power line projects

not radically change the shape of the distribution; smaller projects vary more than larger ones.

Several explanations were advanced at meetings with project managers at the Power Board. One was that the larger the project, the higher the financial and personal risks, and hence it becomes more important to avoid cost overrun. Larger projects are therefore given more attention and more experienced project management. In fact, many firms, not just the Power Board, require follow-ups for investment projects above a certain expenditure limit.[17] In absolute terms, more resources are spent on planning and reviewing large projects, and this may in part explain why larger projects are generally affected by cost overrun more often.

Secondly, although more resources are spent on large projects in absolute terms, the percentage of total investment outlay needed to estimate the correct cost is higher for smaller than for larger projects, and, furthermore, smaller investments are more often replacement or additional investments to larger ones. Replacement and additional investments tend to deviate more than new investments, as it is difficult to know exactly what is needed, or it would cost too much to find out beforehand. When disassembling a part of an old plant, one often finds additional parts that need to be replaced. Thus, in relative terms, smaller projects, and especially replacement and additional investments, are costlier to estimate correctly.

Thirdly, it was pointed out that a larger share of the total cost of a transformer project was procured. Power lines were built and maintained by the permanent workforce of the Power Board, and wages make up a larger part of such projects. Therefore, Power Board engineers had knowledge and control of a larger share of the total cost of a power line than of a transformer.

Fourthly, changes in investment plans have more impact on smaller projects. Allan and Norris[18] looked for explanations for the deviations between estimate and outcome for 84 smaller research and development projects but could not identify one single explanatory factor causing cost overrun that was valid for all projects. The average size of these projects in current money value would be in the range of £80–£90,000, and the development time 28 months. One possible explanation is that it might be more difficult to identify explanations of a more general kind in small projects as the percentage-wise outcome of such projects are more easily affected when they are postponed or accelerated due to company politics, terms of payments, changes in R&D priorities, and events outside the control of project management.

A fifth explanation builds on the observation that the performance of individual budget items in budgets for major projects can vary quite a lot even in projects that have been implemented to cost, as was illustrated by Table 2.1. Large projects can usually be divided up into several smaller projects and the variance in outcomes cancelled out when smaller projects are brought together. Although the paper board machine project described in Chapter 2 came in close to budget, some of the sub-projects showed cost overruns of almost 100 per cent. The outcome of smaller projects is more easily affected by occasional events such as delays, budget cuts, payment conditions, and project- and company-specific events. Larger projects vary less as deviations in sub-projects tend to cancel each other out. This is an example of the law of large numbers.

The More Unique a Project Is to the Estimator, the More Cost Tends to Grow

Deviations vary not only by size, but also by type of project. Figure B.3 shows the distribution in cost for 191 major public sector infrastructure projects distinguished as highway, water resource, rapid rail, building, and ad hoc projects. Data was collected by Leonard Merewitz,[19] who showed that cost overrun was on average lower for water resource and road projects than for what he terms 'ad hoc projects', i.e. projects which are unique, one-of-a-kind to the investor making the investment, such as research and new sports facilities.

The tendency for certain kinds of projects and technologies to exhibit larger cost overruns has been shown in a number of studies. Tables A.1 to A.3 give studies showing that military projects exhibited larger cost overruns than civilian projects,[20] pipeline larger than liquefied natural gas projects,[21] nuclear reactors much larger than solar farms,[22] highway larger than railway projects,[23] and railway larger than highway projects.[24] The results can be contradictory, but study after study shows that some types of projects are more prone to increase in cost.

Figure B.3 shows that the distribution of cost for the 191 major public infrastructure projects is positively skewed. This pattern of projects exhibiting major cost overruns is not balanced by an equal number of projects showing cost underruns, as confirmed in most studies of cost overruns. Such a positive skewness exists in, e.g. studies of major public infrastructure projects,[25] roads,[26] mining,[27] weapons development,[28] and computer software projects.[29] The distribution of the deviation of cost for a group of projects is in general positively skewed. Exceptions are few, power lines in Figure B.2 being one.

If we compare Figures B.1 and B.2, we find that the average deviation in cost and the distribution of deviation in cost differ between

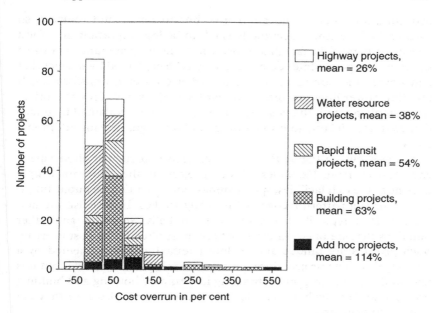

Figure B.3 Cost overrun in 191 major infrastructure projects

transformers and power lines. One explanation for this given by the project managers interviewed was that labour makes up a higher proportion of the cost of power lines than that of transformers. As the Swedish State Power Board had people permanently employed to build and repair their facilities, they required a high and steady capacity utilization. To achieve this, they sometimes used smaller projects to regulate the workload of their employees. The effect of this should be more evident for power lines than for transformer stations, as the latter are more driven by equipment costs than labour.

One simple explanation for positive skewness is that resources spent cannot be fully recovered when changes are made and extra work added. As it is much more likely that changes and additional work will increase rather than decrease cost, changes and additional work will create a positive skewness.

Comparing Figures B.1 and B.2, one can observe that investments in new transformers and power lines vary less than reinvestments and additional investments. One reason for this is that new needs are often discovered when work begins on old machines, needs that were not visible when the machine was operating. Another reason is that renovation is often regarded as a forced investment. When an old machine is in bad condition there is no alternative but to repair and reinvest, so costing the investment accurately is felt to be less important than for a new investment. The fact that transformers show a pronounced positive skewness but power lines do not could thus be explained by the fact that new power lines are more similar to earlier ones than transformers. If building power lines is a more familiar technology with fewer surprises when implemented, the positive skewness could be explained by unanticipated time delays, additional work, and redesigns causing additional costs.

As was shown in Figure B.3, ad hoc projects in particular often experience cost overrun. Examples of such projects in the Merewitz sample were new research facilities, sports arenas, and other unique public buildings. This is a pattern recognized in many studies. In Swedish municipalities, it is typically fire stations, town halls, stadiums and other buildings that are one-of-a-kind that are most often hit by cost overrun. Such projects are unique and seldom planned and implemented by a municipality. The project does not need to be new to the world, but it is new to those planning and estimating it. Ordinary housing and building projects are less likely to be affected by cost overrun because they are familiar to planners.

It was observed in the 1930s in the US aircraft industry that the man hours it took to produce a unit of production decreased by a constant as the number of units produced was doubled. The cost of producing a unit decreases as the total production increases, and this is deemed to be due to the experience gained as more units are produced. This has since been confirmed in all parts of the value chain. However, the learning curve eventually flattens out, and so this phenomenon is steeper at the beginning, but later slows down.

An important precondition for the cost–benefits of learning in this way is standardization. Profiting from the learning effect presupposes production in a long series, impossible unless the parts to be assembled are standardized. The production of parts to small tolerances was essential to reduce re-work and make the assembly line an economic means of production. Standardization of products and work processes also speeds up construction processes.

A lack of standardization, the potential for cost reduction through learning, and little or no historical data help to explain why unique, one-of-a-kind constructions are much more prone to increases in cost than, for instance, apartment blocks. Standardized items and work processes are easier to cost as there is data from earlier, similar projects. Specially produced items do not offer the same possibility for updating and improving cost data.

The Longer the Time Between Estimate and Follow Up, the More Changes There Will Be

The longer the time between an estimate and the follow-up, the larger the cost growth tends to become. This was true for Merewitz's water resources, roads, and rapid transit projects, as well as later infrastructure projects in Nigeria,[30] Saudi Arabia,[31] worldwide,[32] Malaysian[33] construction projects, and the hydroelectric power stations and power lines built by the Swedish State Power Board. It has also been found to apply to both military[34] and civilian[35] research and development projects, and to computer software projects.[36]

One might suspect that cost growth correlates with the length of time between estimate and follow-up due to unanticipated inflation, but this cannot be the whole explanation as the tendency for costs to rise still remains after figures have been adjusted for inflation.[37] In fact, the tendency for cost to rise over time can be even stronger, as unanticipated inflation might have been overestimated in studies where researchers did not have knowledge of price clauses or when payments were made – information that is necessary to estimate the effects of inflation correctly. Thus, the longer the time period between estimate and final cost, the larger the cost growth tends to become, even when figures have been adjusted for inflation.

The Swedish State Power Board had two large hydroelectric power station projects during the 1970s which encountered rather large cost overruns. As larger stations take longer to construct, one could interpret Figure B.4 as proof that larger projects are more prone to overruns. However, the four power stations that showed the highest cost overruns in Figure B.4 were all designed before the first oil crisis in 1973–4. Cost overruns for the other seven, constructed after the first oil crisis, were very modest. Three of them showed a smaller cost overrun of about 10 per cent, and the four others almost no deviation at all.

The cost overruns on the two largest stations made some managers in the Power Board express thoughts that their organization was perhaps not that well suited to carry out large-scale projects. However, a closer look at these projects revealed that it was not the size of the projects as such that had caused their cost overrun, but their redesign and the long time it took to implement them. As energy prices increased, the new power stations were redesigned to utilize the water better. Sharpened environmental and construction standards also contributed to cost increases, as the 1970s was a decade when environmental and safety standards became more stringent.

The economics of a hydroelectric power station is determined by, among other things, the percentage of water utilized and the height of the fall. It is not

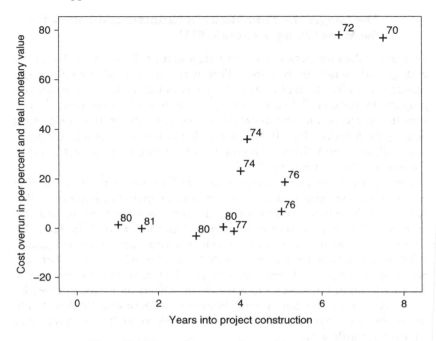

Figure B.4 Time of construction and cost overrun for 11
hydroelectric power stations
Note: Figures such as 72 stands for the year construction started. In
this case 1972. Cost overrun in per percent and real monetary value.

economically justified to make use of all the water when the flow varies a lot
during the year and across different years, because it would require larger
reservoirs. Therefore, project planners put a value on the water utilized and
discount it, in a similar way as is done in discounted cash flow analyses of
capital investments, to determine the optimal design of the power plant.

In this case, the value of the water increased due to the increased price
of competing energy sources, such as fossil power. This made it justifiable
to redesign dams and channels to make better use of available water. This
increased the cost and construction time of the plants, but also their
profitability. Thus, although the plants become more expensive than
anticipated when the board approved them, these changes also made
them more profitable.

The two hydroelectric power stations that took longest to construct
were commenced in 1970 and 1972 and finished in 1978 and 1979,
respectively. The power stations were designed in the late 1960s, which

means that quite a lot of work and funds had been spent by the time the oil price increased three to four times in 1973–4, and then doubled once more in 1978–80. Construction on the other projects with cost overruns began in 1974–7, i.e. between these two sharp price increases, and those without any significant cost overruns after the second oil crisis in 1980–1. The high cost overruns of the earliest projects can be explained by the fact that the cost of making changes in the design increases sharply the closer they are to the end of the project. Making changes on the drawing board does not necessarily make a project more costly, but when construction starts changes become increasingly more expensive. What has been spent cannot be recovered and, in addition, changes contribute to lengthening the time of construction and thus interest expenses.

When a project takes many years to implement, there tend to be changes as project managers want to incorporate new technology, or adjust the project to changing market demand and also competitors' new products. When, for instance, a Swedish heavy truck maker developed a new engine for their heaviest truck, they received the news that their main competitors had developed a slightly stronger engine. They therefore redesigned the engine to have the extra horse power necessary to be able to claim that they offered the strongest engine on the market. Such adjustments in response to competitors and changing market demand will of course lengthen development or construction time and increase the final cost of the project, even though it sometimes can lead to the development of better technical solutions.

Cost overrun has a negative connotation; project managers for the hydroelectric power stations argued that additional investments had increased the capacity of the plants and made them more profitable, and that the projects as implemented could not be compared with the ones approved. That is of course correct, and is almost always the case in projects showing large cost overruns.

What one can claim is that these two power stations should have been re-appraised and a new budget approved before they were redesigned. However, that might have led to discussions on whether and how to make the changes in a project that only became more profitable as the value of the electrical power it would produce increased, which would have caused time delays that would have postponed production. Perhaps this was why it was solved in a more informal way.

A large number of studies have found that the longer the time period between approved budget and follow up, the larger the cost overrun tends to become. The longer the construction period, the larger is the probability that there will be changes in the project; changes add to time and cost partly because accrued expenses cannot be fully recovered, and partly because accrued interest increases.

Deviations in Cost Co-vary with Other Measures of Deviation

The US Government Accountability Office has reviewed government-funded projects for many decades. Cost overruns have decreased since the 1960s but have not gone away, despite stricter methods of control and project management.[38] The reasons are stated to be the same as always – projects are still affected by 'funding instability' (i.e. funds are not allocated as planned) and 'design instability' (i.e. changes in the design of the projects caused by funding instability or other changes external to the project). This lack of continuity and predictability forces project management to make changes in their plans for projects which in the end lead to higher costs.

Such instability is not unique to US government-funded projects. An example is the stopping of the Stockholm bypass project. When the Left won the national election[39] in 2014, they halted the implementation of the project for a couple of months. The bypass project had been estimated to cost SEK 28 billion in 2009 monetary value, and stopping construction certainly added to its final cost. Such 'funding instability' has also been observed elsewhere, for instance in Iranian public investments[40] and development projects in the Swedish manufacturing industry.[41]

Changes in funding, technical standards, and market demand explain why there is a positive covariance between cost overrun and factors such as construction time, volumes of concrete and steel used, man hours, estimated sales volume and price, product mix, and planned capacity. External and internal changes drive costs.

The covariance between deviations of different kinds can be further illustrated by Table B.1 which shows deviations between plan and outcome for 35 new plants.[42] The sample is small but is still of interest as it illustrates the covariance between cost overrun and deviations in other measures of outcome.

About a quarter of the projects reported deviations larger than 5 per cent for the variables listed in Table B.1. Five percent has been chosen as companies' financial protocols typically require project management to go to the board to appropriate new funds when cost exceeds 5–10 per cent of the approved budget. This gives project management a strong incentive to make savings in the budget in order not to have to request more funds. Table B.1 shows that deviations that negatively affected the profitability of a project were more than twice as common as the opposite. That applied not only to estimates of the investment outlay, but also to the length of construction period, technical ambition, plant capacity, operating cost, sales volume, and sales price.

Table B.1 *Deviations in some major investments in industrial plants*

Variable	Negatively 35 projects	Negatively 20 major projects	Positively 35 projects	Positively 20 major projects
Investment outlay	18 (51.4%)	10 (50.0%)	3 (8.6%)	3 (15.0%)
Length of construction period	7	3	6	6
Technical ambition	10	6	1	0
Plant capacity	4	3	5	1
Operating cost	10	7	1	1
Sales volume	10	7	3	1
Sales price	7	5	7	6
Number of deviations larger than 5%	66 (26.9%)	41 (29.3%)	26 (10.6%)	18 (12.9%)

Cost overrun is often associated with deviations in other output measures that indicate changes in plans and the implementation of the project. The project that has been implemented is never exactly the same as that which was originally planned and approved. Still, this survey probably underestimates the true occurrence of deviations, as we can suspect that project managers will tend to play down deviations.

Internal and External Complexity Drives Cost Growth

Major projects can be split up into a number of sub-projects and activities which have to be completed in time so as not to delay other activities. When a time delay large enough to delay another activity happens, it can seldom be cancelled out by an activity being performed in a shorter time than planned. It can propagate and delay other activities, with knock-on effects that add up to a total delay, and thereby higher cost. Richard J. Schonberger[43] claims that this is why projects are 'always' delivered late.

Assume, for instance, a task that has been estimated to take 100 hours to complete. If those performing the task know it well, they might be able to complete it in 80 hours. However, if they do not know exactly what to do or how to perform the task, the time taken can easily slip to more than 120 hours, 150 hours, or even more if they get stuck or make mistakes.

But doing it in less than 80 hours is probably very difficult. There is a limit for how fast a task can be performed, but not for how slowly, which explains why projects with many dependencies are more prone to time and cost overrun. It can also explain positive skewness.

This is not a new observation. Raymond Giguet and G. Morlat[44] argued in 1952 that projects tend to become more expensive than estimated due to the fact that the events that cause deviations are not independent. Engineers determine the probability of various possible events that may occur and try to minimize the risk of undesirable outcomes. However, whenever an unexpected event occurs, this necessitates adjustments and changes that will push the final cost above the previously determined most probable average final cost.

The number of dependencies, their interrelatedness, and their negotiability is by definition a measure of complexity.[45] Observe, however, that a large project is not necessarily more complex than a small one. It is the number of dependencies and the amount of slack in time and trade-offs between requirements that define complexity, not the size of a project. These dependencies can be both internal and external to the project.

High-tech projects are especially susceptible to cost growth due to delays in interrelated activities, as high-performance products are more tightly optimized. Thomas K. Glennen, Jr[46] points out that it can be more difficult to substitute a part in a high-performance product than in an ordinary one, as parts are more tightly optimized in space and functionality, and less standardized.

Using standardized components reduces the risk of having to adjust components to each other, and hence reduces the risk of delays and cost growth. This applies not only to hardware components, but also to software components and suboperations performed by humans. The solutions advanced by Glennen and his contemporaries[47] were parallel product development and more loosely coupled systems. The latter can be achieved by giving components a standardized interface so that they can be easily substituted and rearranged. This reduces the risk of failure[48] and is a principle widely used in complex development projects and complex production systems.[49]

When cost increases, project management can often counteract this to some extent by reducing the size of investment, choosing less costly solutions, or outsourcing certain parts of the investment, as was illustrated by the Frövifors case in Chapter 2. This is not possible in a highly regulated technology such as nuclear energy. If the construction site is short of nuts and bolts of the steel quality specified in approved drawings, work has to be postponed until the correct nuts and bolts arrive. Strict enforcement of safety requirements reduces the options for project management to solving upcoming problems and keep costs down by improvising and choosing second-best solutions.

The cost of production can be reduced if there are economies of scale, i.e. if the cost of producing additional units declines as fixed cost is distributed over more units. The nuclear industry has tried this avenue by building still larger plants to counteract cost growth, but it has not worked either in France,[50] or the US.[51] Operating cost has been relatively unaffected by the increasing size of more recent plants.

Additional safety regulations have made nuclear plants increasingly more complex projects. This, together with increased size, has lengthened construction time, which means more accrued interest. Increased site-specific requirements have also made each new plant a unique project: no two plants are exactly the same. Interrelated factors are many, and many parts are designed for a specific plant, which is why they cannot be substituted with another part filling the same function. This lack of standardization has made it impossible to utilize the learning curve effect to reduce cost. The effects of complexity, size, and construction time have been so great in France and the USA that it has totally offset any economies of scale.

Lower complexity and a higher degree of standardization is one possible explanation as to why the solar and wind farms in Table A.1 have much lower cost growth than nuclear reactors.[52] A solar or wind farm consists of a large number of similar wind generators or solar panels.

Another category of complex projects are large computer software projects. There are internal dependencies between different pieces of software, and there are dependencies between the programme and its user. Early programmers applied the waterfall model to develop software by going from one stage to another, just like a product on an assembly line. This required the previous stage to have been completed before the next could start, which was inappropriate when developing large software systems. The linear model could cause delays, and unsolved problems and user dependencies could cause problems and re-work later on.

A common problem is that customers often are unable to clearly visualize and specify their requirements. This inability causes an instability which programmers try to solve by involving customers in all phases of the development process.[53] Furthermore, major software programmes are composed by a very large number of subcomponents and diverse contributors. The solution to this is to create a modular product architecture that allows several project teams to work in parallel, to avoid blind alleys by attending to problems as fast as they appear through iterative work cycles, and by continuously testing smaller modules and sub-parts of the larger programme in a user environment. A variety of such practices has been developed and goes under the term 'agile programming', often involving measures such as regular and frequent meetings to adapt activities and different parts of the program to each other, and solving problems immediately when they appear, and has proven to reduce both cost and time to market.

Advances in Knowledge Co-vary with Cost Growth

As we saw in Table A.2, research and development projects have a tendency to increase in time and cost, not least for new military weapon systems, which is why US researchers begun to study deviations in military aircraft and missile projects in the 1950s.

One factor which has contributed greatly to making many military aircraft projects more expensive than anticipated, both back in the 1950s and today, has been when fewer planes have been manufactured than originally planned. As the development cost is a large part of the total system cost, reducing the number of aircraft produced significantly increases the cost per aircraft.

Another factor is inflation. As development times are long for new aircraft projects, high inflation can substantially add to development cost. However, after correcting the figures for the number of aircraft manufactured and inflation, the fact remains that development projects are more prone to cost growth than construction projects.[54] This can be seen by comparing Tables A.1 and A.2. Observe that the figures for military aircraft projects in Table A.2 have been adjusted for inflation and the number of aircraft produced. More recent studies of military weapon development[55] have shown that cost overrun is still common.

A third result from early studies of military development projects was that it became clear that cost growth correlates with the degree of technical advance.[56] The larger the advance in technical knowledge, the more the cost tends to increase. This is a maxim that has subsequently been confirmed to apply to development projects in the pharmaceutical industry[57] and in the Swedish manufacturing industry.[58]

The factors causing cost growth in development projects are partly the same as in construction projects. The estimator takes his or her point of departure from the project design available at the moment of the estimate. They estimate the cost of the design and add on a lump sum for contingencies. Then, as the development project progresses, unforeseen technical problems may appear which make it very difficult to achieve the design criteria set up, project requirements may have to be altered as market demand changes, or the design may have to be updated to incorporate new technology.

Such changes lead inevitably to changes in the original design, leading to a new estimate based on the new design. In research and development projects this is natural, as the aim of such a project is to develop new knowledge and specify something. This is very different from a construction project, which takes its point of departure in known technology and thus can be specified before it is implemented.

Burton H. Klein[59] compares building a bridge with a military aircraft project. If the bridge is well designed, the probability is very high that it can be built without making changes in the original design during construction. Military aircraft projects, on the other hand, are seldom implemented as originally planned. Regardless of how much attention had been given to the original design in the cases he studied, there were always surprises later on in the project, and what started with one configuration came out of the process with a different engine, electronic systems, airframe, or tactical role. The essential difference between bridges and aircraft, Klein explains, is that the construction of the former is a question of making best use of existing knowledge while the latter requires a lot of learning.

What Klein described is the distinction between implementation and development projects – that is, projects which can be specified in advance and projects for which the goal partly is to specify something new. Let us assume that we are going to build a new apartment block, a routine project. It should then be possible to estimate the cost of such a project relatively accurately as there are many other similar projects from which cost data can be obtained. We can, if we are thorough, calculate the amount of building material and labour hours needed to build such a block. It is mostly a matter of how much work we decide to spend on planning prior to the construction. If we spend enough resources on planning a standard apartment block then we should be able to estimate the final cost well.

To study whether this was the case also for development projects, Klein used 71 estimates of 22 military aircraft and missile projects. His study found that for some of the projects cost increases were discovered early in the development process, for others late. This differed from project to project, which is why the risk of cost growth in research and development projects cannot be totally eliminated by spending more resources on planning ex ante in an attempt to develop better cost estimates.

Thus, estimating the final cost is partly a question of how much work and money should be spent on project planning prior to implementing the investment. If large resources are invested prior to selecting the final design, then project management has to make early commitments to certain technical solutions. But if they do so, they lose the flexibility that a gradual commitment to technical solutions can offer, perhaps necessitating expensive redesign and causing the final cost of the project to become higher than if certain decisions had been postponed. Some project managers argue that it is easier to keep the final cost low if the project is not specified in too much detail at an early stage because of the high costs of going back and re-specifying should the chosen design not work properly.

Thomas Marschak[60] asked himself why development times for new weapons systems were shorter during World War II than after. Having studied a number of projects, he concluded that the short development time during the war was because project management did not commit themselves to strict design specifications at an early stage, but were allowed to experiment. If they developed a new radar, or a component in a radar or in an engine, it could be immediately installed in an aircraft and tested in action. Sometimes it worked, sometimes it did not. New design ideas were tested in action before excessive resources had been spent on developing them.

In peacetime conditions, this method of development came into conflict with both safety requirements, and civilian and military authorities' need to control their fixed budget. This suggests the conflict between the roles of entrepreneur and controller – the one allocating funds wants to know exactly what the project will cost and how funding will be used, while the entrepreneur relies on their ability to meet new challenges and solve problems as they arise.

Cost Overruns Vary by Organization

It is uncertain as to whether cost overrun is less common today than in the past. It might seem reasonable to assume that increased levels of education and research, better documentation, easier access to information, and experiences from earlier investments would make cost overruns less common today than a few decades ago. But it is doubtful if this is the case, and empirical studies give conflicting results.

Studies of major public transportation projects[61] have not found that recent cost estimates are better than those made 100 years ago or earlier, and this after having transformed their cost data into constant money value and one single currency. Project planners are, on average, equally bad at foreseeing cost overrun today as in the past. However, it is difficult to make such a comparison as currency rates do not adjust perfectly to inflation, and as the practice of contracting and methods of handling inflation in estimates and firms have evolved over time.

Results are also conflicting at the firm level. The earlier study of the State Power Board's investments in power lines and transformers showed that both cost overruns and the variability of outcomes had decreased during the years studied. Studies of research and development projects in two pharmaceutical firms[62] showed that one of them had improved their cost estimates over time, but not the other. Obviously one organization had learnt from their experiences, but the other had not. Similarly, a study of product development in two Swedish manufacturing companies[63] showed that one of the organizations was better at estimating costs than the other. The quality of cost estimates varies, but whether cost estimates produced today are more accurate than cost estimates produced in the past remains unclear.

The planning process matters. Figure B.5 shows the deviation in estimated investment outlay for the 20 largest investments in Table B.1 for which data on first estimate, budget, and follow-up exist. As can be seen, many of the projects that encountered cost overruns also showed cost increases between the first estimate and the approved budget.

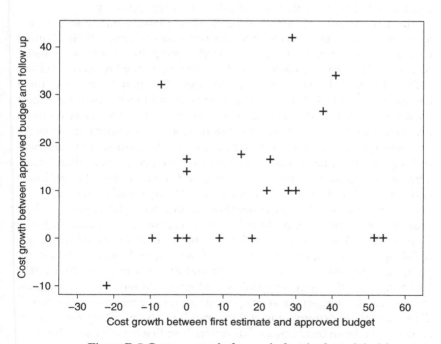

Figure B.5 Cost overrun before and after the formal decision to invest for some major investments in industrial plants

One reason why projects are affected by cost overrun is, as was pointed out earlier, that the decision to go ahead is taken at an early stage when important technical design decisions have not yet been made and any cost estimates are therefore very uncertain. If that was the sole reason, one would expect that the projects in Figure B.5 would show large deviations either between the first estimate and the approved budget, or between the approved budget and follow up. As we can see, this is not always the case. Cost estimates for one of the plants have decreased due to that the firm re-evaluating the market and the strategy for the plant. Moreover, a relatively large number of the projects which encountered large cost overruns did so both between the first estimate and budget and between budget and follow up. This indicates that there must have been changes made in the projects not only after the decision to invest, but also prior to that decision, indicating that the project management team was not in control of the project. The general advice in such situations is not to make additional changes in the project to cut costs, but to go back, specify, and freeze a new design, and to make a new detailed cost estimate and market analysis based on that new design.[64] This is needed to avoid further unanticipated changes that would otherwise drive up costs.

Another pattern sometimes appears when plotting public sector projects. Swedish local governments previously had to report their planned volume of investment during the forthcoming five years to Statistic Sweden. This created a pattern in which projects tended to increase either before the final decision to invest or after. The first hurdle was for a project to be included in the long-term plan, and to be included a cost estimate was required. Then it might have to wait for many years to be properly planned and appraised before it was implemented, as other competing projects were given higher priority. Sometimes the delay was so long that the plan became obsolete and the project was abandoned. This caused public sector projects to increase either between first estimate and approved budget, or between approved budget and follow up.

An extreme example of cost growth in the long-term plan is provided by a project for a new ice rink in Malmö, a town in the south of Sweden opposite Copenhagen. After some discussion, the town council decided to include building a new changing-room at one of their ice rinks in their long-term plan, but after many years of planning and discussions it was found that building a completely new ice rink was a better solution. The project grew from a new changing-room at an open air ice rink to a new indoor ice rink.[65] This example is extreme, but it illustrates how the planning process can sometimes take an unanticipated direction. The first hurdle was to have the project included in the long-term plan, the second was to have the project designed the way one really wanted to see it implemented.

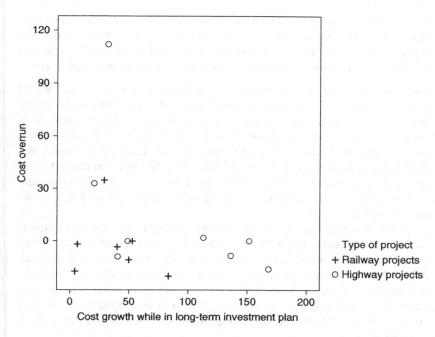

Figure B.6 Deviation in cost estimates before and after the final
decision to invest for some road and railroad projects[66]

This tendency for municipal projects to increase either before or after
their final approval is also visible in major Swedish road and railroad
projects[67]. Figure B.6 shows deviations in cost both when the projects
have been in the long-term plan, and after a budget for the project has
been approved and the project implemented. Budget here stands for the
budget approved before procurement. The project that encountered a
cost overrun of 112 per cent between approved budget and follow up was
a road project that was upgraded from being an expressway to a freeway
after construction work had commenced. This project was, however, an
exception. The largest deviations appeared when the projects in the long-
term plan were waiting to be implemented. Long waiting times, inflation,
and increased construction standards could have contributed to cost
growth.

The private sector abolished the long-term plans that we still find in the
public sector a long time ago. The market changes so fast in a market-
based economy that it is not feasible to make long-term investment plans.
Comparing public and private sector projects, one cannot disregard the
fact that public sector projects sometimes have to wait for five or ten years,

or even longer, to be implemented. Many factors can make an old estimate outdated, including inflation, price changes, new standards, requirements, technical development, and market demand – changes that might make radical changes in the original project plan necessary.

Some organizations are better at estimating costs. In a study of three US utilities[68] referred to in Chapter 5, the Tennessee Valley Authority was consistently better at costing than the other two organizations. The explanation given was that all cost estimates were made by one unit of dedicated project planners working full time on planning and appraising new projects. Letting one unit work full time on project planning and estimating assured better knowledge of up-to-date cost data and opportunities for learning than decentralizing estimates to lower units. Specialization pays off.

Lack of current data is one reason why companies turn to technical consultants to assess major investments. Major consultancy firms which are constantly involved in new investments in a particular industry can thrive on having access to updated cost data. Practice varies by industry, and major consulting firms know how to price their knowledge, but when the board wants to be assured and such an estimate can reduce the risk of surprises, there are strong arguments for paying for such an assessment.

The type of organization seems to be a more important factor determining the accuracy of cost estimates than accumulated knowledge in society, general levels of education, or access to information. Case studies show that some organizations are better at estimating costs than others, and some organizations do not improve, they constantly underestimate costs. A case study[69] of investment reviews in one Swedish manufacturing firm revealed that although project after project exceeded their budget and this was reported upwards in the organization, nothing happened. The overruns were recorded, but only symbolic action was taken. Nothing seems to have been learnt and no action was taken to improve future estimates.

It is well known that organizations are poor at assimilating past experiences, and also that organizations are poor at utilizing the combined knowledge of their employees. Organizations are generally far less knowledgeable than their members. A study[70] of six technical consulting firms documented examples where consultants did not even know that colleagues on the same corridor had already solved the same problem for another customer. In spite of Intranets, meetings, networking, education programmes, and other measures to document and disseminate information, many organizations are still poor at making use of the knowledge of their employees.

Cost overrun is more common in some regions than in others.
Several studies show that cost overrun is more common in certain countries and regions than in others. A few of these are referred to in Table
A.1. Projects in less developed countries have generally been assumed to
shown larger cost overrun than similar projects in industrialized countries. Albert O. Hirschman[71] and other World Bank studies have pointed
out that project planning and appraisal is often based on conditions
prevailing in industrialized countries, and that local conditions in less
developed countries are less well understood.

The propensity for cost increase differs between regions, but exceptions can easily be found. For instance, time and cost overrun of more
than 100 per cent became the norm for new nuclear power plants in the
USA during the 1970s, while nuclear power plants built in Korea during
the same period kept to their timetable and budget.[72] Similarly, plants
constructed in France managed much better,[73] and time and cost overruns for the two Swedish plants reviewed in Chapter 2 were also much
lower.

Many reasons for cost overrun and growth have been advanced in
studies of groups of projects. We have focused here on differences
between projects, and we have also shown that organizational factors
are important. Certain organizations are better at estimating cost than
others, but one does not need to rely on organizational factors and
behavioural biases to explain cost growth. The factors we have identified –
the length of the time period between estimates, project type, uniqueness,
complexity, and advance in new knowledge needed – can explain[74] most
of the cost overrun for a sample of projects.

Appendix C   Actors and Processes

In Appendix B, we reviewed studies comparing groups of projects to find similarities when it comes to cost overrun and deviations between estimate and outcome. Such studies usually relate explanations of cost overrun and growth to the technology of the project. The earlier the decision to go ahead is made, the longer it takes to implement the project, the more complex the project is, the larger the advance in technical knowledge, and the more changes that are made, the more time and cost tend to increase. These are explanations that describe a tendency in a larger number of similar projects, and researchers of this tradition often search for rational explanations to these tendencies, as we did in Appendix B.

There are also numerous case studies advancing different theories and ideas about the causes of cost overrun and why investors and managers put more money into failing projects instead of abandoning them. Thus, there are case studies of such projects, questionnaire studies asking respondents about their reactions to and causes of cost growth and cost overrun, and studies in which people's reaction to cost growth in experimental situations is recorded – studies which try to explain the phenomena by applying theories borrowed from social sciences. They assume that decision makers have limited information and ability to process information, and they often come close to what we term 'bounded rationality'. It is a large and diverse area of research.

In Appendix C, we will review this literature as we previously did with studies of groups of projects. The explanations for, and perspectives on, cost overrun and growth in these studies are many. They can be categorized according to research methodology, from which branch of social science the perspective originates, or key themes, and we will focus here on three such themes – namely: cognitive biases, information asymmetry, and path dependence.

Optimistic bias relates to the well-established fact that most people believe they stand a smaller risk of losing than other people do. An example is the boxer who believes that he will defeat his opponent, although only one can win. It is a bias more common in entrepreneurs than in managers, and in Western and Chinese cultures than in Japanese, and it offers one way of explaining why cost and problems are constantly underestimated.

Self-serving bias refers to the tendency to enhance self-esteem by attributing success to one's own capabilities while attributing failures to others and unforeseeable events. This tendency is also more pronounced in Western and Chinese cultures than in Japanese.

Later estimates are related to the first bias. This anchoring bias makes the first estimate important.

Information asymmetry exists when actors do not have access to the same information, which creates many obstacles which must be tackled if the project is to be implemented at its anticipated cost. It may be that the proponents of the project and those appropriating funding do not have access to the same information and knowledge, or that the procurer does not have the same information and knowledge as the contractors.

To bring a project from idea to decision, various choices have to be made which reduce the number of options available in the next step. Later decisions are restricted by earlier ones, restrictions that can be created by both technology and social factors. The project and those engaged in it become locked in to a project-specific path, which makes it difficult to revise estimates or abandon plans and projects.

Cost Overrun and Decision Biases

Optimistic bias. As was clear from Tables A.1, 2 and 4, cost overrun is considerably more common than cost underrun. Similarly, there is a lot of research showing that people in different situations tend to underestimate the time and the cost required to implement what they plan to do. People making estimates are generally overoptimistic. Researchers use the term 'optimistic bias', which they define as a tendency to overestimate the probability of a certain outcome to occur, a tendency which is often accompanied by an inability to interpret and accept new, contradicting information and modify the original estimate accordingly.

Such overoptimism has been confirmed in a number of different types of decisions which we normally do not see as a lottery, although they might be, such as economic forecasts, stock market estimates, starting a company, investing in a new venture or in an existing company, and buying decisions. There are numerous studies confirming decision makers being overoptimistic.[1] One could claim that decision makers tend to have more confidence in their own judgement than reason suggests they should have.

With regard to investment decisions, optimistic bias has been confirmed to exist in experimental situations in which decision makers are subjected to cost estimates for investments,[2] new products,[3] and market growth rate.[4] Lawrence Pruitt and Stephen Gitman[5] take their point of departure from Edward Miller,[6] who formulated the hypothesis that business managers generally believe that investment estimates are over-optimistic and that they therefore compensate for this overoptimism when they assess investment requests. Pruitt and Gitman found support for this in a mail questionnaire sent to Fortune 500 companies. As many as 78.5 per cent of the managers who responded to the questionnaire thought that those requesting investment typically overestimated reven-ues, and 43.0 per cent thought that they also underestimated costs in their requests. Furthermore, 86.5 per cent thought that marketing overesti-mated sales, 61.9 per cent that research and development underestimated development costs, 81.5 per cent that development cost deviates more when the proposed project represented a major step in production or research, and 61.2 per cent that the actual profit tended to become lower than estimated. A lot of business managers seem to believe that there is an optimistic bias in investment estimates.

An optimistic bias has also been confirmed with regard to financial markets, as demonstrated in, for instance, macro-economic prognoses issued by US authorities,[7] profit estimates of American stock market analysts,[8] and among investors,[9] CEOs,[10] consumers,[11] and project managers.[12] Profit estimates are largely dependent on sales estimates, which financial analysts tend to overestimate, although[13] the optimistic bias is larger for profit than for sales forecasts. Rules of disclosure seem to play a role here. In a comparison of estimates made by financial analysts in different countries,[14] overoptimistic profit estimates were less common in countries with more complete financial disclosure rules.

One area where overoptimism is especially obvious is entrepreneurship and new ventures. Many studies have confirmed that entrepreneurs – people starting new businesses – are overoptimistic,[15] that they are more optimistic than managers,[16] and that they start their companies when they do not fully realize all the risks involved.[17] They overestimate the possibility of being right and generalize on fewer observations[18] than non-entrepreneurs do. Other studies show that entrepreneurs seldom con-template what else they could have done, or admit or express regret concerning a mistake.[19] This optimistic bias is not balanced by venture capitalists as similar studies have found that they too exhibit an optimistic bias.[20] Optimistic bias among entrepreneurs has been shown to have a partly cultural bias,[21] so optimistic bias could be one of the factors explaining differences in the propensity to start new firms in different cultures. For instance, both optimistic bias and the propensity to start new companies are high in the USA and China, but low in Japan. Europe can be found somewhere in between these extremes.

Other studies[22] show that less knowledgeable people have more confidence in their own abilities than more knowledgeable people. Their ignorance seems to make them more optimistic and thereby more likely to commit themselves to new ventures without knowing what these actually imply. One can wonder how many ventures fail because of ignorance and overoptimism.[23] The failure rate of new firms is extremely high. In the USA, only 45 per cent of new companies are estimated to last for more than five years, and only 30 per cent for 10 years,[24] and the figures do not seem to be much higher in other countries. The fact that some new firms become very successful although costs and problems were greatly underestimated at the outset might sometimes be explained by the fact that the windows of opportunity would have closed had not the entrepreneur sized the chance without first properly investigating it. This ability to disregard problems and to act on vague and incomplete information could also explain why entrepreneurs often do not function very well as managers in established organizations, and perhaps it can also explain speculative bubbles.[25]

Behavioural studies have identified a number of biases, but few are as well-documented as optimistic bias. Humans underestimate the chance of being involved in a car accident or getting cancer, and overestimate the possibility of winning the lottery, succeeding in their daily work, and how much of their life remains (the latter to the benefit of pension funds and life insurance companies). Some 80 per cent of the population do this. Mildly depressed people hold a more realistic view, but optimism seems to be an advantage as optimists live longer and are healthier.

Optimistic bias has been explained as a consequence of natural selection and an advantage in the evolution of species[26] and also as a prerequisite for the development of human civilization. The anthropologist Lionel Tiger[27] goes as far as to speculate that optimistic bias has been a driving force in human evolution as it presupposes thinking about and making plans about the future. Doing so created fear of the unknown that could be partly counteracted by being overoptimistic. An obstacle to the latter reasoning is that optimistic bias is not unique to human beings. Biologists have shown that many animals, even pigeons, also exhibit an optimistic bias. It seems like evolution has favoured the development of an optimistic bias. Those that have underestimated future work, problems, and dangers have fared better than those that have held more realistic images of the future.

Leaving the reasons behind optimistic bias, we can conclude that planners tend to underestimate the time and resources needed when estimating the cost of implementing their plans. We can also conclude that entrepreneurs are more optimistic than managers. Entrepreneurs tend to underestimate the actual time, cost, and resources needed to implement the projects they want to achieve, and in many cases this optimism, sometimes based on ignorance, seems to have been a precondition for their decision to go forward with their business idea.

Self-serving bias. Another well-established bias which could contribute to cost growth is self-serving bias. It can be defined as a distortion of the cognitive process in order to maintain and enhance self-esteem.[28] We absorb positive feedback and reject the negative, forget past failures and errors, and credit ourselves for the success and achievements of those we work and associate ourselves with, all to enhance our self-esteem.

The support for the existence of self-serving bias is very strong. A meta-analysis[29] based on 266 studies of self-serving bias found it to be high in Western and Chinese cultures, unnoticeable in Japanese culture, and moderate in Indian culture. Disregarding seven Japanese studies, this type of bias was confirmed to exist in all parts of the world. People have a tendency to attribute positive outcomes to themselves and negative outcomes to others or unforeseeable events. They tend to have a positively distorted image of their own role and performance. There are many studies confirming this, and there are also studies showing that self-serving bias is associated with greater perceived happiness, less depression, better problem-solving skills, stronger immune systems, and lower mortality, and that this distortion of reality is more pronounced during childhood and after the age of 55.

Self-serving bias is more difficult to study than optimistic bias. It is often difficult to establish whether an observed self-serving bias is due to overconfidence, hopes to recover sunk cost, a need to sustain a positive image so as to maintain good relations and access to resources, or some other reason. There is also an interaction between these biases, since they are mostly self-reinforcing. An unconscious drive to enhance one's self can unconsciously affect the decision to maintain a course of action to recover sunk cost or a presentation to stock analysts at the same time as these acts will reinforce the presenter's self, and the other way round. Consequently, self-serving bias is a recurring theme behind many reasons advanced to explain escalating commitment,[30] i.e. why people invest more money in ventures where estimated costs keep increasing in the hope of regaining their previous investment. Explanations for why people throw good money after bad, such as the hope to recover sunk cost, the tendency to seek data that confirms one's assumptions, the need to justify past decisions and actions, and the need to conform to perceived expectations and save face, can all be seen as manifestations of self-serving bias.

There has been a long debate over whether self-serving bias can be explained by cognitive causes or motivational reasons, and recent research in social psychology indicates that the latter might be more important.[31] People highly committed to a project are more likely to overestimate its positive outcome. A cultural trait exists in both optimistic and self-serving biases, and it can sometimes be difficult to distinguish these two biases, but self-serving bias is considered by many to be the main explanation behind optimistic bias.[32] It has, for instance, been shown that those initiating a project are more likely to continue to invest in a project when cost increases than later managers managing the same project,[33] which is in line with studies showing that entrepreneurs are more optimistic than managers. Thus, there is a connection between optimistic and self-serving biases.

Whether this tendency to blame failures on others and unforeseeable events, and to credit success to oneself, is due to a cognitive bias or a conscious effort to influence others' image of oneself or the focal organization is mostly impossible to know. A study of annual report narratives[34] shows that the frequency of self-serving formulations increases in crisis situations, and that impression management is more important than self-serving attributional bias in this case. Companies need to maintain a positive image towards customers and financial analysts to sell products and to keep share prices up. Limited companies are dependent on selling a positive image of the company's prospects. However difficult it is to separate impression management from self-serving bias, one cannot disregard that the latter also exists in companies.

It has been shown that most drivers consider themselves to have above-average driving skills.[35] A similar overconfidence and self-serving attribution has been established in many other areas, including among business leaders.[36] On average, people consider themselves to be a little better than average. We recognize this from stories told by well-known leaders in the business press. When companies are successful, the outcome is ascribed to the foresight and competence of the CEO and top management; when expectations are not met, as is usually the case in economic recession, failures are ascribed to external factors which nobody foresaw or could have foreseen. Explaining failures as due to unforeseeable events and denying responsibility is often probably not a conscious attempt to explain away a failure, but more often an unconscious effort to protect one's own well-being. Responsibility is claimed for success, but rarely for failures.

Some high-ranking political and business leaders have been described not only as overconfident but also as exhibiting narcissistic traits, i.e. they have an unrealistic image of their own importance. They like – or need – to be admired, and to receive attention and positive reinforcement from others. It is better to be confirmed than criticized, although we know that flattery does not foster learning. However, learning and re-evaluation of old assumptions requires negative feedback, something some leaders prefer to avoid. This can lead to a single-minded search for information that supports the project and estimates the leader is in favour of, or that planners and cost estimators presume to be favoured by their superior.

Craig Galbraith and Gregory Merrill[37] sent a questionnaire to senior managers asking them whether they asked subordinates to revise their sales forecasts and cost estimates after having reviewed these. The replies showed that almost 50 per cent claimed to have done so, and that half of these made the revision themselves. A third had asked for 'backcasts', i.e. forecasts that fulfilled a certain pre-specified outcome. Galbraith and Merrill underline that estimating and costing is a political process. Top management do not always want the best possible estimate, but rather the estimate that serves their purpose and needs at the time.

Careerists know that it pays to agree. They tend to provide their bosses with information that confirms the bosses' beliefs. Honesty is highly prized, but honest people tend to be impossible to sway and as a result risk becoming seen as trouble makers. This can create room for a 'yes' culture, populated by careerists who hope to aid their chances of promotion by agreeing and supplying the positive reinforcement that their boss craves,[38] and others who just agree because it is easier to agree than to disagree.

Groups have to reach some kind of agreement as otherwise it is difficult to cooperate. The problem is that good decisions on projects require accurate and undistorted information not only on the estimated cost, but also on factors that may make changes necessary later and thus cause costs to increase, such as realistic market estimates, competitors' strength, and the knowledge and skills available in the organization. Once the project is finished, it can be beneficial to forget or conceal mistakes, as everyone involved will have to cooperate in the future, so a form of conflict avoidance is practised that can lead to a culture of distorting facts and groupthink[39] if it goes too far. The solution is rules of conduct: in politics, a constitution that prohibits leaders from developing dictatorial traits, and in business, professionalism and good corporate governance.

Self-serving bias thrives in ambiguity, as it is easier to maintain alternative views when there is room for alternative interpretations. When a cost estimate can be based on historical records, such as in replacement or closures of plants, there is not much room for alternative interpretations if one accepts the norm of economic rationality. It is much more different when estimating the cost and revenues for an investment into a new market, especially if the technology is also new. Entering new markets and implementing new technology typically encounters unforeseen problems that delay the venture, making costs grow and delaying revenues. There are many possible outcomes, and this ambiguity creates room for alternative views; thus, although proponents and opponents might have exactly the same information, they might draw different conclusions. The less we know about the cost, the more the strength of our belief in the investment becomes, and hence the importance of our self-serving bias to enable us to justify decisions. Ventures in new areas are examples of projects more often based on belief in a vision than hard data.

Ambiguity opens up possibilities for negotiating data. It makes it easier to find options that might favour our interests and formulate rational explanations to support these interests. It makes it easier for those that work on or are committed to the venture in other ways to search for and find evidence confirming estimates that favour the venture, and for those that are against the venture to search for and find evidence to stop it. Ambiguity can also be used deliberately to make it difficult to evaluate and assess the outcomes of estimates. Project managers might tend to emphasize the uniqueness of their project, try to include cushions in estimates, and avoid specifying budgets more than necessary, all to make it more difficult to compare budget and outcome. That gives them flexibility and makes it easier to achieve the budget.

Anchoring bias. The third bias we need to cover in this section is anchoring, which means that later pieces of information are anchored in earlier information. Once one establishes an estimate, this figure serves as the basis for future estimates. Individuals have a tendency to attach more belief to this first estimate than they have reason to and to downplay new information that conflicts with it. Thus, the level of the first offer in a negotiation affects the final level agreed on. The first offer defines the range of possible counteroffers and where the deal will end. Property buyers decide how much they can pay based on the price paid for similar properties. Earlier experiences limit our search for information and solutions. We search for solutions in the glow of the streetlight.

The phenomenon is well known in budgeting. Most budgets are just last year's budget updated with incremental changes. The same weather as last year, perhaps a little colder or warmer, but no perfect storm. Similarly, forecasters may prefer to modify their forecasts so that they don't deviate too much from other forecasters' prognoses.[40] To anchor your estimate on competitors' estimates or historical data are two strategies a forecaster uses to avoid the risk of being criticized if the forecast turns out to be wrong. It is common to play down change as it is difficult to foresee the consequences of change and make others share that view of the future. Simple budgeting works well in stable environments, but needs frequent updates in more fast-changing business environments; also, the purpose of budgeting is not only forecasting for planning, but to specify responsibility and compensation, and create commitment and motivation.

It takes several years of planning to implement a major project, and several cost estimates are usually made before such a project is given the go-ahead. Major cost increases typically appear early in the process. The first estimate can be very simple and based on comparisons with earlier similar projects, or rules of thumb used to estimate cost, but it is still very important as it will serve as an anchor in negotiating funding. It will be remembered and compared with later estimates. If costs increase, project management will have to be able to explain why cost has increased. That might not be a problem in a private company, where management and the board have experience of similar industrial projects, but it can be very difficult to explain to a public that does not have such knowledge. The first estimate can then be compared with the final cost even if it means comparing apples and oranges, when, for instance, most of the cost increase can be explained by the fact that size of the project has increased or by high inflation. The public will not buy the excuse that the first estimate was very vague, so it can be wise not to let grossly uncertain figures be made public.

Cost Overrun and Lack of Information and Information Asymmetry

Investments have to satisfy the needs and requirements of many actors within and outside the organization to be approved and receive funding. Marketing people have the best knowledge of the market and engineers of the technical choices made, but to have their project approved they must be able to sell their idea, they must convince top management that their investment is of greater importance to the company than competing projects in search of funding.

One problem in this selling and commitment process is that those designing the projects have more and better information about project details, making it difficult for those approving the funding to question technical choices. We refer to this as an information asymmetry between those selling and those approving the project, and many (if not most) of the explanations for intentional underestimation in the literature are based on the presence of information asymmetry between two or more actors.

Raymond Giguet and G. Morlat,[41] who postulated that the events causing cost overruns are not independent (see Appendix B), also postulated that when two investment alternatives filling the same purpose are competing for limited funds, the one underestimating the investment outlay stands a better chance of getting funded than the one that correctly estimates the investment outlay. From this, they concluded that underestimated investments will be over-represented in the capital budget, and the total investment budget thereby exceeded.

Based on statistics, one can also postulate that the more bids there are, the lower the lowest bid will be, and the higher the highest bid will be. The one who wins a popular auction will pay too much, and the one winning a much-wanted assignment tends to have underestimated the cost of delivering that assignment.

Not only does the lowest offer stand a better chance of being funded, there is also an incentive to accept the lowest offer when projects compete for discretionary grants from a limited budget. This has been pointed out in studies of both military[42] and civilian public sector procurement.[43] It is especially a problem in public organizations as these are often obliged to accept the lowest offer. They have no choice unless they can argue that a higher offer fulfils their specifications better, meaning that they have to specify quality requirements clearly.

Underbidding is not a new problem. A 100 years ago it was perceived as a major problem causing unfair competition, especially in the new electro-mechanical engineering industry. Costing was more difficult in this new industry, which appeared in the 1880s, as products were assembled by parts manufactured at different manufacturing units. As is usually the case in a new industry, many new and relatively small firms were soon competing for contracts, and many of these small firms did not have the knowledge to properly cost their products. As the procurers tended to choose the lowest offer, many of the firms that had been too optimistic went bankrupt, which caused problems for both the producer and the buyer. Costing practices needed to be improved, and that was done in the USA by creating calculating cartels which collected data to help member firms to make more accurate cost calculations, and by standardizing cost accounting.[44] Standardization meant first standardizing the terminology, and later the principles of cost accounting.[45] It was a process that took several decades and, in the depression, the unfair competition argument resurfaced in the National Industrial Recovery Act passed in 1933. As a part of President Roosevelt's New Deal, this Act prescribed 'fair competition' as meaning that firms were forbidden to set prices so low that competitors went into bankruptcy.[46]

Many bidders with poor information about the real cost no doubt create a risk of underbidding and cost overrun, but Giguet and Morlat's conclusion that underbidding would also cause the total investment budget to exceed its limits does not receive conclusive support in empirical studies. It seems to be more common[47] that the investment budget is not used up as there are always projects where implementation will be postponed or never happen. We are overoptimistic and plan to achieve more during the coming year than we actually manage to achieve. It has been reported that some companies are aware of this and therefore accept more projects than the investment budget allows so as not to miss out on lucrative investment opportunities.

One question which has been discussed in the literature[48] is whether underestimation is unintentional or the result of a deliberate act to make a project look more appealing. If the estimator has developed an optimistic bias then the underestimate is unintentional; if the estimator realizes that the estimate is unrealistically low but still submits it to get the investment approved, then it is a deliberate act. The requestor or project planner may be convinced of the merits of the investment but cannot prove it in the way the company prescribes in its investment processes, or the investment may be in the interest of the planner. The first alternative has already been discussed, so now we turn to investment costs that are deliberately underestimated.

Case studies from both the public[49] and the private sectors[50] give examples of project costs that have been deliberately underestimated in order to have them investigated and even approved. An example was given in the second section of Chapter 4. The managing director of Frövifors Bruk AB said the new mill would cost 300 million to gain approval to do a feasibility study, well aware that the board would probably find it wiser to build a larger and more expensive machine to better utilize economies of scale later on. Because of this information asymmetry '[y]ou have to go about things gradually so that you don't get a negative answer', as the MD of Frövifors put it in Chapter 4.

The use of (or, more correctly, the misuse of) cost-plus contracts, which guarantee the contractor full compensation for costs plus a certain markup in military development projects, has long been criticized[51] for not giving contractors incentives to keep costs down. Tougher competition has encouraged contractors to put in lower offers for cost-plus contracts as the benefit is far larger than the cost of not being able to meet the contract. As public authorities are forced to choose the lowest offer due to the rules for public procurement, and sometimes also lack the competence to assess offers correctly, they risk giving the contract to a contractor who consciously or unconsciously has put in a bid that is too low.

Furthermore, the penalties for not being able to meet technical requirements are higher than the penalties for not meeting time and cost requirements. Hence, problems in meeting technical requirements are taken as
time and cost overrun.[52] This causes military authorities to reduce the
amount of development work done on a cost-plus basis, and to supplement contracts with incentives to hold costs down.

To curb high and rising costs, President Reagan appointed David
Packard to chair a commission on US government military procurement.
The Packard Commission[53] concluded that the problems with cost
growth, delays, and performance shortfalls remained as documented in
earlier studies, and recommended changes in the acquisition process and
in the contracts used. However, this does not seem to have significantly
reduced cost overrun in defence contracts. A study of 269 defence acquisition contracts during the period from 1988 to 1995 did not show
improvements, and in fact Air Force contracts worsened.[54]

Developing new military technologies carries substantial technological
risks, and Kenneth Arrow[55] has argued that the primary reason for using
cost-plus contracts in weapon development and acquisition has not been
to reduce cost growth but to allocate risk between industry and government. Developing new military technology that government deems
necessary is associated with such high risk and uncertainty that industry
needs to share these risks with government. However, this type of contract
has also allowed certain defence industry firms to take advantage of the
situation by ignoring the financial risk, as they have a guarantee preventing bankruptcy. An instrument applied by government to reduce the risk
firms have to take when developing new technology has been exploited by
some firms for profit.

In civilian projects, there might also be an incentive for sellers to underestimate the real cost. However, cost can also increase when cost-plus
contracts are not used if the seller is more knowledgeable about the
project than the buyer. Construction companies sometimes accept deals
that do not look profitable on paper because they foresee that the buyer
will probably need to ask for additional work or changes in the agreed plan
and therefore can be expected to want to renegotiate the deal later on.[56]
The construction company's information and knowledge advantage
allows them to sign unrealistic plans because they know that profitable
additional work will be needed as the other party learns more about their
own plans. Therefore, the procurer needs to match the seller in competence and knowledge, otherwise the seller might take advantage of the
situation. If the procurer lacks the necessary competence, it can be better
to let a consultancy firm evaluate offers, as well as handle procurement
and contracts.

One might expect lenders to be aware when there is information asymmetry between procurers and sellers, but that is not the case. Even when a project is affected by very large cost overruns, lenders almost never make a loss. If it is a public project or company, then the state, and ultimately the taxpayers, take the risk. If it is a private company, then lenders look at the company's ability to pay back the loan. The important thing is the borrowers' ability to repay their loan, not their ability to avoid cost increases. Lenders do not usually evaluate projects; it is easier and cheaper for them to evaluate companies and management.

Information asymmetry exists not only between those proposing and approving a project, but also within organizations. However, removing this asymmetry is not always the best solution because cooperation is built on trust. An approved cost estimate is an agreement between two parties, and a commitment on behalf of those that have requested funding and, in particular, the project manager responsible for implementing the decision, as they have all signed the funding request and by doing so confirmed their belief in it. If those approving the funding question what is in the request too closely, this can be interpreted as questioning the qualifications and loyalty of those making the request. The higher the number of managers who have scrutinized and approved a request, the more difficult it becomes to stop it. Top management cannot reject projects approved lower down the organization without them losing face.[57] Nor is it is always in the best interest of the company to show distrust openly, as that can damage the trust needed to cooperate in the future.

A questionnaire[58] sent to Fortune 500 companies showed that management were aware that some proposers were more optimistic than others, and adjusted their profitability estimates downwards to compensate for this optimism. Managers accept projects even when they know that the true cost is underestimated, as they do not want to disbelieve committed project proposers. Company management is aware that investment requests are often too optimistic and learn to compensate for the optimistic biases of requestors.

It is also a widely held view in industry[59] that it is better to approve a tight budget and be prepared to provide additional funding if needed, as all budgets tend to be used up. 'Wasn't cost overrun larger? I expected twice as much', as the CEO of ASSI is said to have exclaimed when he got the follow-up review of the Frövifors investment. By approving a budget he thought was too small, he got more out of project management and ensured that funds were put to the most efficient use. Not surprisingly, it is extremely unusual for a project to be implemented below cost and unused funding returned; project management always seem to find a way to spend what has been approved.

This can also be an argument for keeping the estimates low in the planning process, and for being prepared for cost to rise gradually, as low-cost estimates put a pressure on project management to find economic solutions. Whether this is effective is another issue. Requesters who know that those responsible for approving requests will always make cuts in the budget can be expected to sneak in extra funds to counteract such cuts. Budgeting is called a game for good reasons.

Cost Overrun and Path Dependency

All projects need finance to be implemented, which means that there are always at least two processes involved in project planning. One is solving technical and economic challenges, and the other is the process through which finance is secured and approved. These two processes are often interconnected, as finance puts restrictions on the size of the project, and the design might have to be altered to attract support and finance. During the process, the number of alternatives is usually reduced to one, and consensus around a specific design and project is gradually built up through commitments from all the interested parties. These commitments are based not only on rational choices but also on emotions. In fact, emotions always come first. Rational choices are reconstructions, efforts to test and prove visions which are sometimes associated with strong emotions. People engaging in getting projects implemented, or indeed stopped, can become very emotionally involved, and assessments and decisions become a mixture of emotions and reason.

The formal investment decision is seldom between different projects. The alternatives are gradually discarded until only one remains. Many different design alternatives, technical solutions, sizes, and localizations can be studied; however, cost estimates are still undetailed and based on comparisons with earlier investments and rough estimates. Only when the board approve the invitation of tenders can reliable estimates be made, and then the choice is not between different localization options but whether to proceed with the alternative chosen or not. The early decisions and choices that are necessary to push the project idea towards implementation can create a path dependency by imposing restrictions on future decisions.

Furthermore, projects are learning processes. We shall not delve into the many theories of learning, but, for learning to take place, there must be some motivation or goal and some form of negative feedback that makes us aware when there is something in our assumptions or images that is not as we assumed. To learn something new, we need to be made aware of the difference between what we think we know and what we do not know. An important supplier of such feedback is the control systems that exist in organizations. They force estimators to learn more about the project before they are allowed to implement it.

Another important aspect of learning is that it has to be focused. One cannot investigate and solve all problems at the same time. To move the project forward, it is necessary to focus on one or a few problems at a time. This typically gives planning processes a sequential character. Richard Cyert and James March termed it 'sequential attention to goals. ... Organizations resolve conflict among goals, in part, by attending to different goals at different times'[60].

Trying to solve all problems simultaneously would make the level of uncertainty unmanageable. Instead, one has to focus on solving one or a few problems at a time and assume that other factors will remain constant. The same applies when there are multiple and possibly conflicting interpretations of the information available. One has to proceed in steps to keep perceived uncertainty at a manageable level. Keeping some goals or solutions constant while experimenting with others also means that some solutions will be developed before others, and so project planning becomes an iterative process. All this – early decisions, commitments, learning, and many other factors reducing alternatives – can create a path dependency that will drive cost.

Path dependency connects our next step with where we come from.[61] It explains how past decisions limit the choice of future possible decisions. Such path dependence can create cost growth both before and after the decision to invest. We have so far focused on commitments to early decisions created by an interconnection between definition and funding processes, and the reduction of alternatives in the definition process. Path dependence can also be inherent in the technology, be a consequence of specialization, driven by hopes of re-couping sunk cost, and individual commitments, causes that are not always easy to distinguish from each other.

A concept related to path dependence is escalating commitments,[62] often expressed as the tendency to 'throw good money after bad', particularly when this action cannot be ascribed to impartial rational reasoning. The reasons advanced for escalating commitments are much the same as for path dependence, and vary from expectations of good profit, to social pressure from peers and the role, and a hope to recover investment already made, i.e. sunk cost. The term 'escalating commitment' is not an explanation but a symptom. The explanations given vary in the relatively rich literature around this topic. We have already described how the definition and impetus processes are interlinked and that those advocating the project must convince those allocating resources of the merit of the project, and get their commitment to the cause. This process of committing support starts right at the beginning of the project, and is one of several explanations for escalating commitment. A related term is 'entrapment', which can be defined as instances of escalating commitment leading to an ineffective course of action.[63] Escalating commitment can lead to both effective and ineffective courses of action.

Starting with technology as a cause of path dependence, an often cited example is the QWERTY keyboard layout which, due to its early dominance in the market, has been able to retain its dominance in spite of better layouts. The more people using it the more difficult it becomes to switch to another layout, a fact well known in the IT industry, where the number of users creates an increasing rate of return. The concept is not new. Harry Turner Newcomb,[64] for instance, showed in 1898 that 'the law of increasing returns' in industries with low operating costs which did not need to increase their investments or increase them in proportion to increases in production, such as the railway industry, leads to the firm with the largest network out-competing other firms. But W. Brian Arthur[65] presented the first formal theory showing how increasing rate of return can lead to 'lock-in due to historical events' to a less efficient technology. Characteristic here is that there are several possible future paths, that the outcome is unpredictable, that the choices made limit future possible choices, and that the path dependency can lead to inefficient ends.

Specialization is another factor that places a firm on a certain path, or commits an individual to a certain profession. Gary Becker[66] distinguishes between general and firm-specific human capital. The former is applicable to firms in general, while the latter is of more value to a specific firm in creating an incentive to remain in the organization. Managers and workers with more specialized, firm-specific skills are of lower value outside the firm, which is why they have fewer options to leave the firm. This could make them more prone to continue investing in failing courses of action.[67]

When it comes to investments, this is true also in a broader sense. Competing firms can be expected to have almost the same information about the market. What makes an investment more profitable for one firm over another is that it has capabilities, i.e. firm-specific resources, better suited to making it profitable. Firms have to specialize and invest in developing capabilities further in areas where they have a competitive advantage, which often implies assets that are so firm-specific that they cannot be traded. Thus, specialization locks the firm into a certain path of investment, in the same way that specialized employees become locked into their firm. This also means that the first investment is the most important. Later investment utilizes earlier investment.

To the employee, firm-specific skills become sunk cost when leaving the firm. Sunk cost is gone and irrelevant, and cannot be recovered. It should not influence future decisions, but can in fact do so due to psychological factors. The gambler makes yet another bet to recover earlier losses, investors make additional investments in the hope of recovering earlier investment, or a bank gives additional loans to recover earlier loans. Hopes of recovering losses can lock an investor into path dependence.

Sunk cost should not matter, but financial obligations can make sunk cost relevant. Investments can be divided into basic and additional investment. The basic investment can be a new plant or production unit. Basic investments can be very expensive and may be partly financed by borrowed capital which has to be repaid. The company therefore becomes locked in to making the basic investment profitable. This forces the company onto a path of making additional investments to be able to pay rents and loans back. The basic investment has several names: in the vehicle and software industry, for instance, it is called a platform. A platform is developed upon which several car models, or many customer software projects, can be based. The principle is the same. A platform is not profitable if it is used only to develop one car model or software for one customer one time only. It has to be made profitable by additional investments.

Sunk cost can also be used intentionally to gain additional funding and investments. An extreme example is the Peruvian regional director referred to by Albert O. Hirschman[68] who, due to lack of funding, used up all his funds to build bridges, which were useless if, later on, funding was not also appropriated to build roads connecting the bridges. Similarly, there is the tale of a regional director in the south of Sweden who spent all his funding on secondary roads, knowing that this would give him strong arguments for extra funding to build highways catering for long-distance transport. This has been claimed to have been behind the Swedish Road Administration developing a fairer allocation system in the 1960s based on cost–benefit analysis.

The world of ideas that exist in organizations can also create path dependence. Gothenburg, the second largest city in Sweden, decided to turn its railway station into a drive-through station by constructing an underground railway loop with two new stations. In the 1980s, a local politician had proposed an underground line connecting three local transport junctions which was considered too expensive, but it later reappeared as a railway line project.[69] However, it turned out to be too difficult and costly to build a whole railway station underneath one of the three local traffic junctions, due partly to space but also to the blue clay substrata underneath the junction, so the station was moved eastwards where it could be constructed in rock. This then made it necessary to scrap another junction, whereby the new loop did not serve the purpose the original underground line was supposed to fill. Still, this did not stop the project. Some project ideas are the result of a search process and others an idea imported from outside, but many are just based on ideas that have been around for a long time. Such ideas are found in both public organizations and private firms, and can create their own path dependency.

Individual actors may also be locked into a course of action. An ambitious entrepreneurial managing director of a public utility saw an opportunity to reverse the downward economic development in his region by developing a biomass energy industry system. He was not alone in promoting this venture, but became identified with it as he promoted it widely in the media. However, as project planning proceeded and more became known about the risks involved, he became gradually more hesitant, and was already doubtful about the prospects for the project when he made his presentation to the board to get the go ahead:

I had this unpleasant feeling that it was going to be difficult. . . . It was said then that the oil price would increase in real terms by two per cent. We had the government's word for that. . . . I've realized since then that we were whistling in the dark, that's what we wanted to believe. We put great store on them saying that the oil price would never go down to such a low level as to make domestic energy sources uncompetitive. That was an additional reason we believed in this. Deep inside I was very worried about this part. One should probably have trusted one's intuitive feelings that this was bloody risky and slammed on the brakes at an earlier stage, but by then the contracts for the project had already been placed.[70]

His fears came true, and, on top of the economics, serious technical problems emerged. The project was shut down, and the entrepreneurial managing director had to shoulder much of the blame as he had become personally associated with the venture through the media. It was seen as his project.

We might wonder why no one hits the brake before a seemingly impossible business idea crashes. Maybe it is not always easy to stop momentum when an idea has become widely accepted as truth, and, as in this case, many people have attached great hopes to the venture. As the highly engaged entrepreneur, our managing director had built up expectations. When he started to doubt his earlier promises, he did not want to make those that had believed in him disappointed, which is why he had to go through with the project and try to make it succeed.

Key actors can become locked in to the promises they make in order to get their project implemented. Even if they realize that the assumptions they have made do not hold, it is often difficult and painful to re-evaluate these assumptions, especially if they were the ones selling the assumptions in the first place. It is easier to hope that they are right and that everything will solve itself.

We started by explaining how emotions, visibility, and rigid decision processes can lock decision makers and other actors in to early estimates and commitments, and make it difficult to revalue old ones and make objective assessments of new information. An estimate needs approval in order to develop an idea further. In this respect, there is no difference between the private and public sectors but, as has been pointed out, it can be more difficult to explain cost growth in the public sector as the requirement for transparency is higher. Large sunk cost and many actors committed to a project can make it more difficult to terminate the project if the cost estimates increases. However, it is not only the organizational context that creates commitments and rigidity. Key actors can become locked in to commitments that they made earlier in the process. Those that have been working with the project for a long time and have put their name on the figures become committed to achieving the figures promised. Personal commitments are built up and can by themselves become a force that helps overcome doubts and drive plans forward, making it difficult to stop plans once they have gathered enough momentum. All these factors mean that plans can be approved even when they should not have been.

Notes

INTRODUCTION

1. Northland Resources S.A., Press release, Luxembourg, 27 September 2010.
2. Northland Resources S.A., Press release, 'Positive Update on Northland's Kaunisvaara Project Confirming the Logistic Solution and a NPV of USD 934 million', Luxembourg, 18 May 2011.
3. Northland Resources S.A., Press release, Luxembourg, 24 January 2013.
4. Northland Resources S.A., Press release, Luxembourg, 30 June 2014.
5. Northland Resources S.A., Press release, Luxembourg, 14 October 2014.
6. Northland Resources S.A., Press release, Luxembourg, 8 December 2014.
7. The trustee estimated assets minus debts at more than SEK 12 billion, or SEK 12,138,613,471.36. See *Norrbottens Kuriren*, 20 March 2015. The currency translation is uncertain as the SEK per US $ rate since 2010 has varied between 6.0 and 8.8, during the last ten years between 6 and 9, and since 1972 from 3.87 in March 1975 to 11.03 in June 2001. Furthermore, our source does not state how much of the debt is in US $.
8. The South African Anglo American Corporation moved its headquarter to London after its merger with Minorco in 1999 and formed the mining giant Anglo American plc.
9. Alex MacDonald, 'Anglo American takes $4 billion charge on mine', *The Wall Street Journal*, 29 January 2013.
10. J. Bertisen and G. A. Davis, 'Bias and error in mine project capital cost estimation', *The Engineering Economist*, vol. 53, no. 2, 2008, 118–39.
11. B. Flyvbjerg and A. Stewart, Olympic proportions: Cost and cost overrun at the Olympics 1960–2012, Oxford: Saïd Business School working papers, June 2012.
12. P. W. G. Morris and G. H. Hough, *Preconditions of Success and Failure in Major Projects* (Oxford: Major Project Association, 1986).
13. B. Flyvbjerg, M. Skamris Holm, and S. Buhl, 'Underestimating costs in public works projects: Error or lie', *Journal of the American Planning Association*, vol. 68, no. 3, 2002, 279–95.
14. E. Mansfield, J. Rapoport, J. Schnee, S. Wagner, and M. Hamburger, *Research and Innovation in the Modern Corporation* (New York: Norton, 1971).
15. Government Accountability Office, *Status of Major Acquisitions as of September 30 1982*, GAO/NS IAD-83-32 (Washington, DC: General Accounting Office, 1983).
16. D. Arditi, G. T. Akan, and S. Gurdamar, 'Cost overruns in public projects', *Project Management*, vol. 3, no. 4, 1985, 218–24.

17. S. Morris, 'Cost and time overruns in public sector projects', *Economic and Political Weekly*, vol. 25, no. 47, 1990, M-154–68.

18. P. Svensson, *Styrning av produktutvecklingsprojekt: En studie av förutsättningarna för planering av produktutvecklingsprojekt i några svenska verkstadsföretag* (Göteborg: Institutionen för Industriell organisation och ekonomi, Chalmers tekniska högskola, 1990).

19. F. Bergeron and J.-Y. St-Arnaud, 'Estimation of information systems development efforts: A pilot study', *Journal of Information and Management*, vol. 22, no. 4, 1992, 239–54.

20. Flyvbjerg, Skamris Holm and Buhl, 'Underestimating costs in public works projects: Error or lie'.

21. Bertisen and Davis, 'Bias and error in mine project capital cost estimation'.

22. J.-K. Lee, 'Cost overrun and cause in Korean social overhead capital projects: Roads, rails, airports, and ports', *Journal of Urban Planning and Development*, vol. 134, no. 2, 2008, 59–62.

23. A. Jenpanitsub, Cost Overruns in Transport Projects: Experience from Sweden, Master of Science Thesis, Stockholm: The Royal Institute of Technology, 2011.

24. J. Odeck, 'Do reforms reduce the magnitude of cost overruns in road projects? Statistical evidence from Norway', *Transportation Research Part A*, vol. 65, July 2014, 68–79.

25. B. K. Sovacool, D. Nugent, and A. Gilbert, 'Construction cost overruns and electricity infrastructure: An unavoidable risk?', *Electricity Journal*, vol. 27, no. 4, 2014, 112–20.

26. Ernst and Young, Spotlight on oil and gas megaprojects, 2014: available at www.ey.com/Publication/vwLUAssets/EY-spotlight-on-oil-and-gas-mega projects/$FILE/EY-spotlight-on-oil-and-gas-megaprojects.pdf.

27. Although cost growth has become a recommended term in project management there is no consensus on what the components of cost growth are and therefore what should be considered as contributing to cost growth. When M. F. Cancian (Cost growth: Perception and reality, A Publication of the Defence Acquisition University, July 2010, 389–404) reviewed the use of the term in four US organizations he found that what was included in their estimates of cost growth differed from organization to organization. The project management literature tends to focus on costs that project management can influence. Thus, a cost overrun due to that, e.g. the firm made losses due to the way the department of finance had chosen to finance the project, is not always considered as cost growth.

28. See e.g. National Audit Office, *North Sea Cost Escalation Study* (London: Her Majesty's Stationary Office, 1976); A. Likierman, 'Analysing project cost escalation: The case study of North Sea oil, *Accounting and Business Research*, vol. 8, no. 29, 1977, 51–7; Flyvbjerg, Skamris Holm, and Buhl, 'Underestimating costs in public works projects: Error or lie'; N. Davies, A. Eager, M. Maier and L. Penfold, *Intergenerational equipment cost escalation, A Ministry of Defence economic research paper on the increasing cost of UK defence equipment*, Ministry of Defence, 18 December 2012; and I. N. Kessides, 'The future of the nuclear industry reconsidered: Risks, uncertainties, and continued promise', *Energy Policy*, vol. 48, 2012, 185–208. One could argue that the term cost escalation would have been a more

appropriate term to be used in this book as we will view cost increases from the perspective of the firm or society making the investment, as an individual investment project thereby becomes a cost item by itself that might increase or decrease in cost relative to other investment alternatives open to the investor.

PROJECT PLANNING, COST ESTIMATES, AND DEVIATIONS IN MAJOR PROJECTS

1. The press section example is borrowed from O. Eriksson, *Tre stora industriella investeringar: Om investeringskalkyleringens bristande ändamålsenlighet vid stora investeringar* (Västerås: Mälardalen University Press, 2002), pp. 573–85.

2. The Frövifors Bruk AB's reorientation and investment in a new paper board machine builds on two earlier studies: E. Segelod, *Kalkylering och avvikelser: Empiriska studier av stora projekt i kommuner och industriföretag* (Malmö: Liber, 1986), and E. Segelod, *Renewal through Internal Development* (Aldershot: Avebury, 1995).

3. The review is reported in E. Segelod, *Kostnadsuppföljning med analys för Genastorp vattenkraftstation, Karlshamnsverkets första oljekraftverk samt för Barsebäcksverkets båda kärnkraftsaggregat,* FE-rapport 187, Göteborg: Företagsekonomiska institutionen, Göteborgs Universitet, 1982.

4. A. Grubler, 'The costs of the French nuclear scale-up: A case of negative learning by doing', *Energy Policy*, vol. 38, 2010, 5174–88.

5. International Energy Agency, *Projected Costs of Generating Electricity, 2010 Edition* (Paris: International Energy Agency, 2010).

6. Government Accountability Office, *Nuclear Regulation. NRC Needs More Effective Analysis to Ensure Accumulation of Funds to Decommission Nuclear Power Plants,* Report to the Honorable Edward J. Markey, Report GAO-04-32, 2004.

7. E. Segelod, 'The cost of the Swedish nuclear waste program', *Progress in Nuclear Energy*, vol. 48, no. 4, 2006, 314–24.

8. Swedish Nuclear Fuel and Waste Management Company, *Plan 2013, Costs from and including 2015 for the radioactive residual products from nuclear power. Basis for fees and guarantees for the period 2015–2017,* Technical Report TR-14-16 (Stockholm: Swedish Nuclear Fuel and Waste Management Co., May 2014).

9. Swedish Government Official Reports, *Spent Nuclear Fuel and Radioactive Waste. A Summary of a Report Given by the Swedish Government Committee on Radioactive Waste,* SOU 1976:32 (Stockholm, 1976).

10. Swedish Government Official Reports, *Kärnkraftens avfall: Organisation och finansiering,* SOU 1980:14 (Stockholm: Liber Förlag, 1980).

11. Swedish Government Official Reports, *Kärnkraftens avfall: Organisation och finansiering.*

12. M. Elam and G. Sundqvist, 'Meddling in Swedish success in nuclear waste management', *Environmental Politics*, vol. 20, no. 2, 2011, 246–63.

13. Swedish Government Official Reports, *Översyn av lagstiftningen på kärnenergiområdet,* SOU 1991:95 (Stockholm: Allmänna förlaget, 1991), Swedish Government Official Reports, *Säkrare finansiering av framtida kärnavfallskostnader,* SOU 1994:107 (Stockholm: Fritze, 1994), and Swedish

Government Official Reports, *Betalningsansvaret för kärnavfallet* (Stockholm: SOU 2004:125, Norstedts Juridik, 2004).

14. The Nuclear Waste Fund, *Activity Report 2014*.
15. The taxes can be estimated at roughly SEK 0.06 per kWh, and production cost excluding taxes and fees for nuclear waste at about SEK 0.20 per kWh.
16. Swedish Radiation Safety Authority, Angående OKG AB:s och Ringhals AB:s beslut om förtida avställning av visa kärnkraftsreaktorer, SSM2015-1198–3, 2015.
17. Ramöverenskommelse mellan Socialdemokraterna, Moderaterna, Miljöpartiet de gröna, Centerpartiet och Kristdemokraterna, 2016–06-10.
18. F. Tchapga, Overview and comparison of international practices on funding mechanisms, Topical Session on Funding Issues in Connection with Decommissioning of Nuclear Power Plants, Paris: Nuclear Energy Agency and OECD, 2004.
19. P. Högselius, 'Spent nuclear fuel policies in historical perspective: An international comparison', *Energy Policy*, vol. 37, no. 1, 2009, 254–63.
20. Elam and Sundqvist, 'Meddling in Swedish success in nuclear waste management'.
21. 'Finnish regulator approves Posiva's waste repository plan', *World Nuclear News*, 12 November 2015.
22. R. C. Callen, 'Congress's nuclear waste "contract with America": Where do we go from here?', *Electricity Journal*, vol. 8, no. 5, 1995, 45–55.
23. Government Accountability Office, Institutional Relations Under the Nuclear Waste Policy Act of 1982, DC: RCED-87–14 (Washington DC: General Accounting Office, 1987).
24. Government Accountability Office, *Nuclear Waste: Technical, Schedule, and Cost Uncertainties of the Yucca Mountain Repository Project*, Report to Congressional Requesters, GAO-02–191 (Washington DC: General Accounting Office, 2001), and Government Accountability Office, *Nuclear Waste: Uncertainties About the Yucca Mountain Repository Project*, Testimony Before the Committee on Energy and Natural Resources, GAO-02-765T (Washington DC: General Accounting Office, 2002).
25. Requires that the asset is tradable.
26. More probable when the asset is firm-specific.
27. For an example of such an analysis, see e.g. S. N. Woodward, 'Performance in planning a large project', *Journal of Management Studies*, vol. 19, no. 2, 1982, 183–98.

THE CONSEQUENCES OF COST OVERRUN

1. E. Segelod, *Kalkylering och avvikelser: Empiriska studier av stora projekt i kommuner och industriföretag* (Malmö: Liber, 1986).
2. C. N. Parkinson, *The Law and the Profit*, Penguin edition, 1965 (London: John Murray, 1960), p. 11.
3. See e.g. National Audit Office, *North Sea Cost Escalation Study* (London: Her Majesty's Stationary Office, 1976); M. Statman and T. T. Tyebjee, 'Optimistic capital budgeting forecasts: An experiment', *Financial*

Management, vol. 13, Autumn 1985, 27–33; Segelod, *Kalkylering och avvikelser: Empiriska studier av stora projekt i kommuner och industriföretag.*

4. E. Segelod, Kostnadsuppföljning med analys för Genastorp vattenkraftstation, Karlshamnsverkets första oljekraftverk samt för Barsebäcksverkets båda kärnkraftsaggregat. *FE-rapport 187*, Företagsekonomiska institutionen, Göteborgs Universitet, 1982.

5. E. Lundberg, *Produktivitet och räntabilitet* (Stockholm: SNS, 1961).

6. A. L. Morner, 'For SOHIO it was Alaskan oil – or bust', *Fortune*, August 1977, 173–84.

7. V. E. Hauck and G.A. Geistauts, 'Construction of the trans-Alaska oil pipeline', *Omega*, vol. 10, no. 3, 1982, 259–65.

8. See e.g. E. Segelod, *Renewal through Internal Development* (Aldershot: Avebury, 1995).

9. A. D. Chandler, Jr., *Scale and Scope: The Dynamics of Industrial Capitalism* (Cambridge, MA: The Belknap Press of Harvard University Press, 1990).

10. U. Bengtsson, *Stora investeringar i mindre kommuner: Scope, scale och stage construction som strategier* (Göteborg: BAS, 2013).

11. For additional examples of stepwise or stage construction, as it is also called, see H. L. Beenhakker and J. G. Danskin, 'Economies of stage construction for transport facilities', *Transportation Research*, vol. 7, no. 2, 1973, 163–78, and U. Bengtsson, *Stora investeringar i mindre kommuner: Scope, scale och stage construction som strategier*. Stepwise construction has to do with the optimal timing of irreversible investments. For an early treatment of the timing decision see S. Marglin, *Approaches to Dynamic Investment Planning*, Amsterdam: North-Holland, 1963, and for the real option approach to the same issue, see A. K. Dixit and S. R. Pindyck, *The Options Approach to Capital Investments*, Princeton, NJ: Princeton University Press, 1995.

12. BillerudKorsnäs, press release, 26 August 2014.

13. O. Eriksson, *Tre stora industriella investeringar: Om investeringskalkyleringens bristande ändamålsenlighet vid stora investeringar* (Västerås: Mälardalen University Press, 2002) has analysed this case and we will draw on his analysis.

14. Eriksson, *Tre stora industriella investeringar*, p. 240.

15. Estimates made by Eriksson, *Tre stora industriella investeringar*.

16. See e.g. T. K. McCraw, ed., *Creating Modern Capitalism: How Entrepreneurs, Companies, and Countries Triumphed in Three Industrial Revolutions* (Cambridge, MA: Harvard University Press, 1997).

17. B. Carlsson and S. Nachemson-Ekwall, *Livsfarlig ledning: Historien om kraschen i ABB* (Stockholm: Ekerlids, 2003).

18. J. E. Sawyer, 'Entrepreneurial error and economic growth', *Explorations in Entrepreneurial History*, vol. 4, no. 2, 1952, 199–204.

19. A. O. Hirschman, *Development Projects Observed* (Washington DC: The Brookings Institution, 1967).

20. Hirschman, *Development Projects Observed*, p. 13–34.

21. C. Freeman, *The Economics of Industrial Innovation* (Harmondsworth: Penguin Books, 1974), p. 233.

22. R. R. Nelson, 'The simple economics of basic scientific research', *Journal of Political Economy*, vol. 67, no. 3, 1959, 297–306.

23. Segelod, *Kalkylering och avvikelser*, or Segelod, *Renewal Through Internal Development*.
24. Segelod, *Renewal through Internal Development*.
25. Segelod, *Renewal through Internal Development*, p. 67.
26. Segelod, *Renewal through Internal Development*, p.67.
27. In fact, there is research showing that less knowledgeable people tend to have more confidence in their own abilities than more knowledgeable people. See e.g. J. Kruger and D. Dunning, 'Unskilled and unaware of it: How difficulties in recognizing one's own incompetence lead to inflated self-assessments', *Journal of Personality and Social Psychology*, vol. 77, no. 6, 1999, 1121–34, and J. Ehrlinger, K. Johnson, M. Banner, D. Dunning, and J. Kruger, 'Why the unskilled are unaware: Further explorations of (absent) self-insight among the incompetent', *Organizational Behavior and Human Decision Processes*, vol. 105, no. 1, 2008, 98–121.
28. Segelod, *Kalkylering och avvikelser*.

A MODEL OF COST OVERRUN AND GROWTH

1. When cost overrun is explained as a consequence of a deliberate underestimation to have a project approved that is in the interest of the estimator, this is usually termed a political explanation. So, e.g. B. Flyvbjerg, M. Skamris Holm, and S. Buhl, 'Underestimating costs in public works projects: Error or lie', *Journal of the American Planning Association*, vol. 68, no. 3, 2002, 279–95. This use of the political and politics is consistent with its use in organizational theory. See e.g. B. T. Mayes and R. W. Allen, 'Toward a definition of organizational politics', *Academy of Management Review*, vol. 2, no. 4, 1977, 672–8, and A. Drory and T. Romm, 'The definition of organizational politics: A review', *Human Relations*, vol. 43, no. 11, 1990, 1133–54. The term 'political explanation' will be used in a slightly different meaning when we in Chapter 5 analyze differences between the logics of politics and economics, and the process by which collective action is achieved.
2. In a study of 52 so-called mega-projects (*Understanding the Outcomes of Megaprojects: A Qualitative Analysis of Very Large Civilian Projects* (Santa Monica, CA: The RAND Corporation, 1988), p. 66), E. W. Merrow, L. McDonnell, and R. Y. Argüden, estimated that economic-technical explanations could explain more than 75 per cent of the variance in outcome.
3. See e.g. S. W. Pruitt and L. J. Gitman, 'Capital budgeting forecast biases: Evidence from the *Fortune* 500', *Financial Management*, vol. 15, Spring 1987, 46–51, D. H. Pickrell, 'A desire named streetcar: Fantasy and fact in rail transit planning', *Journal of the American Planning Association*, vol. 8, no. 2, 1990, 158–76, and Flyvbjerg, Skamris Holm and Buhl, 'Underestimating costs in public works projects: Error or lie'.
4. See e.g. M. Wachs, 'When planners lie with numbers', *Journal of the American Planning Association*, vol. 55, no. 4, 1989, 476–9.
5. See e.g. E. Segelod, *Kalkylering och avvikelser: Empiriska studier av stora projekt i kommuner och industriföretag* (Malmö: Liber, 1986), and E. Segelod, *Renewal through Internal Development* (Aldershot: Avebury, 1995).

6. See e.g. W. Ouchi, 'The conceptual framework for the design of organizational control mechanisms', *Management Science*, vol. 25, no. 9, 1979, 833–48, W. Ouchi and A. Berry, 'Control, organization and accounting', *Accounting, Organization and Society*, vol. 5, no. 2, 1980, 231–44, and T. Malmi and D. A. Brown, 'Management control systems as a package: Opportunities, challenges and research directions', *Management Accounting Research*, vol. 19, 2008, 287–300.

7. See e.g. E. Segelod, 'Investments and investment processes in professional service groups', *International Journal of Production Economics*, vol. 67, no. 2, 2000, 135–54.

8. See e.g. G. F. Davis, *Managed by the Markets: How Finance Reshaped America* (Oxford: Oxford University Press, 2009).

9. Most major corporations have a divisionalized structure with one or several intermediate levels between the head office and the businesses.

10. See e.g. J. L. Bower, 'Planning within the firm', *American Economic Review*, vol. 60, no. 2, 1970, 186–94, J. L. Bower, *Managing the Resource Allocation Process* (Boston, MA: Division of Research, Graduate School of Business Administration, Harvard University, 1970), E. Segelod, *Resource Allocation in Divisionalized Groups: A Study of Investment Manuals and Corporate Level Means of Control* (Aldershot: Avebury, 1996), and J. L. Bower and C. G. Gilbert, eds., *From Resource Allocation to Strategy* (Oxford; Oxford University Press, 2005).

11. G. Wramsby and U. Österlund, *Svenska fastighetsinvesteringar inom EG 1987–1990: Investeringsbedömning, kreditbedömning och hyrespåverkande variabler* (Göteborg: Handelshögskolan vid Göteborgs Universitet, 1995).

12. Wramsby and Österlund, *Svenska fastighetsinvesteringar inom EG 1987–1990*. The Swedish banking sector had been deregulated 1983–5.

13. J. C. Ericsson, *Utan omsvep: Mitt berikande liv med Consafe* (Stockholm: Timbro, 1987).

14. R. Nelson, ed., *The Rate and Direction of Inventive Activity: Economic and Social Factors* (Princeton, NJ: Princeton University Press, 1962), and T. Marschak, T. K. Glennan, Jr., and R. Summers, eds., *Strategy for R&D* (Berlin: Springer Verlag, 1967).

15. B. H. Klein, 'The decision making problem in development', in Nelson, ed., *The Rate and Direction of Inventive Activity*, pp. 477–508.

16. D. Dörner, *The Logic of Failure: Recognizing and Avoiding Error in Complex Situations* (New York: Metropolitan Books, 1996).

17. See R. J. Schonberger 'Why projects are "always" late: A rationale based on manual simulation of a PERT/CPM network', *Interfaces*, vol. 11, no. 5, 1981, 66–70, p. 66.

18. In this we will build on B. H. Klein and W. Meckling, 'Application of operations research to development projects', *Operations Research*, vol. 6, no. 3, 1958, 352–63, B. H. Klein, 'The decision making problem in development', in Nelson, ed., *The Rate and Direction of Inventive Activity*, pp. 477–508, and T. K. Glennan, Jr., 'Issues in the choice of development policies', in T. Marschak, T. K. Glennan Jr. and R. Summers, eds., *Strategies for R&D: Studies in the Microeconomics of Development* (Berlin: Springer Verlag, 1967), pp. 13–48.

19. This is a distinction made by e.g. P. Stangert, *Information, Uncertainty and Adaptive Planning* (Stockholm: FOA P Rapport C8392-M3, 1974), and L. Brigelius and P. Rosén, *Risk och Försäkring* (Göteborg: BAS, 1988).

20. Also, internal factors can contribute to static uncertainty in a world of political uncertainty, as will be shown in Chapter 5.

21. National Audit Office, *North Sea Cost Escalation Study* (London: Her Majesty's Stationary Office, 1976).

22. Konglige olje- og energidepartement, Kostnadsanalysen – norsk kontinentalsokkel (Oslo: Konglige olje- og energidepartement, 1980).

23. See e.g. J. H. Crowley, *Nuclear energy: What's next?* Monterey, CA: The work shop on the electric imperative atomic industrial forum Inc., 14–17 June 1981.

24. A. Grubler, 'The costs of the French nuclear scale-up: A case of negative learning by doing', *Energy Policy*, vol. 38, 2010, 5174–88.

25. M. Cooper, *Policy Challenges of Nuclear Reactor Construction: Cost Escalation and Crowding Out Alternatives. Lessons from the US and France for the Effort to Revive the US Industry with Loan Guarantees and Tax Subsidies*, South Royalton, VT: Vermont Law School, September 2010.

26. A. Grubler, 'The costs of the French nuclear scale-up'.

27. Cooper, *Policy Challenges of Nuclear Reactor Construction*. See also, e.g. M. Berthélemy and L. Escobar Rangel, 'Nuclear reactors' construction costs: The role of lead-time, standardization and technological progress', *Energy Policy*, vol. 82, July 2015, 118–30.

28. I. N. Kessides, 'The future of the nuclear industry reconsidered: Risks, uncertainties, and continued promise', *Energy Policy*, vol. 48, 2012, 185–208.

29. J. H. Crowley, Nuclear energy – What's next? Monterey, CA: The work shop on the electric imperative atomic industrial forum Inc., 14–17 June 1981.

30. See Nelson, ed., *The Rate and Direction of Inventive Activity*, M. S. Peck and F. M. Scherer, The Weapon Acquisition Process: An Economic Analysis (Boston, MA: Harvard University, Graduate School of Business Administration, 1962), and Marschak, Glennan Jr., and Summers, eds., *Strategies for R&D*.

31. P. Pugh, *The Cost of Sea Power: The Influence of Money on Naval Affairs from 1815 to the Present Day* (London: Conway Maritime Press, 1986).

32. M. V. Arena, I. Blickstein, O. Younossi, and C. A. Grammich, *Why Has the Cost of Navy Ships Risen? A Macroscopic Examination of the Trends in US Naval Ship Costs Over the Past Several Decades* (Santa Monica, CA: RAND Corporation, 2006), and M. V. Arena, O. Younossi, K. Brancato, I. Blickstein, and C. A. Grammich, *Why Has the Cost of Fixed-Wing Aircraft Risen? A Macroscopic Examination of the Trends in US Military Aircraft Cost over the past Several Decades* (Santa Monica, CA: RAND Corporation, 2008).

33. Pugh, *The Cost of Sea Power*.

34. See e.g. W. Adams, 'The military-industrial complex and the new industrial state', *American Economic Review*, vol. 58, no. 2, 1968, 652–65, A. Alptekin and P. Levine, 'Military expenditure and economic growth: A meta-analysis', *European Journal of Political Economy*, vol. 28, no. 4, 2012, 636–50, J. Castillo, J. Lowell, A. J. Tellis, J. Muñoz and B. Zycher, *Military Expenditures and Economic Growth* (Santa Monica, CA: RAND, 2001), and V. W. Ruttan, *Is*

War Necessary for Economic Growth? Military Procurement and Technology Development (New York: Oxford University Press, 2006).

35. O. Granstrand, E. Bohlin, C. Oskarsson, and N. Sjöberg, 'External technology acquisition in large multi-technology corporations', *R&D Management*, vol. 22, no. 2, 1992, 111–33, or O. Granstrand and S. Sjölander, 'Managing innovation in multi-technology corporations', *Research Policy*, vol. 19, no. 1, 1990, 35–60.

36. See e.g. R. R. Nelson, 'Uncertainty, learning and the economics of parallel research and development efforts', *Review of Economics and Statistics*, vol. 43, no. 4, 1961, 351–64, T. K. Glennan, Jr., 'Issues in the choice of development policies', in Marschak, Glennan Jr., and Summers, eds., *Strategies for R&D*, pp. 13–48, C. Y. Baldwin and K. B. Clark, *Design Rules, Volume 1: The Power of Modularity* (Cambridge, MA: MIT Press, 2000), C. Y. Baldwin and C. J. Woodard, 'The architecture of platforms: A unified view', in Annabelle Gawer, ed., *Platforms, Markets and Innovation* (Cheltenham, UK and Northampton, MA, US: Edward Elgar, 2009), pp. 19–44, and C. Y. Baldwin and J. Henkel, 'Modularity and intellectual property protection', *Strategic Management Journal*, vol. 36, no. 11, 2015, 1637–55.

37. See A. L. Morner, 'For SOHIO it was Alaskan oil, or bust', *Fortune*, August 1977, 173–84. At least $3.1 million of the $9,300 million was estimated to be due to inflation. See O. P. Kharbanda and E. A. Stallworthy, *How to Learn from Project Disasters* (Aldershot: Gower, 1983), p. 179.

38. Government Accountability Office, *Lesson Learned from Constructing the Trans-Alaska Oil Pipeline*, Report to the Congress by the Comptroller General of the United States, EMD-78-52 (Washington DC: General Accounting Office, 1978).

39. Government Accountability Office, *Lesson Learned from Constructing the Trans-Alaska Oil Pipeline*, pp. 11–12.

40. Government Accountability Office, *Lesson Learned from Constructing the Trans-Alaska Oil Pipeline*, p. i.

41. V. E. Hauck and G. A. Geistauts, 'Construction of the trans-Alaska oil pipeline', *Omega*, vol. 10, no. 3, 1982, 259–65.

42. A. D. Chandler, Jr., *Scale and Scope: The Dynamics of Industrial Capitalism* (Cambridge, MA: The Belknap Press of Harvard University Press, 1990).

43. U. Bengtsson, *Stora investeringar i mindre kommuner: Scope, scale och stage construction som strategier* (Göteborg: BAS, 2013.) studied 20 such major investments in 9 Swedish municipalities with a size of 20–50,000 inhabitants, and the impression is that it has become a common strategy to lower cost. Smaller municipalities cooperate both with each other and with private interest to build larger, more cost-efficient facilities, especially for district heating and energy production, water purification, waste treatment, and transportation investments.

44. This statement is most easily proved on the stock market, where investors lose money due to unrelated emotions and feelings affecting their trading. For a brief introduction, see e.g. J. R. Nofsinger, *The Psychology of Investing*, 5th edn. (Upper Saddle River, NJ: Pearson Prentice Hall, 2016). Behavioural finance is today a major research area within finance.

45. A. Smith, *The Theory of Moral Sentiments* (6th edn. 1790, London: A. Millar, 1759), Part II, i., ch. 2, § 2.
46. Smith, *The Theory of Moral Sentiments*, Part III, ch. 3, § 4.
47. Smith, *The Theory of Moral Sentiments*, Part III, ch. 3, § 4.
48. For a more detailed description of Smith as a behavioural scientist see e.g. W. Grampp, 'Adam Smith and the Economic Man', *Journal of Political Economy*, vol. 56, no 4, 1948, 315–36, N. Ashraf, C. F. Camerer, and G. Loewenstein, 'Adam Smith, behavioral economist', *Journal of Economic Perspectives*, vol. 19, no. 3, 2005, 131–45, and E. L. Khalil, 'Self-deceit and self-serving bias: Adam Smith on "General Rules"', *Journal of Institutional Economics*, vol. 5, no. 2, 2009, 251–8.
49. M. Toda, 'Emotion and decision making', *Acta Psychologica*, vol. 45, 1980, 133–55.
50. See e.g. A. Bechara, 'The role of emotion in decision-making: Evidence from neurological patients with orbitofrontal damage', *Brain and Cognition*, vol. 55, no. 1, 2004, 30–40, and A. Coricelli, R. J. Dolan, and A. Sirigu, 'Brain, emotion and decision making: The paradigmatic example of regret', *TRENDS in Cognitive Science*, vol. 11, no. 6, 2007, 258–65.
51. A. Smith, *An Inquiry into the Nature and Causes of the Wealth of Nations* (London: W. Strahan; and T. Cadell, in the Strand, 1776), book I, ch. x, p. 132.
52. Smith, *An Inquiry into the Nature and Causes of the Wealth of Nations*, book I, ch. x, p. 133.
53. Smith, *An Inquiry into the Nature and Causes of the Wealth of Nations*, book I, ch. x, p. 132.
54. For a review, see e.g. B. Fischhoff, S. Lichtenstein, P. Slovic, R. Keeney, and S. Derby, *Acceptable Risk* (Cambridge: Cambridge University Press, 1980), R. M. Hogarth, 'Beyond discrete biases: Functional and dysfunctional aspects of judgemental heuristics', *Psychological Bulletin*, vol. 90, no. 2, 1981, 197–217, R. M. Hogarth and S. Makridakis, 'Forecasting and planning: An evaluation', *Management Science*, vol. 27, no. 2, 1981, 115–38, or D. Kahneman, 'Maps of bounded rationality: Psychology for behavioural economics', *American Economic Review*, vol. 93, no. 5, 2003, 1449–75. On overconfident consumers: M. D. Grubb, 'Overconfident consumers in the marketplace', *Journal of Economic Perspective*, vol. 29, no. 4, 2015, 9–35. On overconfident CEOs: U. Malmendier and T. Geoffrey, 'Behavioral CEOs: The role of managerial overconfidence', *Journal of Economic Perspective*, vol. 29, no. 4, 2015, 37–60. On overconfident investors: K. Daniel and D. Hirshleifer, 'Overconfident investors, predictable returns, and excessive trading', *Journal of Economic Perspective*, vol. 29, no. 4, 2015, 61–87.
55. Daniel and Hirshleifer, 'Overconfident investors, predictable returns, and excessive trading'.
56. See U. Malmendier and G. Tate, 'CEO overconfidence and corporate investment' *Journal of Finance*, vol. 60, no. 6, 2005, U. Malmendier and G. Tate, 'Does overconfidence affect corporate investment? CEO overconfidence measures revisited', *European Financial Management*, vol. 11, no. 5, 2005, 649–59,

and Malmendier and Geoffrey, 'Behavioral CEOs: The role of managerial overconfidence'.

57. Grubb, 'Overconfident consumers in the marketplace'.

58. See e.g. J. A. Hornaday, 'Research about living entrepreneurs', in C. A. Kent, D. L. Sexton, and K. L. Vesper, eds., *Encyclopedia of Entrepreneurship* (Engelwood Cliffs, NJ: Prentice Hall, 1982), pp. 281–90, A. C. Cooper, W. C. Dunkelberg, and C. Y. Woo, 'Optimists and pessimists: 2994 entrepreneurs and their perceived chances for success', *in Frontiers of Entrepreneurship Research* (Wellesey, MA: Babson College, 1986), pp. 563–77, and K. A. Egge, 'Expectations vs. reality among founders of recent start-ups', in Frontiers of Entrepreneurship Research (Wellesley, MA: Babson College, 1992), pp. 322–36.

59. G. Fabricius and M. Büttgen, 'Project managers' overconfidence: How is risk reflected in anticipated project success', *Business Research*, vol. 8, no. 2, 2015, 239–63.

60. See e.g. J. Kruger and D. Dunning, 'Unskilled and unaware of it: How difficulties in recognizing one's own incompetence lead to inflated self-assessments', *Journal of Personality and Social Psychology*, vol. 77, no. 6, 1999, 1121–34, and J. Ehrlinger, K. Johnson, M. Banner, D. Dunning, and J. Kruger, 'Why the unskilled are unaware: Further explorations of (absent) self-insight among the incompetent', *Organizational Behavior and Human Decision Processes*, vol. 105, no. 1, 2008, 98–121.

61. C. Darwin, *The Descent of Man* (London: John Murray), p. 3, quoted in Kruger and Dunning, 'Unskilled and unaware of it', p. 1121.

62. Pruitt and Gitman, 'Capital budgeting forecast biases'.

63. See e.g. L. Tiger, *Optimism: The Biology of Hope* (New York: Simon & Schuster, 1979), D. M. Buss, 'Evolutionary personality psychology', *Annual Review of Psychology*, vol. 42, February 1991, 459–91, M. Waldman, 'Systematic errors and the theory of natural selection', *American Economic Review*, vol. 84, no. 3, 1994, 482–97, A. Postlewaite and O. Compte, 'Confidence enhanced performance', *American Economic Review*, vol. 83, no. 5, 2005, 1536–57, and T. Sharot, 'The optimism bias', *Current Biology*, vol. 21, no. 23, 2011, R941-5.

64. Smith, *The Theory of Moral Sentiments*, Part III, ch. 4, § 5–6.

65. See e.g. D. R. Forsyth, 'Self-serving bias', in W. A. Darity, ed., *International Encyclopedia of the Social Sciences*, Vol. 7, 2nd edn. (New York: Macmillan Reference, 2008), p. 429.

66. A. H. Mezulis, L. Y. Abramson, J. S. Hyde, and B. L. Hankin, 'Is there a universal positivity bias in attributions? A meta-analytic review of individual, developmental, and cultural differences in the self-serving attributional bias', *Psychological Bulletin*, vol. 130, no. 5, 2004, 711–47.

67. Anchoring is a concept introduced by Amon Tversky and David Kahneman in their article: 'Judgment under uncertainty: Heuristics and biases', *Science*, vol. 185, no. 4157, 1974, 1124–31.

68. H. A. Simon, *Administrative Behavior* (New York: The Macmillan Company, 1947). See also H. A. Simon, 'A behavioural model of rational choice', *Quarterly Journal of Economics*, vol. 69, no. 1, 1955, 99–118, and H. A.

Simon, 'Theories of decision-making in economics and behavioral science', *American Economic Review*, vol. 49, no. 3, 1959, 253–83.

69. Daniel Kahneman was awarded the Sveriges Riksbank Prize in Economic Sciences in Memory of Alfred Nobel Nobel for his work on prospect theory. See D. Kahneman and A. Tversky, 'Prospect theory: An analysis of decisions under risk', *Econometrica*, vol. 47, no. 2, 1979, 313–27. The notion of anchoring was advanced in Tversky and Kahneman, 'Judgment under uncertainty'. Kahneman has summarized his research in his bestseller *Thinking, Fast and Slow* (New York: Farrar, Straus & Giroux, 2011).

THE LOGIC OF ECONOMICS VERSUS THE LOGIC OF POLITICS

1. We will not go into the discussion of to what extent political parties are ideological or governed by pragmatism and vote-maximization, neither that complex organizations such as democratic parties tend to develop into oligarchies ruled by an elite, a leadership class, in order to be successful, as Robert Michels has so well exemplified with historical examples and termed 'the Iron Law of Oligarchy'. See Robert Mitchels, *Zur Soziologie des Parteiwesens in der modernen Demokratie. Untersuchungen über die oligarchischen Tendenzen des Gruppenlebens* (Leipzig: Verlag von Dr. Werner Klinkhardt, 1911), or Robert Mitchels, *Political Parties: A Sociological Study of the Oligarchial Tendencies of Modern Democracy* (Kitchener, ON: Batoche Books, 2001). For a more literary depiction of the same phenomenon see e.g. Joan Didion, *Political Fictions* (New York: Alfred A. Knopf, 2001), and Peter Oborne, *The Triumph of the Political Class* (London: Simon & Schuster, 2007).

2. For a comprehensive exploration of the way emotions, collective emotions, and morality differ across cultures and supporters of political parties see Jonathan Haidt, *The Righteous Mind: Why Good People Are Divided by Politics and Religion* (New York: Pantheon Books, 2012).

3. K. Polanyi, *The Great Transformation: The Political & Economic Origins of Our Time* (New York: Rinehart & Company, Inc., 1944).

4. D. H. Lasswell, *Politics: Who Gets What, When, How* (New York: Whittlesey House, 1936).

5. See e.g. K. Asp, *Mäktiga massmedier: Studier av politisk opinionsbildning* (Stockholm: Akademilitteratur, 1986), G. Mazzoleni and W. Schulz, 'Mediatization" of politics: A challenge for democracy?', *Political Communication*, vol. 16, no. 3, 1999, 247–61, and S. Hjarvard, 'The mediatisation of society. A theory of the media as agents of social and cultural change', *Nordicom Review*, vol. 29, no. 2, 2008, 105–34.

6. Empirical observations give support to the so-called salience theory formulated by R. K. Mitchell, B. R. Agle, and D. J. Wood, 'Toward a theory of stakeholder identification and silence: Defining the principle of who and what really counts', *Academy of Management Review*, vol. 22, no. 4, 1997, 853–86. Salience theory centres around the five concepts of stakeholders, power, legitimacy, urgency, and salience, and propose that priority given to stakeholders is high if all three of power, legitimacy and urgency are present, low if only one is present, and moderate if two of these are present. Furthermore, that what the

authors term dominant stakeholders can have their will based on only power and a legitimate claim to exercise influence, dependent stakeholders on legitimacy and urgency, and dangerous stakeholders on power and urgency.

7. This table and Section 5.2 are mainly based on informal discussions with some local government politicians.

8. President John F. Kennedy's 'Special Message to the Congress on Urgent National Needs', 25 May 1961.

9. See e.g. G. M. Steinberg, 'Large-scale national projects as political symbols: The case of Israel', *Comparative Politics*, vol. 19, no. 3, 1987, 331–46.

10. For examples see, e.g. E. Segelod, *Renewal Through Internal Development* (Aldershot: Avebury, 1995).

11. National Auditing Agency, *Varför blev det dyrare? Kostnadsutvecklingen för statliga reformer*, Dnr 1983:334 (Stockholm: Riksrevisionsverket, 1983).

12. National Auditing Agency, *Varför blev det dyrare?*, p. 14.

13. N. R. F. Maier, *Problem-solving Discussions and Conferences: Leadership Methods and Skills* (New York: MacGraw-Hill Book Company, 1963).

14. B. Jacobsson, *Kraftsamling: Politik och företagande i parallella processer* (Lund: Studentlitteratur, 1994).

15. See A. R. Prest and R. Turvey, 'Cost-benefit analysis: A survey', *Economic Journal*, vol. 75, no. 300, 1965, 683–735, M. M. Hufschmidt, 'Benefit-cost analysis, 1933-1985', *Water Resources Update*, vol. 116, 2000, 42–9, or J. Persky, 'Retrospectives. Cost-benefit analysis and the classical creed', *Journal of Economic Perspectives*, vol. 15, no. 4, 2001, 199–208.

16. See e.g. John Roberts, 'No one is perfect: The limits of transparency and an ethic for "intelligent! Accountability', *Accounting, Organizations and Society*, vol. 34, no. 8, 2009, 957–70, and also M. Messner, 'The limits of accountability', *Accounting, Organizations and Society*, vol. 34, no. 8, 2009, 918–38.

17. R. L. Carson, *Silent Spring* (Boston: Houghton Mifflin Company, 1962).

18. *Kongl. Maj:ts Nådige Förordning, Angående Skrif- och Tryck-friheten; Gifwen Stockholm i Råd-Cammaren then 2 Decembr. 1766* (Stockholm: Kongl. Tryckeriet, 1766).

19. J. Conrad, *The Secret Agent* (Leipzig: Bernhard Tauchnitz, 1907), p. 139.

20. For a review of accountability in politics, see A. Przeworski, S. C. Stokes, and B. Manin, eds., *Democracy, Accountability, and Representation* (Cambridge: Cambridge University Press, 1999), and R. Grant and R. O. Keohane, 'Accountability and abuses of power in world politics', *American Political Science Review*, vol. 99, no. 1, 2005, 29–43.

21. Accountability can be more or less clearly specified, and be individually or collectively based. Two contrasting examples can illustrate this. Bergman and Beving (today B&B Tools) is a trading company providing the industrial sector with industrial consumables and components. Twenty years ago the group had some 250 profit centres buying and selling a large number of products. The head office was small and decisions on what these business units should buy and sell were decentralized to divisions and businesses. Investments in customer relations were high but small in fixed assets, as they usually are in trading companies. The market for industrial products can change very fast as

products become obsolete, and the market for an individual product or type of product can virtually disappear. The head office relied on strict financial control. If a profit centre made losses for a couple of month it had to find some other products to sell, or risk being dissolved. The head office did not interfere in what the centres were trading as it did not have the knowledge to do so. The strict focus on financial performance often found in trading groups makes the profit centre and its manager accountable, at the same time as it delegates the authority to change the product mix and thereby the strategy of the business unit. Who is accountable becomes very clear.

Accountability is usually attached less well to individuals in capital-intensive groups. A good example is AGA, a multinational gas company with plants and distribution systems in Europe and the USA, today a part of the Linde Group. It is a very capital-intensive business, and investments accounted for about 10 per cent of sales. As all plants used the same technology regardless of where they were located, conditions were good for central staff to accumulate, coordinate, and disseminate knowledge about gas technology. However, investment requests were generated in the businesses as it knew the markets best.

AGA had a very comprehensive capital investment manual which not only explained the process, who is responsible for what, and how to put together a request, but also contained a lot of gas-technology-specific information. Investment appraisals were made in the companies, but priorities were set and investments ranked in cooperation with staff visiting from the head office once a year to review the investment plans of the company. This direct face-to-face contact made it less important for the request to achieve a pre-determined cut-off rate or payback period. There was no limit of authorization, and no strict financial performance measure by which companies were evaluated, but a set of target criteria, e.g. the volume of sales and investments, and operating income before depreciation. The close contacts between the head office and businesses enabled a more flexible control, often found in similar capital-intensive groups, which, however, also tends to make accountability less well attached to a specific manager. Accountability becomes more collective.

Accountability can be more or less specified, and most multinational groups try to combine clear accountability with more direct communication between head offices and businesses. In large diverse organizations it becomes difficult for the head office to know more about the business than the business itself. Hence, financial measures become more important means of control, and by that accountability is decentralized. Similarly, in smaller municipalities politics tends to be driven more by pragmatism, and in larger ones more by ideology. For further examples see M. Goold and A. Campbell, *Strategies and Styles: The Role of the Centre in Managing Diversified Corporations* (Oxford: Basil Blackwell, 1987).

22. See E. Segelod, *Kalkylering och avvikelser: Empiriska studier av stora projekt i kommuner och industriföretag* (Malmö: Liber, 1986).

23. M. M. Hufschmidt and J. Gerin, 'Systematic errors in cost estimates for public investment projects', in J. Margolis, ed., *The Analysis of Public Output* (New York, Columbia University Press, 1970), pp. 267–315.

24. O. P. Kharbanda and E. A. Stallworthy, *How to Learn from Project Disasters* (Aldershot: Gower, 1983).

25. See e.g. R. K. Fleischman and T. N. Tyson, 'The evolution of standard costing in the UK and US: From decision making to control', *Abacus*, vol. 34, no. 1, 1998, 92–119, R. K. Fleischman and T. N. Tyson, 'The history of management accounting in the US', in C. S. Chapman, A. G. Hopwood, and M. D. Shields, eds., *Handbook of Management Accounting Research, Volume 2* (Amsterdam: Elsevier, 2007), pp. 1071–89, and E. Segelod and L. Carlsson, 'The emergence of uniform principles of cost accounting in Sweden 1900-36', *Accounting, Business, and Financial History*, vol. 20, no. 3, 2010, 327–63.

26. E. T. Svedenstierna and C. J. Lidbeck, 'Utdrag af byggnads-räkningen öfver Tunkarsbo nya masugn, år 1805', *Samlingar i bergsvettenskapen*, vol. 3, no. 1, 1811, 44–9.

27. See J. K. Hollmann, ed., *Total Cost Management Framework: An Integrated Approach to Portfolio, Program, and Project Management*, 1st edn. revised (Morgantown: AACE International, The Association for the Advancement of Cost Engineering, 2012), p. 147.

28. See B. Flyvbjerg, 'Curbing optimism bias and strategic misrepresentation in planning: Reference class forecasting in practice', *European Planning Studies*, vol. 16, no. 1, 2008, 3–21.

29. See e.g. B. Flyvbjerg, 'From Nobel prize to project management: Getting risks right', *Project Management Journal*, vol. 37, no. 3, 2006, 5–15, Flyvbjerg, 'Curbing optimism bias and strategic misrepresentation in planning', or B. Flybjerg, 'Over budget, over time, over and over again', in P. W. Morris, J. K. Pinto, and J. Söderlund, eds., *The Oxford Handbook of Project Management* (Oxford: Oxford University Press, 2012), pp. 321–44.

30. See L. Liu, G. Wehbe, and J. Sisovic, 'The accuracy of hybrid estimating approaches: A case study of an Australian State Road & Traffic Authority', *The Engineering Economist*, vol. 55, no. 3, 2010, 225–45.

31. See J. Odeck, 'Do reforms reduce the magnitude of cost overruns in road projects? Statistical evidence from Norway', *Transportation Research Part A*, vol. 65, July 2014, 68–79, and J. Odeck, M. Welde, and G. H. Volden, 'The impact of external quality assurance of costs estimates on cost overruns: Empirical evidence from the Norwegian road sector', *European Journal of Transportation Infrastructure Research*, vol. 15, no. 3, 2015, 286–303.

32. See Flyvbjerg, 'Curbing optimism bias and strategic misrepresentation in planning'.

33. Segelod, *Kalkylering och avvikelser*.

34. See K. J. Arrow and R. C. Lind 'Uncertainty and the evaluation of public investment decisions', *American Economic Review*, vol. 60, no. 3, 1970, 364–78, who advance another argument for omitting the risk premium, namely that the cost of a risk to an individual public project becomes negligible when these risks are spread across all taxpayers.

35. For an example of such an analysis, see e.g. S. N. Woodward, 'Performance in planning a large project', *Journal of Management Studies*, vol. 19, no. 2, 1982, 183–98.

36. Maier, *Problem-solving Discussions and Conferences*, p. 7.

EXPLAINING COST OVERRUN, SUMMARY, AND CONCLUSIONS

1. In his book *The Joyless Economy: An Inquiry into Human Satisfaction and Consumer Dissatisfaction* (New York: Oxford University Press, 1976), Tibor Scitovsky showed how these fields of research could be integrated.

2. A. Smith, *The Theory of Moral Sentiments*, 6th edn., 1790 (London: A. Millar, 1759), Part I, iii. ch. 2, § 3.

3. See K. A. Wittfogel, *Oriental Despotism: A Comparative Study of Total Power* (New Haven: Yale University Press, 1957), and M. Harris, *Cannibals and Kings: The Origin of Cultures* (New York: Random House, 1977).

4. Smith, *The Theory of Moral Sentiments*, Part III, ch. 2, § 5.

5. E. Becker, *The Denial of Death* (New York: Simon & Schuster, 1973).

6. See e.g. J. Greenberg, T. Pyszczynski, and S. Solomon, 'The causes and consequences of a need for self-esteem: A terror management theory', in R. F. Baumeister, ed., *Public Self and Private Self* (New York: Springer Verlag, 1986), pp. 189–212, T. Pyszczynski, J. Greenberg, S., Solomon, J. Arndt, and J. Schimel, 'Why do people need self-esteem? A theoretical and empirical review', *Psychological Bulletin*, vol. 130, no. 3, 2004, 435–68, and S. Solomon, J. Greenberg, J. Schimel, J. Arndt, and T. Pyszczynski, 'Human awareness of mortality and the evolution of culture', in M. Schaller and C. S. Crandell, eds., *The Psychological Foundation of Culture* (Mahwah: Lawrence Erlbaum Associates, Inc.), 2004, pp. 15–40.

7. B. L. Burke and E. H. Faucher, 'Two decades of terror management theory: A meta-analysis of mortality salience research', *Personality and Social Psychology Review*, vol. 14, no. 2, 2010, 155–95.

8. An article often referred to is Robert K. Merton's 'The unanticipated consequences of purposive social action', *American Sociological Review*, vol. 1, no. 6, 1936, 894–904.

9. G. Hardin, 'The tragedy of the commons', *Science*, vol. 162, 1968, 1243–8.

10. Adam Smith, *An Inquiry into the Causes and Effects of the Wealth of Nations* (London: W. Strahan; and T. Cadell, in the Strand, 1776), Book IV, ch. II, p. 35.

11. See D. Dörner, *The Logic of Failure: Recognizing and Avoiding Error in Complex Situations* (New York: Metropolitan Books, 1996).

12. C. Freeman and F. Louçã, *As Time Goes By: From the Industrial Revolutions to the Information Revolution* (Oxford: Oxford University Press, 2001), p. 197.

13. BillerudKorsnäs, press release, 26 August 2014.

14. For a review, see e.g. G. Ahuja, C. Morris Lampert, and E. Novelli, 'The second face of appropriability: Generative appropriability and its determinants', *Academy of Management Review*, vol. 38, no. 2, 2013, 248–69, and R. Conti, A. Gambardella, and E. Novelli, 'Research on markets for inventions and implications for R&D allocation strategies', *Academy of Management Annals*, vol. 7, no. 1, 2014, 717–74.

15. See e.g. Z. Griliches, 'Issues in assessing the contribution of R&D to productivity growth', *Bell Journal of Economics*, vol. 10, no. 1, 1979, 92–116, A. Jaffe, 'Technological opportunity and spillovers of R&D', *American Economic Review*, vol. 76, no. 5, 1986, 984–1001, and J. I. Bernstein and M. I. Nadiri,

'Interindustry R&D spillovers, rate of return, and production in high-tech industries', *American Economic Review*, vol. 78, no. 2, 1988, 429–34.
16. Society's return on R&D has been estimated (e.g. by Bernstein and Nadiri, 'Interindustry R&D spillovers, rate of return, and production in high-tech industries', p. 264) at 30 per cent for machinery, 67 per cent for chemicals, 90 per cent for instruments, and 123 per cent for petroleum.

APPENDIX A

1. The Assessors' report in P. Jones, *Ove Arup: Masterbuilder of the Twentieth Century* (New Haven, CT: The Yale University Press, 2006), p. 188.
2. P. Jones, 'Ove Arup: The outsider and the art of the impossible', in K. Powell, ed., *The Great Builders* (London: Thames & Hudson, 2011), p. 222.
3. The Pritzker Architecture Prize press release, 'Danish Architect Jørn Utzon Becomes 2003 Pritzker Architecture Prize Laureate', 2003.
4. This very brief description is based on an analysis of cases reported in inter alia P. Hall, *Great Planning Disasters* (London: Weidenfeld & Nicolson, 1980), P. D. Henderson, 'Two British Errors: Their probable size and some possible lessons', *Oxford Economic Papers*, vol. 28, July 1977, 159–205, and D. Pope, *Nuclear Implosions: The Rise and Fall of the Washington Public Power Supply System* (Cambridge: Cambridge University Press, 2008).
5. M. M. Hufschmidt and J. Gerin, 'Systematic errors in cost estimates for public investment projects', in J. Margolis, ed., *The Analysis of Public Output* (New York: Columbia University Press, 1970), pp. 267–315. The 34 projects implemented by TVA consisted of 61 sub-projects, whereof one-third showed cost overruns. Dams and reservoirs showed cost overruns of 21.7 per cent; stem-powered power plants showed underruns of −9.3 per cent.
6. L. Merewitz, 'Cost overruns in public works', in W. Niskanen, ed., *Benefit-Cost and Policy Analysis 1972: An Aldine Annual on Forecasting, Decision-making, and Evaluation* (Chicago: Aldine Pub. Co., 1973), pp. 278–95, and L. Merewitz, 'How do urban rapid transit projects compare in cost estimating experience?' Proceedings of the International Conference on Transportation Research, Brugge, June 1973, 484–93. All projects implemented in the USA, with the exception of most of the rapid transit projects.
7. Konglige olje- og energidepartement, *Kostnadsanalysen – norsk kontinentalsokkel* (Oslo: Konglige olje- og energidepartement, 1980).
8. Government Accountability Office, *Status of Major Acquisitions as of September 30 1982*, GAO/NS IAD-83-32 (Washington DC, General Accounting Office, 1983). Inflation was found to be the main reason for cost growth in the civilian projects, and in the military projects project growth, inflation, underestimates, additional cost of support, design changes, and changes in the time table. Observe that the study concerns ongoing projects.
9. D. Arditi, G. T. Akan, and S. Gurdamar, 'Cost overruns in public projects', *Project Management*, vol. 3, no. 4, 1985, 218–24. The study is based on a

questionnaire. The authors suspect that the low figures for public sector projects are caused by an unwillingness in the public sector to report large cost overruns. The reasons advanced for cost overrun are delays, design changes, project growth, miscalculations, and inflation. Only 25–30 per cent of the cost overrun is estimated to have been caused by inflation.

10. E. Segelod, *Kalkylering och avvikelser: Empiriska studier av stora projekt i kommuner och industriföretag* (Malmö: Liber, 1986).

11. Segelod, *Kalkylering och avvikelser: Empiriska studier av stora projekt i kommuner och industriföretag*. The values given within parentheses are somewhat uncertain as some budget items, but not all, included a provision for anticipated price increases.

12. S. Morris, 'Cost and time overruns in public sector projects', *Economic and Political Weekly*, vol. 25, no. 47, 1990, M-154–68. Extreme projects excluded. Time overrun varied between 0 and 204 per cent, with an average of 70.5 per cent.

13. The data comes from the National Auditing Agency, *Infrastrukturinvesteringar: En kostnadsjämförelse mellan plan och utfall i 15 större projekt inom Vägverket och Banverket*, RRV 1994:23 (Stockholm: Riksrevisionsverket, 1994). Public projects can spend many years in a long-term plan until they are implemented, and cost can grow both in the long-term plan and during implementation. In this study cost overrun from when the project was included in the long term-term plan until follow-up of finished project was +86 per cent for road projects and 17 per cent for railway projects; from approved project budget to follow up +9.8 per cent for road projects and −8.3 per cent for railway projects. Thus the railway projects became less expensive than anticipated. The largest cost growth appeared in the long-term plan when the projects were waiting to be finally approved and implemented.

14. B. Flyvbjerg, M. Skamris Holm, and S. Buhl, 'Underestimating costs in public works projects: Errors of lie', *Journal of the American Planning Association*, vol. 68, no. 3, 2002, 279–95. Costs have been converted to constant money value and comparable exchange rates.

15. J. Odeck, 'Cost overruns in road construction: What are their sizes and determinants?', *Transport Policy*, vol. 11, no. 1, 2004, 43–53.

16. J. Bertisen and G. A. Davis, 'Bias and error in mine project capital cost estimation', *The Engineering Economist*, vol. 53, no. 2, 2008, 118–39.

17. J.-K. Lee, 'Cost overrun and cause in Korean social overhead capital projects: Roads, rails, airports, and ports', *Journal of Urban Planning and Development*, vol. 134, no. 2, 2008, 59–62.

18. A. Jenpanitsub, *Cost Overruns in Transport Projects: Experience from Sweden*, Master of Science Thesis, Stockholm: The Royal Institute of Technology, 2011. The standard deviation for rail was 50.5 and for roads 24.6, and the distribution for rail is more positively skewed. Outliers with exceptional high cost overrun were stations and rail yards.

19. J. Odeck, J., 'Do reforms reduce the magnitude of cost overruns in road projects? Statistical evidence from Norway', *Transportation Research Part A*, vol. 65, 2014, 68–79.

20. B. K. Sovacool, D. Nugent, and A. Gilbert, 'Construction cost overruns and electricity infrastructure: An unavoidable risk?', *Electricity Journal*, vol. 27, no. 4, 2014, 112–20. Project cost data compiled from various sources, with 66 per cent of the projects from North America and Europe. All cost data updated to current monetary value first by using historical currency conversion data, then US historical inflation data.

21. Ernst and Young, 'Spotlight on oil and gas megaprojects', 2014; available at www.ey.com/Publication/vwLUAssets/EY-spotlight-on-oil-and-gas-mega projects/$FILE/EY-spotlight-on-oil-and-gas-megaprojects.pdf. Percentage figures are based on cost data from 205 of 365 projects.

22. A. W. Marshall and W. H. Meckling, 'Predictability of the costs, time, and success of development', in R. Nelson, ed., *The Rate and Direction of Inventive Activity: Economic and Social Factors* (Princeton, NJ: Princeton University Press, 1962), pp. 461–75.

23. R. Summers, 'Cost estimates as predictors of actual costs: A statistical study of military developments', in T. Marschak, T. K. Glennan, Jr., and R. Summers, eds., *Strategy for R&D* (Berlin: Springer Verlag, 1967), pp. 140–89.

24. Marshall and Meckling, 'Predictability of the costs, time, and success of development'.

25. R. Summers, 'Cost estimates as predictors of actual costs: A statistical study of military developments'. When cost data has been adjusted for the true number of aircraft produced and inflation average cost overrun decreases from 226 per cent to 79 per cent, and the standard deviation from 5.39 to 1.34.

26. E. Mansfield, J. Rapoport, J. Schnee, S. Wagner, and M. Hamburger, *Research and Innovation in the Modern Corporation* (New York: Norton, 1971), and J. E. Schnee, 'Development cost: Determinants and overruns', *Journal of Business*, vol. 45, no. 3, 347–74. The standard deviation for company A was 0.74, and for company B 3.18.

27. P. Svensson, *Styrning av produktutvecklingsprojekt: En studie av förutsättningarna för planering av produktutvecklingsprojekt i några svenska verkstadsföretag* (Göteborg: Chalmers tekniska högskola, 1990). The standard deviation for company A was 1.1 and for company B 0.5.

28. M. S. Peck and F. M. Scherer, *The Weapons Acquisition Process: An Economic Analysis* (Boston, MA: Division of Research, Graduate School of Business Administration, Harvard University, 1962).

29. Mansfield, Rapoport, Schnee, Wagner, and Hamburger, *Research and Innovation in the Modern Corporation*.

30. Arena, Younossi, Brancato, Blickstein, and Grammich, *Why Has the Cost of Fixed-Wing Aircraft Risen? A Macroscopic Examination of the Trends in US Military Aircraft Cost over the past Several Decades*.

31. Nordlund, Åkerström, Öström and Löfstedt, Kostnadsutveckling för försvarsmateriel.

32. Davies, Eager, Maier, and Penfold, *Intergenerational equipment cost escalation, A Ministry of Defence economic research paper on the increasing cost of UK defence equipment*.

33. M. V. Arena, I. Blickstein, O. Younossi, and C. A. Grammich, *Why Has the Cost of Navy Ships Risen? A Macroscopic Examination of the Trends in US Naval*

Ship Costs Over the Past Several Decades (Santa Monica, CA: RAND Corporation, 2006), and M. V. Arena, O. Younossi, K. Brancato, I. Blickstein, and C. A. Grammich, *Why Has the Cost of Fixed-Wing Aircraft Risen? A Macroscopic Examination of the Trends in US Military Aircraft Cost over the past Several Decades* (Santa Monica, CA: RAND Corporation, 2008).

34. P. Pugh, *The Cost of Sea Power: The Influence of Money on Naval Affairs from 1815 to the Present Day* (London: Conway Maritime Press, 1986), and N. Davies, A. Eager, M. Maier, and L. Penfold, *Intergenerational Equipment Cost Escalation, A Ministry of Defence Economic Research Paper on the Increasing Cost of UK Defence Equipment*, Ministry of Defence, 18 December 2012.

35. S. Kvalvik and P. Johansen, *Enhetskostnadsvekst på forsvarsinvesteringer*, Forsvarets Forskningsinstitutt, Rapport 2008/01129, 2008, and K. Hove and T. Lillekvelland, 'Investment cost escalation: An overview of the literature and revised estimates', *Defence and Peace Economics*, vol. 27, no. 2, 2015, 208–30.

36. P. Nordlund, J. Åkerström, B. Öström, and H. Löfstedt, Kostnadsutveckling för försvarsmateriel, Report FOI-R-3213-SE (Stockholm: Totalförsvarets forskningsinstitut, 2011).

37. The Standish Group Report, *The CHAOS Report*, first published in 1995; most recent in 2015.

38. K. Molökken and M. Jörgensen, 'A review of surveys on software effort estimation', Proceedings of the 2003 International Symposium on Empirical Software Engineering, *IEEE Computer Society*, 2003, 223–30, M. Jörgensen and K. Molökken, How large are software cost overruns? Critical comments on the Standish Group's CHAOS Reports. Working paper, 2003, and J. L. Eveleens and C. Verhoef, 'The rise and fall of the Chaos report figures', *IEEE Software*, vol. 27, no. 1, 2008, 30–6.

39. A. M. Jenkins, J. D. Naumann, and J. C. Wetherbe, 'Empirical investigation of systems development practices and results', *Information & Management*, vol. 7, 1984, 73–82.

40. D. Phan, D. Vogel, and J. Nunamaker, 'The search for perfect project management', *Computerworld*, vol. 22, no. 39, 1988, 95–100.

41. F. Bergeron and J.-Y. St-Arnaud, 'Estimation of information systems development efforts: A pilot study', *Information & Management*, vol. 22, no. 4, 1992, 239–54.

42. F. J. Heemstra, 'Software cost estimation', *Information and Software Technology*, vol. 34, no. 10, 1992, 627–39.

43. The Standish Group Report, *The CHAOS Report*, 1995.

44. M. Keil and J. Mann, 'The nature and extent of IT-project escalation: Results from a survey of IS audit and control professionals', *IS Audit & Control Journal*, vol. 1, 1997, 40–8, and M. Keil and J. Mann, 'Understanding the nature and extent of IS project escalation: Results from a survey of IS audit and control professionals', *IEEE, Proceedings of the Thirtieth Hawaii International Conference on System Sciences*, 1997, 139–48.

45. T. Little, 'Schedule estimation and uncertainty surrounding the cone of uncertainty', *IEEE Software*, vol. 23, no. 3, 2006, 48–54.

46. J. L. Eveleens, P. van der Pas, and C. Verhoef, C., 'Quantifying forecast quality of IT business value', *Science of Computer Programming*, vol. 77, no. 3, 2012, 314–54.
47. B. W. Boehm, *Software Engineering Economics* (Englewood Cliffs, NJ: Prentice Hall, 1981).
48. E.g. J. M. Stecklein, J. Dabney, D. Brandon, B. Haskins, R. Lowell, and G. Moroney, *Error cost escalation through the project life cycle*, Report JSC-CN-8435 (Houston, TX: NASA Johnson Space Center, 2004).
49. E. Segelod and G. Jordan, 'The use and importance of external sources of knowledge in the software development process', *R&D Management*, vol. 34, no. 3, 2004, 239–52.
50. Eveleens, van der Pas, and Verhoef, 'Quantifying forecast quality of IT business value'.
51. Little, 'Schedule estimation and uncertainty surrounding the cone of uncertainty'.

APPENDIX B

1. P. W. G. Morris and G. H. Hough, *Preconditions of Success and Failure in Major Projects* (Oxford: Major Project Association, 1986).
2. See A. W. Marshall and W. H. Meckling, 'Predictability of the costs, time, and success of development', in R. Nelson, ed., *The Rate and Direction of Inventive Activity: Economic and Social Factors* (Princeton: Princeton University Press, 1962), pp. 461–75, and R. Summers, 'Cost estimates as predictors of actual costs: A statistical study of military developments', in T. Marschak, T. K. Glennan, Jr., and R. Summers, eds., *Strategy for R&D* (Berlin: Springer Verlag, 1967), pp. 140–89.
3. See D. S. Christenson, 'An analysis of cost overruns on defense acquisition contracts', *Project Management Journal*, vol. 19, no. 3, 1993, 43–8, and D. S. Christensen, D. A. Searle, and C. Vickery, 'The impact of the Packard Commission's recommendation on reducing cost overruns on defense acquisition contracts', *Acquisition Review Quarterly*, vol. 6, Summer 1999, 251–62.
4. See E. Mansfield, J. Rapoport, J. Schnee, S. Wagner, and M. Hamburger, *Research and Innovation in the Modern Corporation* (New York: Norton, 1971), and J. Schnee, 'Development cost: Determinants and overruns', *Journal of Business*, vol. 45, no. 3, 1972, 347–74.
5. M. O. Federle and S. C. Pigneri, 'Predictive models of cost overruns', Annual Meeting, American Association of Cost Engineers, *1993 AACE Transactions*, 1993, L.7.1–9.
6. These five reasons have all been advanced in interviews to the author by project managers, and have most likely also been mentioned in earlier literature.
7. See Summers, 'Cost estimates as predictors of actual costs', 140–89, J. M. Allen and K. P. Norris, 'Project estimates and outcomes in the electricity generation research', *Journal of Management Studies*, vol. 7, October 1970, 271–87, F. D. Clark and A. B. Lorenzoni, *Applied Cost Engineering*, 3rd edn. (New York: Marcel Dekker, Inc., 1985), O. P. Kharbanda and E. A.

Stallworthy, 'Lessons from project disasters', *Industrial Management & Data Systems*, vol. 92, no. 3, 1992, 1–46, and C. C. Cantarelli, E. J. E. Molin, B. van Wee, and B. Flyvbjerg, 'Characteristics of cost overruns for Dutch transport infrastructure projects and the importance of the decision to build and project phases', *Transport Policy*, vol. 22, 2012, 49–56.

8. D. S. Remer and H. R. Buchanan, 'Estimating the cost for doing a cost estimate', *International Journal of Production Economics*, vol. 66, no. 2, 2000, 101–4.

9. O. P. Kharbanda and E. A. Stallworthy, *How to Learn from Project Disasters* (Aldershot: Gower, 1983), p. 252.

10. E. Segelod, *Renewal through Internal Development* (Aldershot: Avebury, 1995).

11. See e.g. P. Hall, *Great Planning Disasters* (London: Weidenfeld & Nicolson. 1980), and Kharbanda and Stallworthy, *How to Learn from Project Disasters.*

12. See M. M. Hufschmidt and J. Gerin, 'Systematic errors in cost estimates for public investment projects', in J. Margolis, ed., *The Analysis of Public Output* (New York: Columbia University Press, 1970), pp. 267–315, and E. Segelod, *Kalkylering och avvikelser: Empiriska studier av stora projekt i kommuner och industriföretag* (Malmö: Liber, 1986).

13. See Cantarelli, Molin, van Wee, and Flyvbjerg, 'Characteristics of cost over-runs for Dutch transport infrastructure projects', and C. C. Cantarelli, B. van Wee, E. J. E. Molin, and B. Flyvbjerg, 'Different cost performance: Different determinants? The case of cost overruns in Dutch transport infrastructure projects', *Transport Policy*, vol. 22, 2012, 88–95.

14. J. Odeck, 'Cost overruns in road construction: What are their sizes and determinants?', *Transport Policy*, vol. 11, no. 1, 2004, 43–53.

15. See Mansfield, Rapoport, Schnee, Wagner, and Hamburger, *Research and Innovation in the Modern Corporation*, and Schnee, 'Development cost: Determinants and overruns'.

16. Segelod, *Kalkylering och avvikelser.*

17. E. Segelod, *Resource Allocation in Divisionalized Groups: A Study of Investment Manuals and Corporate Level Means of Control* (Aldershot: Avebury, 1996).

18. Allen and Norris, 'Project estimates and outcomes in the electricity genera-tion research'.

19. All projects and sources are listed in L. Merewitz, 'How do urban rapid transit projects compare in cost estimating experience?' Proceedings of the International Conference on Transportation Research, Brugge, June 1973, 484–93.

20. Government Accountability Office, *Status of Major Acquisitions as of September 30 1982*, DC: GAO/NS IAD-83–32 (Washington DC, General Accounting Office, 1983).

21. Ernst and Young, *Spotlight on oil and gas megaprojects*, 2014; available at www.ey.com/Publication/vwLUAssets/EY-spotlight-on-oil-and-gas-mega projects/$FILE/EY-spotlight-on-oil-and-gas-megaprojects.pdf.

22. B. K. Sovacool, D. Nugent, and A. Gilbert, Construction cost overruns and electricity infrastructure: An unavoidable risk? *Electricity Journal*, vol. 27, no. 4, 2014, 112–20.

23. National Auditing Agency, *Infrastrukturinvesteringar: En kostnadsjämförelse mellan plan och utfall i 15 större projekt inom Vägverket och Banverket*, RRV 1994:23 (Stockholm: Riksrevisionsverket, 1994).

24. See B. Flyvbjerg, M. Skamris Holm, and S. Buhl, 'Underestimating costs in public works projects: Error or lie', *Journal of the American Planning Association*, vol. 68, no. 3, 2002, 279–95, and J.-K. Lee, 'Cost overrun and cause in Korean social overhead capital projects: Roads, rails, airports, and ports', *Journal of Urban Planning and Development*, vol. 134, no. 2, 2008, 59–62.

25. See L. Merewitz, 'Cost overruns in public works', Merewitz, 'How do urban rapid transit projects compare in cost estimating experience?', and Flyvbjerg, Skamris Holm, and Buhl, 'Underestimating costs in public works projects: Error or lie'.

26. Odeck, 'Cost overruns in road construction: What are their sizes and determinants?'

27. J. Bertisen and G. A. Davis, 'Bias and error in mine project capital cost estimation', *The Engineering Economist*, vol. 53, no. 2, 2008, 118–39.

28. Summers, 'Cost estimates as predictors of actual costs'.

29. T. Little, 'Schedule estimation and uncertainty surrounding the cone of uncertainty', *IEEE Software*, vol. 23, no. 3, 2006, 48–54.

30. A. Aibinu and G. Jagboro, 'The effects of construction delays on project in Nigeria Construction industry', *International Journal of Project Management*, vol. 20, no 8, 2002, 593–9.

31. S. Assaf and S. Al-Hejji, 'Causes of delay in large construction projects', *International Journal of Project Management*, vol. 24, no. 4, 2006, 349–57.

32. See B. Flyvbjerg, M. K. Skamris Holm, and S. L. Buhl, 'What causes cost overrun in transport infrastructure projects?', *Transport Review*, vol. 24, no. 1, 2004, 3–18, C. C. Cantarelli, B. Flyvbjerg, and S. L. Buhl, 'Geographical variation in project cost performance: The Netherlands versus worldwide', *Journal of Transportation Geography*, vol. 24, 2012, 324–31, and Cantarelli, Molin, van Wee, and Flyvbjerg, 'Characteristics of cost overruns for Dutch transport infrastructure projects'.

33. A. H. Memon, I. A. Rahman, M. R. Abdullah, A. Asmi, and A. Azis, 'Factors affecting construction cost in Mara Large Construction Project: Perspective of project management consultant', *International Journal of Sustainable Construction Engineering & Technology*, vol. 1, no 2, 2010, 41–54.

34. Summers, 'Cost estimates as predictors of actual costs.

35. See Mansfield, Rapoport, Schnee, Wagner, and Hamburger, *Research and Innovation in the Modern Corporation*, and Schnee, 'Development cost: Determinants and overruns'.

36. Little, 'Schedule estimation and uncertainty surrounding the cone of uncertainty'.

37. See Summers, 'Cost estimates as predictors of actual costs', Segelod, *Kalkylering och avvikelser*, Flyvbjerg, Skamris Holm, and Buhl, 'What causes cost overrun in transport infrastructure projects?', Cantarelli, Molin, van Wee, and Flyvbjerg, 'Characteristics of cost overruns for Dutch transport infrastructure projects', and Cantarelli, van Wee, Molin, and Flyvbjerg, 'Different cost performance: Different determinants?'.

38. Government Accountability Office, *Major Acquisitions – Summary of Recurring Problems and Systemic Issues: 1960–1987*, GAO/NSIAD-88-135BR (Washington DC: General Accounting Office, 1988).

39. The left, socialists, and green parties won the election and could form a minority government as neither the left nor the right, liberal, and conservative parties wanted to cooperate with a reactionary party which received 12.86 per cent of the votes.

40. A. N. Mashayekhi, 'Project cost dynamics for development policy-making', *Journal of the Operational Research Society*, vol. 51, no. 3, 2000, 301–10.

41. P. Svensson, *Styrning av produktutvecklingsprojekt: En studie av förutsättningarna för planering av produktutvecklingsprojekt i några svenska verkstadsföretag* (Göteborg: Institutionen för Industriell organisation och ekonomi, Chalmers tekniska högskola, 1990).

42. Segelod, *Kalkylering och avvikelser*.

43. R. J. Schonberger 'Why projects are "always" late: A rationale based on manual simulation of a PERT/CPM network', *Interfaces*, vol. 11, no. 5, 1981, 66–70, p. 66.

44. R. Giguet and G. Morlat, 'Les causes d'erreur systématique dans la prévision du prix des travaux', *Annales des Ponts et Chaussées. Mémoires et documents relatifs à l'art des constructions et au service de l'ingénieur*, vol. 122, no. 5, 1952, 543–62.

45. D. Dörner, *The Logic of Failure: Recognizing and Avoiding Error in Complex Situations* (New York: Metropolitan Books, 1996).

46. T. K. Glennan, Jr., 'Issues in the choice of development policies', in T. Marschak, T. K. Glennan Jr., and R. Summers, eds., *Strategies for R&D: Studies in the Microeconomics of Development* (Berlin: Springer Verlag, 1967), pp. 13–48.

47. See R. R. Nelson, 'Uncertainty, learning and the economics of parallel research and development efforts', *Review of Economics and Statistics*, vol. 43, no. 4, 1961, 351–64, and Glennan, 'Issues in the choice of development policies'.

48. See C. R. Perrow, *Normal Accident: Living with High Risk Technologies* (New York: Basic Books, 1984), C. R. Perrow, 'Organizing to reduce the vulnerabilities of complexity', *Journal of Contingencies and Crisis Management*, vol. 7, no. 3, 1999, 150–5, and C. R. Perrow, 'Complexity, catastrophe, and modularity', *Sociological Inquiry*, vol. 78, no. 2, 2008, 162–73.

49. See C. Y. Baldwin and K. B. Clark, *Design Rules, Volume 1: The Power of Modularity* (Cambridge: MIT Press, 2000), C. Y. Baldwin and Joachim Henkel, 'Modularity and intellectual property protection', *Strategic Management Journal*, vol. 36, no. 11, 2015, 1637–55, and C. Y. Baldwin and C. J. Woodard, 'The architecture of platforms: A unified view', in A. Gawer, ed., *Platforms, Markets and Innovation* (Cheltenham, UK, and Northampton, MA: Edward Elgar, 2009), pp. 19–44.

50. Grubler, A., 'The costs of the French nuclear scale-up: A case of negative learning by doing', *Energy Policy*, vol. 38, 2010, 5174–88.

51. !M. Cooper, *Policy Challenges of Nuclear Reactor Construction: Cost Escalation and Crowding Out Alternatives. Lessons from the US and France for the Effort to Revive the US Industry with Loan Guarantees and Tax Subsidies* (South Royalton: Vermont Law School, September 2010).

52. Sovacool, Nugent, and Gilbert, 'Construction cost overruns and electricity infrastructure: An unavoidable risk?'

53. See E. Segelod and G. Jordan, 'The use and importance of external sources of knowledge in the software development process', *R&D Management*, vol. 34, no. 3, 2004, 239–52.

54. Summers, 'Cost estimates as predictors of actual costs'.

55. See P. Pugh, *The Cost of Sea Power: The Influence of Money on Naval Affairs from 1815 to the Present Day* (London: Conway Maritime Press, 1986), Government Accountability Office, *Major Acquisitions*, Christenson, 'An analysis of cost overruns on defense acquisition contracts', Christensen, Searle, and Vickery, 'The impact of the Packard Commission's recommendation on reducing cost overruns', M. V. Arena, I. Blickstein, O. Younossi, and C. A. Grammich, *Why Has the Cost of Navy Ships Risen? A Macroscopic Examination of the Trends in US Naval Ship Costs Over the Past Several Decades* (Santa Monica: RAND Corporation, 2006), M. V. Arena, O. Younossi, K. Brancato, I. Blickstein, and C. A. Grammich, *Why Has the Cost of Fixed-Wing Aircraft Risen? A Macroscopic Examination of the Trends in US Military Aircraft Cost over the past Several Decades* (Santa Monica: RAND Corporation, 2008), P. Nordlund, J. Åkerström, B. Öström, and H. Löfstedt, *Kostnadsutveckling för försvarsmateriel*, Report FOI-R-3213-SE (Stockholm: Totalförsvarets forskningsinstitut, 2011), and N. Davies, A. Eager, M. Maier, and L. Penfold, *Intergenerational equipment cost escalation, A Ministry of Defence economic research paper on the increasing cost of UK defence equipment*, Ministry of Defence, 18 December 2012.

56. See Marshall and Meckling, 'Predictability of the costs, time, and success of development', Summers, 'Cost estimates as predictors of actual costs'.

57. See Mansfield, Rapoport, Schnee, Wagner, and Hamburger, *Research and Innovation in the Modern Corporation*, and Schnee, 'Development cost: Determinants and overruns'.

58. Svensson, *Styrning av produktutvecklingsprojekt*.

59. B.H. Klein, 'The decision making problem in development', in Nelson, ed., *The Rate and Direction of Inventive Activity*, pp. 477–508.

60. T. Marschak, 'The role of project histories in the study of R&D', in Marschak, Glennan, and Summers, eds., *Strategies for R&D*, pp. 49–139.

61. See B. Flyvbjerg, M. Skamris Holm, and S. Buhl, 'Underestimating costs in public works projects: Error or lie', and B. Flyvbjerg, N. Bruzelius, and W. Rothengatter, *Megaprojects and Risk: An Anatomy of Ambition* (Cambridge: Cambridge University Press, 2003).

62. See Mansfield, Rapoport, Schnee, Wagner, and Hamburger, *Research and Innovation in the Modern Corporation*, and Schnee, 'Development cost: Determinants and overruns'.

63. Svensson, *Styrning av produktutvecklingsprojekt*.

64. D. Davis, 'New projects: Beware of false economies', *Harvard Business Review*, vol. 63, no. 2, 1985, 95–101.

65. U. Odenmar, *Kommunal budgetprocess och projektadministration för byggprojekt* (Malmö: Avdelningen för Byggproduktionsteknik, Lunds Tekniska högskola, 1983).

66. National Auditing Agency, *Infrastrukturinvesteringar: En kostnadsjämförelse mellan plan och utfall i 15 större projekt inom Vägverket och Banverket.*

67. National Auditing Agency, *Infrastrukturinvesteringar: En kostnadsjämförelse mellan plan och utfall i 15 större projekt inom Vägverket och Banverket.*

68. Hufschmidt and Gerin, 'Systematic errors in cost estimates for public investment projects'.

69. See I. Hägg, 'Reviews of capital investments: Empirical studies', *Finnish Journal of Business Economics*, vol. 28, no. 3, 1979, 211–25.

70. P.-A. M. Sverlinger, *Managing Knowledge in Professional Service Organizations: Technical Consultants Serving the Construction Industry* (Göteborg: Department of Service Management, Chalmers University of Technology, 2000).

71. A. O. Hirschman, *Development Projects Observed* (Washington DC: The Brookings Institution, 1967).

72. Kharbanda and Stallworthy, *How to Learn from Project Disasters.*

73. P. W. G. Morris, *The Management of Projects* (Telford: London, 1994).

74. In a study of 52 so-called mega-projects (i.e. very large projects), E. W. Merrow, L. McDonnell, and R. Y. Argüden found that factors similar to those advanced in this chapter explained more than three-quarters of the variation in outcomes. Technology is no doubt a very important explanation for time and cost growth: *Understanding the Outcomes of Megaprojects: A Qualitative Analysis of Very Large Civilian Projects* (Santa Monica: The RAND Corporation, 1988), p. 66.

APPENDIX C

1. For a review of behavioural biases see e.g. B. Fischhoff, S. Lichtenstein, P. Slovic, R. Keeney, and S. Derby, *Acceptable Risk* (Cambridge: Cambridge University Press, 1980), R. M. Hogarth, 'Beyond discrete biases: Functional and dysfunctional aspects of judgemental heuristics', *Psychological Bulletin*, vol. 90, no. 2, 1981, 197–217, R. M. Hogarth and S. Makridakis, 'Forecasting and planning: An evaluation', *Management Science*, vol. 27, no. 2, 1981, 115–38, D. Kahneman, 'Maps of bounded rationality: Psychology for behavioural economics', *American Economic Review*, vol. 93, no. 5, 2003, 1449–75, and D. Kahneman, J. L. Knetsch, and R. H. Thaler, 'Anomalies: The Endowment Effect, Loss Aversion, and Status Quo Bias', *Journal of Economic Perspectives*, vol. 5, no.1, 1991, 193–206.

2. See M. Statman and T. T. Tyebjee, 'Optimistic capital budgeting forecasts: An experiment', *Financial Management*, vol. 13, Autumn 1985, 27–33, and C. S. Galbraith and G. B. Merrill, 'The politics of forecasting: Managing the truth', *California Management Review*, vol. 38, no. 2, 1996, 29–43.

3. T. T. Tyebjee, 'Behavioral biases in new product forecasting', *International Journal of Forecasting*, vol. 3, 1987, 393–404.

4. J. Mahajan, 'The overconfidence effect in marketing management predictions', *Journal of Marketing Research*, vol. 19, no. 4, 1992, 329–42.

5. S. W. Pruitt and L. J. Gitman, 'Capital budgeting forecast biases: Evidence from the *Fortune* 500', *Financial Management*, vol. 15, Spring 1987, 46–51.

6. E. M. Miller, 'Uncertainty induced bias in capital budgeting', *Financial Management*, Fall 1978, 12–18.

7. S. K. McNees, 'An assessment of the "official" economic forecasts', *New England Economic Review*, July–August 1995, 13–24.

8. D. N. Dreman and M. A. Berry, 'Analyst forecasting errors and their implications for security analysis', *Financial Analysts Journal*, vol. 51, no. 3, 1995, 30–40.

9. K. Daniel and D. Hirshleifer, 'Overconfident investors, predictable returns, and excessive trading', *Journal of Economic Perspective*, vol. 29, no. 4, 2015, 61–87.

10. See U. Malmendier and G. Tate, 'CEO overconfidence and corporate investment' *Journal of Finance*, vol. 60, no. 6, 2005, 2660–700, U. Malmendier and G. Tate, 'Does overconfidence affect corporate investment? CEO overconfidence measures revisited', *European Financial Management*, vol. 11, no. 5, 2005, 649–59, and U. Malmendier and T. Geoffrey, 'Behavioral CEOs: The role of managerial overconfidence', *Journal of Economic Perspective*, vol. 29, no. 4, 2015, 37–60.

11. M. D. Grubb, 'Overconfident consumers in the marketplace', *Journal of Economic Perspective*, vol. 29, no. 4, 2015, 9–35.

12. G. Fabricius and M. Büttgen, 'Project managers' overconfidence: How is risk reflected in anticipated project success', *Business Research*, vol. 8, no. 2, 2015, 239–63.

13. D. P. Mest and E. Plummer, 'Analysts' rationality and forecast bias: Evidence from sales forecasts', *Review of Quantitative Finance and Accounting*, vol. 21, no. 2, 2003, 103–22.

14. H. N. Higgins, 'Analyst forecasting performance in seven countries', *Financial Analysts Journal*, vol. 54, no. 3, 1998, 58–62.

15. J. A. Hornaday, 'Research about living entrepreneurs', in C. A. Kent, D. L. Sexton, and K. L. Vesper, eds., *Encyclopedia of Entrepreneurship* (Engelwood Cliffs: Prentice Hall, 1982), 281–90, A. C. Cooper, W. C. Dunkelberg, and C. Y. Woo, 'Optimists and pessimists: 2994 entrepreneurs and their perceived chances for success', in *Frontiers of Entrepreneurship Research* (Wellesey: Babson College, 1986), pp. 563–77, and K. A. Egge, 'Expectations vs. reality among founders of recent start-ups', in *Frontiers of Entrepreneurship Research* (Wellesley: Babson College, 1992), pp. 322–36.

16. See L. W. Busenitz and J. B. Barney, 'Differences between entrepreneurs and managers in large organizations: Biases and heuristics in strategic decision-making', *Journal of Business Venturing*, vol. 12, no. 1, 1997, 9–30, and G. Arabsheibani, D. de Meza, J. Maloney, and B. Pearson, 'And a vision appeared unto them of a great profit: evidence of self-deception among the self-employed', *Economic Letters*, vol. 67, no. 1, 2000, 35–41.

17. M. Simon, S. M. Houghton, and K. Aquino, 'Cognitive bias, risk perception, and venture formation: How individuals decide to start companies', *Journal of Business Venturing*, vol. 15, no. 2, 1999, 113–34.

18. Busenitz and Barney, 'Differences between entrepreneurs and managers in large organizations'.

19. R. A. Baron, 'Counterfactual thinking and venture formation: The potential effects of thinking about "what might have been"', *Journal of Business Venturing*, vol. 15, no. 1, 1999, 79–91.

20. A. L. Zacharakis and D. A. Shepherd, 'The nature of information and over-confidence on venture capitalists' decision making', *Journal of Business Venturing*, vol. 16, no. 4, 2001, 311–32.

21. J. F. Yates, J.-W. Lee and H. Shinotsuka, 'Beliefs about over-confidence, including its cross-national variation', *Organizational Behavior and Human Decision Processes*, vol. 65, no. 2, 1996, 138–47.

22. See e.g. J. Kruger and D. Dunning, 'Unskilled and unaware of it: How difficulties in recognizing one's own incompetence lead to inflated self-assessments', *Journal of Personality and Social Psychology*, vol. 77, no. 6, 1999, 1121–34, and J. Ehrlinger, K. Johnson, M. Banner, D. Dunning, and J. Kruger, 'Why the unskilled are unaware: Further explorations of (absent) self-insight among the incompetent', *Organizational Behavior and Human Decision Processes*, vol. 105, no. 1, 2008, 98–121.

23. See e.g. J. E. Sawyer, 'Entrepreneurial error and economic growth', *Explorations in Entrepreneurial History*, vol. 4, no. 2, 1952, 199–204, A. O. Hirschman, *Development Projects Observed* (Washington, DC: The Brookings Institution, 1967), and Busenitz and Barney, 'Differences between entrepreneurs and managers in large organizations'.

24. S. A. Shane, *The Illusions of Entrepreneurship: The Costly Myths That Entrepreneurs, Investors, and Policy Makers Live* (New Haven: Yale University Press, 2010), p. 98.

25. Busenitz and Barney, 'Differences between entrepreneurs and managers in large organizations'.

26. See e.g. L. Tiger, *Optimism: The Biology of Hope* (New York: Simon & Schuster, 1979), D. M. Buss, 'Evolutionary personality psychology', *Annual Review of Psychology*, vol. 42, February 1991, 459–91, M. Waldman, 'Systematic errors and the theory of natural selection', *American Economic Review*, vol. 84, no. 3, 1994, 482–97, or T. Sharot, 'The optimism bias', *Current Biology*, vol. 21, no. 23, 2011, R941-5.

27. Tiger, *Optimism: The Biology of Hope*.

28. See e.g. D. R. Forsyth, 'Self-serving bias', in W. A. Darity, ed., *International Encyclopedia of the Social Sciences, Vol. 7*, 2nd edn. (New York: Macmillan Reference, 2008), p. 429.

29. A. H. Mezulis, L. Y. Abramson, J. S. Hyde, and B. L. Hankin, 'Is there a universal positivity bias in attributions? A meta-analytic review of individual, developmental, and cultural differences in the self-serving attributional bias', *Psychological Bulletin*, vol. 130, no. 5, 2004, 711–47.

30. See e.g. B. M. Staw, 'Knee-deep in the big muddy: A study of escalating commitment to a chosen course of action', *Organizational Behavior and Human Performance*, vol. 16, no. 1, 1976, 27–44, B. M. Staw and J. Ross, 'Understanding behaviour in escalation situations', *Science*, vol. 246, no. 4927, 1989, 216–20, B. M. Staw, 'The escalation of commitment: An update ad appraisal', in Z. Shapira, ed., *Organizational Decision Making* (Cambridge: Cambridge University Press, 1997), pp. 191–215, and J. Brockner, R.

Houser, G. Birnbaum, K. Lloyd, J. Deitcher, S. Nathanson, and J. Z. Rubin, 'Escalation of commitment to an ineffective course of action: The effect of feedback having negative implications for self-identity', *Administrative Science Quarterly*, vol. 31, no. 1, 1986, 109–26.

31. See e.g. C. Sedikides, W. K. Campbell, G. Reeder, and A. Elliot, 'Self-serving bias in a relational context', *Journal of Personality and Social Psychology*, vol. 74, no. 2, 1998, 378–86, J. Shepperd, W. Malone, and K. Sweeny, 'Exploring causes of the self-serving bias', *Social and Personality Psychology Compass*, vol. 2, no. 2, 2008, 895–908, or D. A. Shepherd, H. Patzelt, and M. Wolfe, 'Moving forward from project failure: Negative emotions, affective commitment, and learning from the experience', *Academy of Management Journal*, vol. 54, no. 6, 2011, 1229–59.

32. D. T. Miller and M. Ross, 'Self-serving biases in the attribution of causality: Fact or fiction?', *Psychological Bulletin*, vol. 82, no. 2, 1975, 129–65.

33. J. B. Schmidt and R. J. Calantone, 'Escalation of commitment during new product development', *Journal of the Academy of Marketing Science*, vol. 30, no. 2, 2002, 103–18.

34. T. Keusch, L. H. H. Bollen, and H. F. D. Hassink, 'Self-serving bias in annual report narratives: An empirical analysis of the impact of economic crises', *European Accounting Review*, vol. 21, no. 3, 2013, 623–48.

35. O. Svenson, 'Are we all less risky and more skillful than our fellow drivers?', *Acta Psychologica*, vol. 47, 1981, 143–8.

36. See Malmendier and Tate, 'CEO overconfidence and corporate investment', Malmendier and Tate, 'Does overconfidence affect corporate investment?', and U. Malmendier, G. Tate, and J. Yan, 'Overconfidence and early-life experiences: The effect of managerial traits on corporate financial policies', *Journal of Finance*, vol. 66, no. 5, 2011, 1687–733.

37. Galbraith and Merrill, 'The politics of forecasting'.

38. C. Prendergast, 'A theory of "Yes Men"', *American Economic Review*, vol. 83, no. 4, 1993, 757–70.

39. See I. L. Janis, *Victims of Groupthink: A Psychological Study of Foreign Policy Decisions and Fiascoes* (Boston: Houghton Mifflin, 1972), which offers a number of examples of groupthink in politics.

40. D. W. Williams, 'The politics of forecast bias: Forecaster effect and other effects in New York City revenue forecasting', *Public Budgeting & Finance*, vol. 32, no. 4, 2012, 1–18.

41. R. Giguet and G. Morlat, 'Les causes d'erreur systématique dans la prévision du prix des travaux', *Annales des Ponts et Chausssées. Mémoires et documents relatifs à l'art des constructions et au service de l'ingénieur*, vol. 122, no. 5, 1952, 543–62.

42. See e.g. V. Gaspar and A. P. N. Leite, 'Selection bias induced cost overruns', *Information Economics and Policy*, vol. 4, 1989/90, 175–87, and D. S. Christensen, D. A. Searle, and C. Vickery, 'The impact of the Packard Commission's recommendation on reducing cost overruns on defense acquisition contracts', *Acquisition Review Quarterly*, vol. 6, Summer 1999, 251–62.

43. See e.g. D. H. Pickrell, 'A desire named streetcar: Fantasy and fact in rail transit planning', *Journal of the American Planning Association*, vol. 8, no. 2,

1990, 158–76, and J. Eliasson and M. Fosgerau, 'Cost overruns and demand shortfalls: Deception or selection?', *Transportation Research Part B*, vol. 57, 2013, 105–13.

44. F. Mitchell and S. P. Walker, 'Market pressures and the development of costing practice: The emergence of uniform costing in the UK printing industry', *Management Accounting Research*, vol. 8, no. 1, 1997, 75–101.

45. E. Segelod and L. Carlsson, 'The emergence of uniform principles of cost accounting in Sweden 1900-36', *Accounting, Business, and Financial History*, vol. 20, no. 3, 2010, 327–63.

46. See R. K. Fleischman and T. N. Tyson, 'The evolution of standard costing in the UK and US: From decision making to control', *Abacus*, vol. 34, no. 1, 1998, 92–119, and R. Fleischman and T. Tyson, 'The history of management accounting in the US', in C. S. Chapman, A. G. Hopwood and M. D. Shields, eds., *Handbook of Management Accounting Research, Volume 2* (Amsterdam: Elsevier, 2007), pp. 1071–89, p. 1080.

47. E. Segelod, *Resource Allocation in Divisionalized Groups: A Study of Investment Manuals and Corporate Level Means of Control* (Aldershot: Avebury, 1996).

48. See e.g. Pruitt and Gitman, 'Capital budgeting forecast biases', D. H. Pickrell, 'A desire named streetcar: Fantasy and fact in rail transit planning', and B. Flyvbjerg, M. Skamris Holm, and S. Buhl, 'Underestimating costs in public works projects: Error or lie', *Journal of the American Planning Association*, vol. 68, no. 3, 2002, 279–95.

49. See M. Wachs, 'When planners lie with numbers', *Journal of the American Planning Association*, vol. 55, no. 4, 1989, 476–9, and M. Wachs, 'Ethics and advocacy in forecasting for public policy', *Business and Professional Ethics Journal*, vol. 9, no 1–2, 1990, 141–57.

50. E. Segelod, *Renewal through Internal Development* (Aldershot: Avebury, 1995).

51. A. W. Marshall and W. H. Meckling, 'Predictability of the costs, time, and success of development', in R. Nelson, ed., *The Rate and Direction of Inventive Activity: Economic and Social Factors* (Princeton: Princeton University Press, 1962), pp. 461–75, and R. Summers, 'Cost estimates as predictors of actual costs: A statistical study of military developments', in T. Marschak, T. K. Glennan, Jr., and R. Summers, eds., *Strategy for R&D* (Berlin: Springer Verlag, 1967), pp. 140–89.

52. A. W. Marshall and W. H. Meckling, 'Predictability of the costs, time, and success of development', in Nelson, ed., *The Rate and Direction of Inventive Activity*.

53. The Packard Commission, *A Quest for Excellence: Final Report to the President's Blue Ribbon Commission on Defense Management* (Washington DC, June 1986).

54. Christensen, Searle, and Vickery, 'The impact of the Packard Commission's recommendation on reducing cost overruns on defense acquisition contracts'.

55. K. J. Arrow, 'Economic welfare and the allocation of resources for invention', in Nelson, ed., *The Rate and Direction of Inventive Activity*, pp. 609–26.

56. E. Segelod, *Kalkylering och avvikelser: Empiriska studier av stora projekt i kommuner och industriföretag* (Malmö: Liber, 1986), and Y. Chen and R. Smith,

'Equilibrium cost overruns', *Annals of Economics and Finance*, vol. 2, 2001, 401–14.

57. A. G. Hopwood, *Accounting and Human Behaviour* (New Jersey: Prentice Hall, 1976).
58. Pruitt and Gitman, 'Capital budgeting forecast biases'.
59. National Audit Office, *North Sea Cost Escalation Study* (London: Her Majesty's Stationary Office, 1976), and Segelod, *Resource Allocation in Divisionalized Groups*.
60. R. M. Cyert and J. G. March, *A Behavioural Theory of the Firm* (Englewoodss Cliffs: Prentice Hall, Inc., 1963), p. 118.
61. S. J. Liebowitz and S. E. Margolis, 'Path dependence', in B. Bouckaert and G. Geest, *Encyclopedia of Law and Economics*, eds. (Elgar: Cheltenham, 2000), p. 981.
62. See e.g. Staw, 'Knee-deep in the big muddy', Staw and Ross, 'Understanding behaviour in escalation situations', Staw, 'The escalation of commitment', and Brockner, Houser, Birnbaum, Lloyd, Deitcher, Nathanson, and Rubin, 'Escalation of commitment to an ineffective course of action'.
63. Brockner, Houser, Birnbaum, Lloyd, Deitcher, Nathanson, and Rubin, 'Escalation of commitment to an ineffective course of action'.
64. H. T. Newcomb, *Railway Economics* (Philadelphia: Railway World Pub. Co., 1898), pp. 55–9.
65. A. W. Brian, 'Competing technologies, increasing returns, and lock-in by historical events', *Economic Journal*, vol. 99, no. 394, 1989, 116–31.
66. G. S. Becker, *Human Capital: A Theoretical and Empirical Analysis, with Special Reference to Education* (Chicago, University of Chicago Press, 1964).
67. A. Zardkoohi, 'Do real options lead to escalation of commitment?', *Academy of Management Review*, vol. 29, no. 1, 2004, 111–19.
68. Hirschman, *Development Projects Observed*.
69. The case description is based on an article in the local newspaper *Göteborgsposten* ('Gärna Västlänken – men inte via Haga', 2 February 2016) written by Lars Nordström, professor emeritus and politician representing the liberal party.
70. Segelod, *Renewal through Internal Development*, p. 71.

Bibliography

Acuto, M., 'High-rise Dubai urban entrepreneurialism and the technology of symbolic power', *Cities*, vol. 27, no. 4, 2010, 272–84.

Adams, W., 'The military-industrial complex and the new industrial state', *American Economic Review*, vol. 58, no. 2, 1968, 652–65.

Ahiaga-Dagbui, D. D. and S. D. Smith, 'Rethinking construction cost overruns: Cognition, learning and estimation', *Journal of Financial Management of Property and Construction*, vol. 19, no. 1, 2014, 38–54.

Ahuja, G., C. Morris Lampert, and E. Novelli, 'The second face of appropriability: Generative appropriability and its determinants', *Academy of Management Review*, vol. 38, no. 2, 2013, 248–69.

Aibinu, A. and G. Jagboro, 'The effects of construction delays on project delivery in Nigeria Construction industry', *International Journal of Project Management*, vol. 20, no. 8, 202, 593–99.

Akerlof, G. A. and R. J. Shiller, *Animal Spirits: How Human Psychology Drives the Economy and Why It Matters for Global Capitalism*, Princeton: Princeton University Press, 2009.

Akintoye, A., 'Analysis of factors influencing project cost estimation practice', *Construction Management and Economics*, vol. 18, no. 1, 2000, 77–89.

Allen, J. M. and K. P. Norris, 'Project estimates and outcomes in the electricity generation research', *Journal of Management Studies*, vol. 7, October 1970, 271–87.

Alptekin, A. and P. Levine, 'Military expenditure and economic growth: A meta-analysis', *European Journal of Political Economy*, vol. 28, no. 4, 2012, 636–50.

Altshuler, A. and D. Luberoff, *Mega-Projects: The Changing Politics of Urban Public Investment*, Washington DC: Brooking Institute, 2003.

Andersson, B. and K. S. M. Welde, 'Low estimates – high stakes: Underestimation of costs at the front-end of projects', *International Journal of Managing Projects in Business*, vol. 9, no. 1, 2016, 171–93.

Anheier, H. K., ed., *When Things Go Wrong: Organizational Failures and Breakdowns*, Thousand Oaks: Sage Publications, 1999.

Arabsheibani, G., D. de Meza, J. Maloney, and B. Pearson, 'And a vision appeared unto them of a great profit: Evidence of self-deception among the self-employed', *Economic Letters*, vol. 67, no. 1, 2000, 35–41.

Arditi, D., G. T. Akan, and S. Gurdamar, 'Cost overruns in public projects', *Project Management*, vol. 3, no. 4, 1985, 218–24.

234

Arena, M. V., I. Blickstein, O. Younossi, and C. A. Grammich, *Why Has the Cost of Navy Ships Risen? A Macroscopic Examination of the Trends in US Naval Ship Costs over the Past Several Decades*, Santa Monica: RAND Corporation, 2006.

Arena, M. V., O. Younossi, K. Brancato, I. Blickstein, and C. A. Grammich, *Why Has the Cost of Fixed-Wing Aircraft Risen? A Macroscopic Examination of the Trends in US Military Aircraft Cost over the past Several Decades*, Santa Monica: RAND Corporation, 2008.

Arrow, K. J., 'Functions of a theory of behavior under uncertainty', *Metroeconomica*, vol. 11, no. 1–2, 1959, 12–20.

'Economic welfare and the allocation of resources for invention', in R. Nelson, ed., *The Rate and Direction of Inventive Activity: Economic and Social Factors*, Princeton: Princeton University Press, 1962, pp. 609–26.

'Limited knowledge and economic analysis', *American Economic Review*, vol. 64, no. 1, 1974, 1–10.

Arrow, K. J. and R. C. Lind, 'Uncertainty and the evaluation of public investment decisions', *American Economic Review*, vol. 60, no. 3, 1970, 364–78.

Arthur, B. W., 'Competing technologies, increasing returns, and lock-in by historical events', *Economic Journal*, vol. 99, no. 394, 1989, 116–31.

Arvan, L. and A. P. N. Leite, 'Cost overruns in long term projects', *International Journal of Industrial Organization*, vol. 8, no. 3, 1990, 443–67.

Ashraf, N., C. F. Camerer, and G. Loewenstein, 'Adam Smith, behavioral economist', *Journal of Economic Perspectives*, vol. 19, no. 3, 2005, 131–45.

Asp, K., *Mäktiga massmedier: Studier av politisk opinionsbildning*, Stockholm: Akademilitteratur, 1986.

Assaf, S. and S. Al-Hejji, 'Causes of delay in large construction projects', *International Journal of Project Management*, vol. 24, no. 4, 2006, 349–57.

Baccarini, D., 'The concept of project complexity: A review', *International Journal of Project Management*, vol. 14, no. 4, 1996, 201–4.

Baldwin, C. Y. and K. B. Clark, *Design Rules, Volume 1: The Power of Modularity*, Cambridge, MA: MIT Press, 2000.

Baldwin, C. Y. and J. Henkel, 'Modularity and intellectual property protection', *Strategic Management Journal*, vol. 36, no. 11, 2015, 1637–55.

Baldwin, C. Y. and C. J. Woodard, 'The architecture of platforms: A unified view', in A. Gawer, ed., *Platforms, Markets and Innovation*, Cheltenham, UK and Northampton, MA, US: Edward Elgar, 2009, pp. 19–44.

Baron, R. A., 'Conterfactual thinking and venture formation: The potential effects of thinking about "what might have been"', *Journal of Business Venturing*, vol. 15, no. 1, 1999, 79–91.

Bart, C. K., 'Budgeting gamesmanship', *Academy of Management Executive*, vol. 2, no. 4, 1988, 285–94.

Bazerman, M. H., *Judgement in Managerial Decision-Making*, 2nd edn, New York: John Wiley & Sons, 1990.

Bazerman, M. H., G. Loewenstein, and D. A. Moore, 'Why good accountants do bad audits', *Harvard Business Review*, vol. 97, no. 6, 2002.

Bazerman, M. H., K. P. Morgan, and G. F. Loewenstein, 'The impossibility of auditor independence', *MIT Sloan Management Review*, vol. 38, no. 4, 89–94.

Bechara, A., 'The role of emotion in decision-making: Evidence from neurological patients with orbitofrontal damage', *Brain and Cognition*, vol. 55, no. 1, 2004, 30–40.

Becker, E., *The Denial of Death*, New York: Simon & Schuster, 1973.

Becker, G. S., *Human Capital: A Theoretical and Empirical Analysis, with Special Reference to Education*, Chicago: University of Chicago Press, 1964.

Beenhakker, H. L. and J. G. Danskin, 'Economies of stage construction for transport facilities', *Transportation Research*, vol. 7, no. 2, 1973, 163–78.

Bengtsson, U., *Stora investeringar i mindre kommuner: Scope, scale och stage construction som strategier*, Göteborg: BAS, 2013.

Beniger, J. R., *The Control Revolution: Technological and Economic Origins of the Information Society*, Cambridge, MA: Harvard University Press, 1986.

Bennet, W. L., 'The personalization of politics: Political identity, social media, and changing patterns of participation', *Annals of the American Academy of Political and Social Science*, vol. 644, no. 1, 2012, 20–39.

Bergeron, B. and J.-Y. St-Arnaud, 'Estimation of information systems development efforts: A pilot study', *Information & Management*, vol. 22, no. 4, 1992, 239–54.

Bernstein, J. I. and M. I. Nadiri, 'Interindustry R&D spillovers, rate of return, and production in high-tech industries', *American Economic Review*, vol. 78, no. 2, 1988, 429–34.

Berthélemy, M. and L. Escobar Rangel, 'Nuclear reactors' construction costs: The role of lead-time, standardization and technological progress', *Energy Policy*, vol. 82, July 2015, 118–30.

Bertisen, J. and G. A. Davis, 'Bias and error in mine project capital cost estimation', *The Engineering Economist*, vol. 53, no. 2, 2008, 118–39.

Bleiker, R. and E. Hutchison, 'Fear no more: Emotions and world politics', *Review of International Studies*, vol. 34, Supplement S1, 2008, 115–35.

Bloch, M., S. Blumberg, and J. Laartz, 'Delivering large-scale IT projects on time, on budget, and on value', *McKinsey Quarterly*, October 2012.

Boccard, N., 'The cost of nuclear electricity: France after Fukushima', *Energy Policy*, vol. 66, March 2014, 450–61.

Boehm, B. W. *Software Engineering Economics*, Englewood Cliffs: Prentice Hall, 1981.

Bolton, J. G., R. S. Leonard, M. V. Arena, O. Younossi, and J. M. Sollinger, *Sources of Weapon System Cost Growth: Analysis of 35 Major Defense Acquisition Programs*, Santa Monica: RAND Corporation, 2008.

Bovens, M., *The Quest for Responsibility: Accountability and Citizenship in Complex Organisations*, Cambridge: Cambridge University Press, 1995.

Bower, J. L., *Managing the Resource Allocation Process: A Study of Corporate Planning and Investment*, Boston: Division of Research, Graduate School of Business Administration, Harvard University, 1970.

'Planning within the firm', *American Economic Review*, vol. 60, no. 2, 1970, 186–94.

Bower, J. L. and C. G. Gilbert, eds., *From Resource Allocation to Strategy*, Oxford: Oxford University Press, 2005.

Brandy, T., A. Davies, and P. Nightingale, 'Dealing with uncertainty in complex projects: Revisiting Klein and Meckling', *International Journal of Managing Projects in Business*, vol. 5, no. 4, 2012, 718–36.

Brigelius, L. and P. Rosén, *Risk och Försäkring*, Göteborg: BAS, 1988.

Brockner, J., R. Houser, G. Birnbaum, K. Lloyd, J. Deitcher, S. Nathanson, and J. Z. Rubin, 'Escalation of commitment to an ineffective course of action: The effect of feedback having negative implications for self-identity', *Administrative Science Quarterly*, vol. 31, no. 1, 1986, 109–26.

Brown, L. D., 'Analyst forecasting errors: Additional evidence', *Financial Analysts Journal*, vol. 53, no. 6, 1997, 81–7.

Brüggen, A. and J. L. Luft, 'Capital rationing, competition, and misrepresentation in budget forecasts', *Accounting, Organizations and Society*, vol. 36, no. 7, 2011, 399–411.

'Cost estimates, cost overrun, and project continuation decisions', *Accounting Review*, vol. 91, no. 3, 2016, 793–810.

Burke, B. L. and E. H. Faucher, 'Two decades of terror management theory: A meta-analysis of mortality salience research', *Personality and Social Psychology Review*, vol. 14, no. 2, 2010, 155–95.

Busenitz, L. W. and J. B. Barney, 'Differences between entrepreneurs and managers in large organizations: Biases and heuristics in strategic decision-making', *Journal of Business Venturing*, vol. 12, no. 1, 1997, 9–30.

Buss, D. M., 'Evolutionary personality psychology', *Annual Review of Psychology*, vol. 42, February 1991, 459–91.

Calisir, F. and C. A. Gumussoy, 'Determinants of budget overruns on IT-projects', *Technovation*, vol. 25, no. 6, 2005, 631–6.

Callen, R. C., 'Congress's nuclear waste "contract with America": Where do we go from here?', *Electricity Journal*, vol. 8, no. 5, 1995, 45–55.

Cancian, M. F., 'Cost growth: Perception and reality', A Publication of the Defense Acquisition University, July 2010, 389–403.

Cantarelli, C. C., B. Flyvbjerg, and S. L. Buhl, 'Geographical variation in project cost performance: The Netherlands versus worldwide', *Journal of Transportation Geography*, vol. 24, 2012, 324–31.

Cantarelli, C. C., B. Flyvbjerg, E. J. E. Molin, and B. van Wee, 'Cost overruns in large-scale transportation infrastructure projects: Explanations and their theoretical embeddedness', *European Journal of Transport and Infrastructure Research*, vol. 10, no. 1, 2010, 5–18.

Cantarelli, C. C., E. J. E. Molin, B. van Wee, and B. Flyvbjerg, 'Characteristics of cost overruns for Dutch transport infrastructure projects and the importance of the decision to build and project phases', *Transport Policy*, vol. 22, 2012, 49–56.

Cantarelli, C. C., B. van Wee, E. J. E. Molin, and B. Flyvbjerg, 'Different cost performance: Different determinants? The case of cost overruns in Dutch transport infrastructure projects', *Transport Policy*, vol. 22, 2012, 88–95.

Carlsson, B. and S. Nachemson-Ekwall, *Livsfarlig ledning: Historien om kraschen i ABB*, Stockholm: Ekerlids, 2003.

Carson, R. L., *Silent Spring*, Boston: Houghton Mifflin Company, 1962.

Castillo, J., J. Lowell, A. J. Tellis, J. Muñoz, and B. Zycher, *Military Expenditures and Economic Growth*, Santa Monica: RAND, 2001.

Certo, S. T., B. L. Connelly, and L. Tihanyi, 'Managers and their not-so rational decisions', *Business Horizons*, vol. 51, no. 2, 2008, 113–19.

Chandler, A. D., Jr., *Scale and Scope: The Dynamics of Industrial Capitalism*, Cambridge, MA: The Belknap Press of Harvard University Press, 1990.

Chen, Y., and R. Smith, 'Equilibrium cost overruns', *Annals of Economics and Finance*, vol. 2, no. 2, 2001, 401–14.

Christensen, D. S., 'An analysis of cost overruns on defense acquisition contracts', *Project Management Journal*, vol. 24, no. 3, 1993, 43–8.

Christensen, D. S., 'Cost overrun optimism: Fact or fiction?', *Acquisition Review Quarterly*, vol. 1, Winter 1994, 25–38.

Christensen, D. S., 'Project advocacy and the estimate at completion problem', *Journal of Cost Analysis*, vol. 13, no. 1, 1996, 35–60.

Christensen, D. S., D. A. Searle, and C. Vickery, 'The impact of the Packard Commission's recommendation on reducing cost overruns on defense acquisition contracts', *Acquisition Review Quarterly*, vol. 6, Summer 1999, 251–62.

Clark, F. D. and A. B. Lorenzoni, *Applied Cost Engineering*, 3rd edn., New York: Marcel Dekker, Inc., 1996.

Clements, K. W. and J. Si, 'The investment project pipeline: Cost escalation, lead time, success, failure and speed', *Australian Journal of Management*, vol. 36, no. 3, 2011, 317–48.

Coe, D. T. and E. Helpman, 'International R&D spillovers', *European Economic Review*, vol. 39, no. 5, 859–87.

Cohen, M. D., J. G. March, and J. P. Olsen, 'A garbage can model of organizational choice', *Administrative Science Quarterly*, vol. 17, no. 1, 1972, 1–25.

Conrad, J., *The Secret Agent*, Leipzig: Bernhard Tauchnitz, 1907.

Conti, R., A. Gambardella, and E. Novelli, 'Research on markets for inventions and implications for R&D allocation strategies', *Academy of Management Annals*, vol. 7, no. 1, 2014, 717–74.

Cooper, A. C., W. C. Dunkelberg, and C. Y. Woo, 'Optimists and pessimists: 2994 entrepreneurs and their perceived chances for success', in *Frontiers of Entrepreneurship Research*, Wellesley: Babson College, 1986, pp. 563–77.

Cooper, M., *Policy Challenges of Nuclear Reactor Construction: Cost Escalation and Crowding Out Alternatives. Lessons from the US and France for the Effort to Revive the US Industry with Loan Guarantees and Tax Subsidies*, South Royalton: Vermont Law School, September 2010.

Coricelli, G., R. J. Dolan, and A. Sirigu, 'Brain, emotion and decision making: The paradigmatic example of regret', *Trends in Cognitive Science*, vol. 11, no. 6, 2007, 258–65.

Crowley, J. H., Nuclear energy: What's next? Monterey, CA: The work shop on the electric imperative atomic industrial forum Inc., 14–17 June 1981.

Cyert, R. M. and J. G. March, *A Behavioural Theory of the Firm*, Englewood Cliffs: Prentice Hall, Inc., 1963.

Daniel, K. and D. Hirshleifer, 'Overconfident investors, predictable returns, and excessive trading', *Journal of Economic Perspective*, vol. 29, no. 4, 2015, 61–87.

Davies, N., A. Eager, M. Maier and L. Penfold, *Intergenerational equipment cost escalation, A Ministry of Defence economic research paper on the increasing cost of UK defence equipment*, Ministry of Defence, 18 December 2012.

Davies, A. and M. Hobday, *The Business of Projects: Managing Innovation in Complex Products and Systems*, Cambridge: Cambridge University Press, 2011.

Davis, D., 'New projects: Beware of false economies', *Harvard Business Review*, vol. 63, no. 2, 1985, 95–101.

Davis, G. F., *Managed by the Markets: How Finance Reshaped America*, Oxford: Oxford University Press, 2009.

Denison, C. A., 'Real options and escalation of commitment: A behavioral analysis of capital investment decisions', *The Accounting Review*, vol. 84, no. 1, 2009, 133–55.

Didion, J., *Political Fictions*, New York: Alfred A. Knopf, 2001.

Dixit, A. K. and S. R. Pindyck, *The Options Approach to Capital Investments*, Princeton: Princeton University Press, 1995.

Doloi, H. K., 'Understanding stakeholders' perspective of cost estimation in project management', *International Journal of Project Management*, vol. 29, no. 5, 2011, 622–36.

Dörner, D., *The Logic of Failure: Recognizing and Avoiding Error in Complex Situations*, New York: Metropolitan Books, 1996.

Douglas, M. and A. B. Wildavsky, *Risk and Culture: An Essay on the Selection of Technical and Environmental Dangers*, Berkeley: University of California Press, 1982.

Doukas, J. A. and D. Petmezas, 'Acquisitions, overconfident managers and self-attribution bias', *European Financial Management*, vol. 13, no. 3, 2007, 531–77.

Dreman, D. N. and M. A. Berry, 'Analyst forecasting errors and their implications for security analysis', *Financial Analysts Journal*, vol. 51, no. 3, 1995, 30–40.

Drory, A. and T. Romm, 'The definition of organizational politics: A review', *Human Relations*, vol. 43, no. 11, 1990, 1133–54.

Eden, C., T. Williams, and F. Ackermann, 'Analysing project cost overruns: Comparing the "measured mile" analysis and system dynamics modelling', *International Journal of Project Management*, vol. 23, no. 2, 2005, 135–9.

Eden, C., F. Ackermann, and T. Williams, 'The amoebic growth of project costs', *Project Management Journal*, vol. 36, no. 1, 2005, 15–27.

Egge, K. A., 'Expectations vs. reality among founders of recent start-ups', in *Frontiers of Entrepreneurship Research*, Wellesley: Babson College, 1992, pp. 322–36.

Ehrlinger, J., K. Johnson, M. Banner, D. Dunning, and J. Kruger, 'Why the unskilled are unaware: Further explorations of (absent) self-insight among the incompetent', *Organizational Behavior and Human Decision Processes*, vol. 105, no. 1, 2008, 98–121.

Elam, M. and G. Sundqvist, 'Meddling in Swedish success in nuclear waste management', *Environmental Politics*, vol. 20, no. 2, 2011, 246–63.

Eliasson, J. and M. Fosgerau, 'Cost overruns and demand shortfalls: Deception or selection?', *Transportation Research Part B*, vol. 57, 2013, 105–13.

Transportation Research Part B: Methodological, vol. 57, November 2013, 105–13.

Elster, J., 'Emotions and economic theory', *Journal of Economic Literature*, vol. 36, no. 1, 1998, 47–74.

Engwall, M., 'The futile dream of the perfect goal', in K. Sahlin-Andersson and L. Söderholm, eds., *Beyond Project Management*, Malmö: Daleke Grafiska, 2002, pp. 161–77.

Ericsson, J. C., *Utan omsvep: Mitt berikande liv med Consafe*, Stockholm: Timbro, 1987.

Eriksson, J., *Coping with Decisions on Deviations in Complex Product Development Projects*, Västerås: Mälardalen University Press, 2012.

Eriksson, O., *Tre stora industriella investeringar: Om investeringskalkyleringens bristande ändamålsenlighet vid stora investeringar*, Västerås: Mälardalen University Press, 2002.

Ernst and Young, Spotlight on oil and gas megaprojects, 2014: available from www.ey.com/Publication/vwLUAssets/EY-spotlight-on-oil-and-gas-mega projects/$FILE/EY-spotlight-on-oil-and-gas-megaprojects.pdf

Eveleens, J. L., P. van der Pas, and C. Verhoef, 'Quantifying forecast quality of IT business value', *Science of Computer Programming*, vol. 77, no. 3, 2012, 314–54.

Eveleens, J. L. and C. Verhoef, 'The rise and fall of the Chaos report figures', *IEEE Software*, vol. 27, no. 1, 2008, 30–6.

Fabricius, G. and M. Büttgen, 'Project managers' overconfidence: How is risk reflected in anticipated project success', *Business Research*, vol. 8, no. 2, 2015, 239–63.

Federle, M. O. and S. C. Pigneri, 'Predictive models of cost overruns', Annual Meeting American Association of Cost Engineers, *1993 AACE Transactions*, 1993, L.7.1–9.

Fischhendler, I., G. Cohen-Blankshtain, Y. Shuali, and M. Boykoff, 'Communicating mega-projects in the face of uncertainties: Israeli mass media treatment of the Dead Sea Water Canal', *Public Understanding of Science*, vol. 24, no. 7, 2015, 794–810.

Fischhoff, B., S. Lichtenstein, P. Slovic, R. Keeney, and S. Derby, *Acceptable Risk*, Cambridge: Cambridge University Press, 1980.

Fleischman, R. K. and T. N. Tyson, 'The evolution of standard costing in the UK and US: From decision making to control', *Abacus*, vol. 34, no. 1, 1998, 92–119.

'The history of management accounting in the US', in C. S. Chapman, A. G. Hopwood, and M. D. Shields, eds., *Handbook of Management Accounting Research, Volume 2*, Amsterdam: Elsevier, 2007, pp. 1071–89.

Flinders, M., 'In defence of politics', *Political Quarterly*, vol. 81, no. 3, 2010, 309–25.

Flyvbjerg, B., 'From Nobel Prize to project management: Getting risks right', *Project Management Journal*, vol. 37, no. 3, 2006, 5–15.

'Curbing optimism bias and strategic misrepresentation in planning: Reference class forecasting in practice', *European Planning Studies*, vol. 16, no. 1, 2008, 3–21.

'Cost overruns and demand shortfalls in urban rail and other infrastructure', *Transportation Planning and Technology*, vol. 30, no. 1, 2008, 9–30.

'Over budget, over time, over and over again', in P. W. Morris, J. K. Pinto, and J. Söderlund, eds., *The Oxford Handbook of Project Management*, Oxford: Oxford University Press, 2012, pp. 321–44.

'How planners deal with uncomfortable knowledge: The dubious ethics of the American Planning Association', *Cities*, vol. 32, June 2013, 157–63.

Flyvbjerg, B., N. Bruzelius, and W. Rothengatter, *Megaprojects and Risk: An Anatomy of Ambition*, Cambridge: Cambridge University Press, 2003.

Flyvbjerg, B. and A. Budzier, 'Why your IT project may be riskier than you think', *Harvard Business Review*, vol. 89, no. 9, 2011, 23–5.

Flyvbjerg, B., M. Garvuio, and D. Lovallo, 'Delusion and deception in large infrastructure projects: Two models for explaining and preventing executive disaster', *California Management Review*, vol. 51, no. 2, 2009, 170–93.

Flyvbjerg, B., M. Skamris Holm, and S. Buhl, 'Underestimating costs in public works projects: Error or lie', *Journal of the American Planning Association*, vol. 68, no. 3, 2002, 279–95.

'How common and how large are cost overruns in transport infrastructure projects?', *Transport Review*, vol. 23, no. 1, 2003, 71–88.

'What causes cost overrun in transport infrastructure projects?', *Transport Review*, vol. 24, no. 1, 2004, 3–18.

Flyvbjerg, B. and A. Stewart, *Olympic proportions: Cost and cost overrun at the Olympics 1960–2012*, Oxford: Saïd Business School working papers, June 2012.

Forsyth, D. R., 'Self-serving bias', in W. A. Darity, ed., *International Encyclopedia of the Social Sciences, Vol. 7*, 2nd edn., New York: Macmillan Reference, 2008, p. 429.

Freeman, C., *The Economics of Industrial Innovation*, Harmondsworth: Penguin Books, 1974.

Freeman, C. and F. Louçã, *As Time Goes By: From the Industrial Revolutions to the Information Revolution*, Oxford: Oxford University Press, 2001.

Freeman, C. and L. Soete, *The Economics of Industrial Innovation*, 3rd edn., London and New York: Routledge, 1997.

Galbraith, C. S. and G. B. Merrill, 'The politics of forecasting: Managing the truth', *California Management Review*, vol. 38, no. 2, 1996, 29–43.

Gaspar, V. and A. P. N. Leite, 'Selection bias induced cost overruns', *Information Economics and Policy*, vol. 4, no. 2, 1989/90, 175–87.

Gavetti, G., D. Levinthal, and W. Ocasio, 'Neo-Carnegie: The Carnegie School's past, present, and reconstructing for the future', *Organization Science*, vol. 18, no. 3, 2007, 523–36.

van Genuchten, M., 'Why is software late? An empirical study of reasons for delay in software development', *IEEE Transactions on Software Engineering*, vol. 17, no. 6, 1991, 582–90.

Giguet, R. and G. Morlat, 'Les causes d'erreur systématique dans la prévision du prix des travaux', *Annales des Ponts et Chaussées. Mémoires et documents relatifs à l'art des constructions et au service de l'ingénieur*, vol. 122, no. 5, 1952, 543–62.

Glennan, Jr., T. K., 'Issues in the choice of development policies', in T. Marschak, T. K. Glennan Jr., and R. Summers, eds., *Strategies for R&D: Studies in the Microeconomics of Development*, Berlin: Springer Verlag, 1967, pp. 13–48.

Goold, M. and A. Campbell, *Strategies and Styles: The Role of the Centre in Managing Diversified Corporations*, Oxford: Basil Blackwell, 1987.

Government Accountability Office, *Lesson Learned from Constructing the Trans-Alaska Oil Pipeline*, Report to the Congress by the Comptroller General of the United States, EMD-78-52, Washington DC: General Accounting Office, 1978.

Status of Major Acquisitions as of September 30 1982, GAO/NS IAD-83–32, Washington DC: General Accounting Office, 1983.

Major Acquisitions – Summary of Recurring Problems and Systemic Issues: 1960–1987, Briefing Report to the Chairman, Committee on Armed Services, GAO/NSIAD-88-135BR, Washington DC: General Accounting Office, 1988.

Nuclear Waste: Technical, Schedule, and Cost Uncertainties of the Yucca Mountain Repository Project, Report to Congressional Requesters, GAO-02–191, Washington DC: General Accounting Office, 2001.

Nuclear Waste: Uncertainties About the Yucca Mountain Repository Project, Testimony Before the Committee on Energy and Natural Resources, GAO-02-765T, Washington DC: General Accounting Office, 2002.

Department of Energy: Status of Contract and Project Management Reforms, Testimony Before the Committee on Government Reforms, GAO-03-570T, Washington DC: General Accounting Office, 2003.

Nuclear Regulation. NRC Needs More Effective Analysis to Ensure Accumulation of Funds to Decommission Nuclear Power Plants, Report to the Honorable Edward J. Markey, Report GAO-04–32, Washington DC: General Accounting Office, 2004.

Grampp, W., 'Adam Smith and the Economic Man', *Journal of Political Economy*, vol. 56, no. 4, 1948, 315–36.

Granstrand, O. and S. Sjölander, 'Managing innovation in multi-technology corporations', *Research Policy*, vol. 19, no. 1, 1990, 35–60.

Granstrand, O., E. Bohlin, C. Oskarsson, and N. Sjöberg, 'External technology acquisition in large multi-technology corporations', *R&D Management*, vol. 22, no. 2, 1992, 111–33.

Grant, R. and R. O. Keohane, 'Accountability and abuses of power in world politics', *American Political Science Review*, vol. 99, no. 1, 2005, 29–43.

Greenberg, J., T. Pyszczynski, and S. Solomon, 'The causes and consequences of a need for self-esteem: A terror management theory', in R. F. Baumeister, ed., *Public Self and Private Self*, New York: Springer Verlag, 1986, pp. 189–212.

Griliches, Z., 'Issues in assessing the contribution of R&D to productivity growth', *Bell Journal of Economics*, vol. 10, no. 1, 1979, 92–116.

Grubb, M. D., 'Overconfident consumers in the marketplace', *Journal of Economic Perspective*, vol. 29, no. 4, 2015, 9–35.

Grubler, A., 'The costs of the French nuclear scale-up: A case of negative learning by doing', *Energy Policy*, vol. 38, no. 9, 2010, 5174–88.

Hägg, I., 'Reviews of capital investments: Empirical studies', *Finnish Journal of Business Economics*, vol. 28, no. 3, 1979, 211–25.

Haidt, J., *The Righteous Mind: Why Good People Are Divided by Politics and Religion*, New York: Pantheon Books, 2012.

Hall, P., *Great Planning Disasters*, London: Weidenfeld & Nicolson, 1980.

Hällgren, M., *Avvikelsens mekanismer: Observationer av projekt i praktiken*. Umeå: Umeå University, 2009.
'Mechanisms of deviations: Observations of projects in practice', *International Journal of Managing Projects in Business*, vol. 2, no. 4, 2009, 611–25.

Hällgren, M. and E. Maaninen-Olsson, 'Deviations and the breakdown of project management principles', *International Journal of Managing Projects in Business*, vol. 2, no. 1, 2009, 53–69.

Hällgren, M. and A. Söderholm, 'Orchestrating deviations in global projects: Projects-as-practice observations', *Scandinavian Journal of Management*, vol. 26, no. 4, 2010, 352–67.

Hardin, G., 'The tragedy of the commons', *Science*, vol. 162, 13 December 1968, 1243–48.

Harris, M., *Cannibals and Kings: The Origin of Cultures*, New York: Random House, 1977.

Hauck, V. E. and G. A. Geistauts, 'Construction of the trans-Alaska oil pipeline', *Omega*, vol. 10, no. 3, 1982, 259–65.

Heemstra, F. J., 'Software cost estimation', *Information and Software Technology*, vol. 34, no. 10, 1992, 627–39.

Henderson, P. D., 'Two British Errors: Their probable size and some possible lessons', *Oxford Economic Papers*, vol. 28, July 1977, 159–205.

Higgins, H. N., 'Analyst forecasting performance in seven countries', *Financial Analysts Journal*, vol. 54, no. 3, 1998, 58–62.

von Hippel, W. and R. Trivers, 'The evolution and psychology of self-deception', *Behavioral and Brain Sciences*, vol. 34, February 2011, 1–56.

Hirschman, A. O., *Development Projects Observed*, Washington DC: The Brookings Institution, 1967.

Hjarvard, S. 'The mediatisation of society. A theory of the media as agents of social and cultural change', *Nordicom Review*, vol. 29, no. 2, 2008, 105–34.

Hogarth, R. M., 'Beyond discrete biases: Functional and dysfunctional aspects of judgemental heuristics', *Psychological Bulletin*, vol. 90, no. 2, 1981, 197–217.

Hogarth, R. M. and S. Makridakis, 'Forecasting and planning: An evaluation', *Management Science*, vol. 27, no. 2, 1981, 115–38.

Högselius, P., 'Spent nuclear fuel policies in historical perspective: An international comparison', *Energy Policy*, vol. 37, no. 1, 2009, 254–63.

Hollmann, J. K., ed., *Total Cost Management Framework: An Integrated Approach to Portfolio, Program, and Project Management*, 1st edn. revised, Morgantown: AACE International, The Association for the Advancement of Cost Engineering, 2012.

Hopwood, A. G., *Accounting and Human Behaviour*, Egelwood Cliffs: Prentice Hall, 1976.

Hornaday, J. A., 'Research about living entrepreneurs', in C. A. Kent, D. L. Sexton, and K. L. Vesper, eds., *Encyclopedia of Entrepreneurship*, Engelwood Cliffs: Prentice Hall, 1982, pp. 281–90.

Hove, K. and T. Lillekvelland, 'Investment cost escalation: An overview of the literature and revised estimates', *Defence and Peace Economics*, vol. 27, no. 2, 2015, 208–30.

Hufschmidt, M. M., 'Benefit-cost analysis, 1933-1985', *Water Resources Update*, vol. 116, no. 1, 2000, 42–9.

Hufschmidt, M. M. and J. Gerin, 'Systematic errors in cost estimates for public investment projects', in J. Margolis, ed., *The Analysis of Public Output*, New York: Columbia University Press, 1970, pp. 267–315.

Hutchison, E. and R. Bleiker, 'Theorizing emotions in world politics', *International Theory*, vol. 6, no. 3, 2014, 491–514.

Ingvarsson Munthe, C., L. Uppvall, M. Engwall, and L. Dahlén, 'Dealing with the devil of deviation: Managing uncertainty during product development execution', *R&D Management*, vol. 44, no. 2, 2014, 203–16.

International Energy Agency, *Projected Costs of Generating Electricity, 2010 Edition*, Paris: International Energy Agency, 2010.

Jacobsson, B., *Kraftsamling: Politik och företagande i parallella processer*, Lund: Studentlitteratur, 1994.

Jaffe, A., 'Technological opportunity and spillovers of R&D', *American Economic Review*, vol. 76, no. 5, 1986, 984–1001.

Jamieson, D., 'Scientific uncertainty and the political process', *Annals of the American Academy of Political and Social Science*, vol. 545, May 1996, 35–43.

Janis, I. L., *Victims of Groupthink: A Psychological Study of Foreign Policy Decisions and Fiascoes*, Boston: Houghton Mifflin, 1972.

Jenkins, A. M., J. D. Naumann, and J. C. Wetherbe, 'Empirical investigation of systems development practices and results', *Information & Management*, vol. 7, no. 2, 1984, 73–82.

Jenpanitsub, A., Cost Overruns in Transport Projects: Experience from Sweden, Master of Science Thesis, Stockholm: The Royal Institute of Technology, 2011.

Jones, L. R. and K. J. Euske, 'Strategic misrepresentation in budgeting', *Journal of Public Administration Research and Theory*, vol. 1, no. 4, 1991, 437–60.

Jones, P., *Ove Arup: Masterbuilder of the Twentieth Century*, New Haven: Yale University Press, 2006.

'Ove Arup: The outsider and the art of the impossible', in K. Powell, ed., *The Great Builders*, London: Thames & Hudson, 2011, pp. 217–22.

Jørgensen, M., T. Halkjelsvik, and B. Kitchenham, 'How does project size affect cost estimation error? Statistical artifacts and methodological challenges', *International Journal of Project Management*, vol. 30, no. 7, 2012, 839–49.

Jørgensen, M. and K. Molökken, How large are software cost overruns? Critical comments on the Standish Group's CHAOS Reports, Working paper, 2003.

Kahneman, D., 'Maps of bounded rationality: Psychology for behavioural economics', *Americsan Economic Review*, vol. 93, no. 5, 2003, 1449–75.

Thinking, Fast and Slow, New York: Farrar, Straus & Giroux, 2011.

Kahneman, D., J. L. Knetsch, and R. H. Thaler, 'Anomalies: The endowment effect, loss aversion, and status quo bias', *Journal of Economic Perspectives*, vol. 5, no.1, 1991, 193–206.

Kahneman, D., D. Lovallo, and O. Sibony, 'Before you make that bid decision . . . ', *Harvard Business Review*, vol. 89, no. 6, 2011, 50–60.

Kahneman, D., and A. Tversky, 'Prospect theory: An analysis of decisions under risk', *Econometrica*, vol. 47, no. 2, 1979, 313–27.

Kardes, I., A. Ozturk, S. T. Cavusgil, and E. Cavusgil, 'Managing global megaprojects: Complexity and risk management', *International Business Review*, vol. 22, no. 6, 2013, 905–17.

Keil, M., 'Pulling the plug: Software project management and the problem of project escalation', *MIS Quarterly*, vol. 19, no. 4, 1995, 421–47.

Keil, M. and J. Mann, 'The nature and extent of IT-project escalation: Results from a survey of IS audit and control professionals', *IS Audit & Control Journal*, vol. 1, 1997, 40–8.

'Understanding the nature and extent of IS project escalation: Results from a survey of IS audit and control professionals', *IEEE, Proceedings of the Thirtieth Hawaii International Conference on System Sciences*, 7–10 January 1997, 139–48.

Keil, M., J. Mann, and A. Rai, 'Why software projects escalate: An empirical analysis and test of four theoretical models', *MIS Quarterly*, vol. 24, no. 4, 2000, 631–64.

Kessides, I. N., 'The future of the nuclear industry reconsidered: Risks, uncertainties, and continued promise', *Energy Policy*, vol. 48, 2012, 185–208.

Keusch, T., L. H. H. Bollen, and H. F. D. Hassink, 'Self-serving bias in annual report narratives: An empirical analysis of the impact of economic crises', *European Accounting Review*, vol. 21, no. 3, 2013, 623–48.

Khalil, E. L., 'Self-deceit and self-serving bias: Adam Smith on 'General Rules'', *Journal of Institutional Economics*, vol. 5, no. 2, 2009, 251–8.

Kharbanda, O. P. and E. A. Stallworthy, *How to Learn from Project Disasters*, Aldershot: Gower, 1983.

'Lessons from project disasters', *Industrial Management & Data Systems*, vol. 92, no. 3, 1992, 1–46.

Kirkpatrick, David. L. I., 'Trends in the costs of weapon systems and the consequences', *Defence and Peace Economics*, vol. 15, no. 3, 2004, 259–73.

Klein, B. H., 'The decision making problem in development', in R. Nelson, ed., *The Rate and Direction of Inventive Activity*, Princeton: Princeton University Press, 1962, pp. 477–508.

246   Bibliography

Klein, B. H. and W. Meckling, 'Application of operations research to development projects', *Operations Research*, vol. 6, no. 3, 1958, 352–63.

Knight, F. H., *Risk, Uncertainty and Profit*, Boston, MA: Houghton Mifflin, 1921.

Konglige olje- og energidepartement, *Kostnadsanalysen – norsk kontinentalsokkel*, Oslo: Konglige olje- og energidepartement, 1980.

Krieger, M. H., 'Big decisions and a culture of decision making', *Journal of Policy Analysis and Management*, vol. 5, no. 4, 1986, 779–97.

Kruger, J. and D. Dunning, 'Unskilled and unaware of it: How difficulties in recognizing one's own incompetence lead to inflated self-assessments', *Journal of Personality and Social Psychology*, vol. 77, no. 6, 1999, 1121–34.

Kvalvik, S. and P. Johansen, Enhetskostnadsvekst på försvarsinvesteringer, Forsvarets Forskningsinstitutt, Rapport 2008/01129, 2008.

Landerer, N., 'Rethinking the logics: A conceptual framework for the mediatization of politics', *Communication Theory*, vol. 23, no. 3, 2013, 239–58.

Larwood, L. and W. Whittaker, 'Managerial myopia: Self-serving biases in organizational planning', *Journal of Applied Psychology*, vol. 62, no. 2, 1977, 194–8.

Lasswell, D. H., *Politics: Who Gets What, When, How*, New York: Whittlesey House, 1936.

Lavallo, D. and D. Kahneman, 'Delusions of success: How optimism undermines executives' decisions', *Harvard Business Review*, vol. 81, no. 7, 2003, 56–63.

Lavallo, D. and O. Sibony, 'The case for behavioral strategy', *McKinsey Quarterly*, March 2010, 1–16.

Le Coze, J.-C., '1984–2014. Normal accidents. Was Charles Perrow right for the wrong reasons?', *Journal of Contingencies and Crisis Management*, vol. 23, no. 4, 2015, 275–86.

Lederer, A. L. and J. Prasad, 'Causes of inaccurate software development cost estimates', *Journal of Systems Software*, vol. 21, no. 2, 1995, 125–34.

Lee, J.-K., 'Cost overrun and cause in Korean social overhead capital projects: Roads, rails, airports, and ports', *Journal of Urban Planning and Development*, vol. 134, no. 2, 2008, 59–62.

Lehtonen, J.-M. and J. Anteroinen, 'The capability factors as explanatory variables of equipment unit cost growth: A methodological proposal', *Defence and Peace Economics*, vol. 27, no. 2, 2015, 1–19.

Lewis, S. and T. Grogan, 'A hundred years of ENR Cost Indexes', *Engineering News-Record*, 30 September 2013, 1–2.

Liebowitz, S. J. and S. E. Margolis, eds., 'Path dependence', in B. Bouckaert and G. Geest, *Encyclopedia of Law and Economics*, Elgar: Cheltenham, 2000, pp. 981–98.

Likierman, A., 'Analysing project cost escalation: The case study of North Sea oil', *Accounting and Business Research*, vol. 29, no. 29, 1977, 51–7.

'Avoiding cost escalation on major projects', *Management Accounting*, vol. 58, February 1980, 28–30.

Little, T., 'Schedule estimation and uncertainty surrounding the cone of uncertainty', *IEEE Software*, vol. 23, no. 3, 2006, 48–54.

Liu, L., G. Wehbe, and J. Sisovic, 'The accuracy of hybrid estimating approaches: A case study of an Austrailian State Road & Traffic Authority', *The Engineering Economist*, vol. 55, no. 3, 2010, 225–45.

Love, P. E. D., D. D. Ahiaga-Dagbui, and Z. Irani, 'Cost overruns in transportation infrastructure projects: Sowing the seeds for a probabilistic theory of causation', *Transportation Research Part A*, vol. 92, 2016, 184–94.

Love, P. E. D. and D. J. Edwards, 'Determinants of rework in building construction projects', *Engineering, Construction and Architectural Management*, vol. 11, no. 4, 2004, 259–74.

Love, P. E. D., D. J. Edwards, and Z. Irani, 'Moving beyond optimism bias and strategic misrepresentation: An explanation for social infrastructure project cost overruns', *IEEE Transactions on Engineering Management*, vol. 59, no. 4, 2012, 560–71.

Love, P. E. D., C.-P. Sing, X. Wang, Z. Irani, and D. W. Thawala, 'Overruns in transportation infrastructure projects', *Structure and Infrastructure Engineering*, vol. 10, no. 2, 2014, 141–59.

Love, P. E. D., J. Smith, I. Simpson, M. Regan, and O. Olatunji, 'Understanding the landscape of overruns in transport infrastructure projects', *Environment and Planning B*: Urban Analytics and City Science, vol. 42, no. 3, 2015, 490–509.

Love, P. E. D. and A. S. Sohal, 'Capturing rework costs in projects', *Managerial Audit Journal*, vol. 18, no. 4, 2003, 329–39.

Lundberg, E., *Produktivitet och räntabilitet*, Stockholm: SNS, 1961.

Mahajan, J., 'The overconfidence effect in marketing management predictions', *Journal of Marketing Research*, vol. 29, no. 3, 1992, 329–42.

Maier, N. R. F., *Problem-solving Discussions and Conferences: Leadership Methods and Skills*, New York: MacGraw-Hill Book Company, 1963.

Magnussen, O. M. and N. O. E. Olsson, 'Comparative analysis of cost estimates of major public investment projects', *International Journal of Project Management*, vol. 24, no. 4, 2006, 281–8.

Malmendier, U. and G. Tate, 'CEO overconfidence and corporate investment' *Journal of Finance*, vol. 60, no. 6, 2005, 2661–2700.

'Does overconfidence affect corporate investment? CEO overconfidence measures revisited', *European Financial Management*, vol. 11, no. 5, 2005, 649–59.

'Behavioral CEOs: The role of managerial overconfidence', *Journal of Economic Perspective*, vol. 29, no. 4, 2015, 37–60.

Malmendier, U., G. Tate, and J. Yan, 'Overconfidence and early-life experiences: The effect of managerial traits on corporate financial policies', *Journal of Finance*, vol. 66, no. 5, 2011, 1687–733.

Malmendier, U. and T. Taylor, 'On the verges of overconfidence', *Journal of Economic Perspective*, vol. 29, no. 4, 2015, 3–7.

Malmi, T. and D. A. Brown, 'Management control systems as a package: Opportunities, challenges and research directions', *Management Accounting Research*, vol. 19, no. 4, 2008, 287–300.

Mansfield, E., J. Rapoport, J. Schnee, S. Wagner, and M. Hamburger, *Research and Innovation in the Modern Corporation*, New York: Norton, 1971.

Marglin, S., *Approaches to Dynamic Investment Planning*, Amsterdam: North-Holland, 1963.

van Marrewijk, A., S. R. Clegg, T. S. Pitsis, and M. Veenswijk, 'Managing public-private megaprojects: Paradoxes, complexity, and project design', *International Journal of Project Management*, vol. 26, no. 6, 2008, 591–600.

Marschak, T., 'The role of project histories in the study of R&D', in T. Marschak, T. K. Glennan Jr., and R. Summers, eds., *Strategies for R&D: Studies in the Microeconomics of Development*, Berlin: Springer Verlag, 1967, pp. 49–139.

'Towards a normative theory of development', in T. Marschak, T. K. Glennan Jr., and R. Summers, eds., *Strategies for R&D: Studies in the Microeconomics of Development*, Berlin: Springer Verlag, 1967, pp. 190–221.

Marschak, T., T. K. Glennan Jr. and R. Summers, eds., *Strategies for R&D: Studies in the Microeconomics of Development*, Berlin: Springer Verlag, 1967.

Marshall, A. W. and W. H. Meckling, 'Predictability of the costs, time, and success of development', in R. Nelson, ed., *The Rate and Direction of Inventive Activity: Economic and Social Factors*, Princeton: Princeton University Press, 1962, pp. 461–75.

Mashayekhi, A. N., 'Project cost dynamics for development policy-making', *Journal of the Operational Research Society*, vol. 51, no. 3, 2000, 301–10.

Mayes, B. T. and R. W. Allen, 'Toward a definition of organizational politics', *Academy of Management Review*, vol. 2, no. 4, 1977, 672–8.

Mazzoleni, G. and W. Schulz, '"Mediatization" of politics: A challenge for democracy?', *Political Communication*, vol. 16, no. 3, 1999, 247–61.

McCraw, T. K., ed., *Creating Modern Capitalism: How Entrepreneurs, Companies, and Countries Triumphed in Three Industrial Revolutions*, Cambridge, MA: Harvard University Press, 1997.

McNamara, G., H. Moon, and P. Bromiley, 'Banking on commitment: Intended and unintended consequences of an organization's attempt to attenuate escalation of commitment', *Academy of Management Journal*, vol. 45, no. 2, 2002, 443–52.

McNees, S. K., 'An assessment of the "official" economic forecasts', *New England Economic Review*, July–August 1995, 13–24.

Memon, A. H., I. A. Rahman, M. R. Abdullah, A. Asmi, and A. Azis, 'Factors affecting construction cost in Mara Large Construction Project: Perspective of project management consultant', *International Journal of Sustainable Construction Engineering & Technology*, vol. 1, no. 2, 2010, 41–54.

Merewitz, L., 'Public transportation: Wish fulfillment and reality in the San Francisco bay area', *American Economic Review*, vol. 62, no. 2, 1972, 78–86.

'Cost overruns in public works', in W. Niskanen, ed., *Benefit-Cost and Policy Analysis 1972: An Aldine Annual on Forecasting, Decision-making, and Evaluation*, Chicago: Aldine Pub. Co., 1973, pp. 278–95.

'How do urban rapid transit projects compare in cost estimating experience?' Proceedings of the International Conference on Transportation Research, Brugge, June 1973, pp. 484–93.

Merrow, E. W., K. E. Phillips, and C. W. Myers, *Understanding Cost Growth and Performance Shortfalls in Pioneer Process Plants*, Santa Monica: The Rand Corporation, 1981.

Merrow, E. W., L. McDonnell, and R. Y. Argüden, *Understanding the Outcomes of Megaprojects: A Qualitative Analysis of Very Large Civilian Projects*, Santa Monica: The RAND Corporation, 1988.

Merton, R. K., 'The unanticipated consequences of purposive social action', *American Sociological Review*, vol. 1, no. 6, 1936, 894–904.

Messner, M., 'The limits of accountability', *Accounting, Organization and Society*, vol. 34, no. 8, 2009, 918–38.

Mest, D. P. and E. Plummer, E., 'Analysts' rationality and forecast bias: Evidence from sales forecasts', *Review of Quantitative Finance and Accounting*, vol. 21, no. 2, 2003, 103–22.

Mezias, J. M. and W. H. Starbuck, 'What do managers know, anyway? A lot less than they think. Now, the good news', *Harvard Business Review*, vol. 81, no. 5, 2003, 16–7.

Mezulis, A. H., L. Y. Abramson, J. S. Hyde, and B. L. Hankin, 'Is there a universal positivity bias in attributions? A meta-analytic review of individual, developmental, and cultural differences in the self-serving attributional bias', *Psychological Bulletin*, vol. 130, no. 5, 2004, 711–47.

Miller, D. T. and M. Ross, 'Self-serving biases in the attribution of causality: Fact or fiction?', *Psychological Bulletin*, vol. 82, no. 2, 1975, 129–65.

Miller, E. M., 'Uncertainty induced bias in capital budgeting', *Financial Management*, vol. 7, Fall 1978, 12–18.

Miller, P. and M. Power, 'Accounting, organizing and economizing: Connecting accounting research and organization theory', *Academy of Management Annals*, vol. 7, no. 1, 2014, 557–605.

Mintzberg, H., *The Rise and Fall of Strategic Planning*, New York: Prentice Hall, 1994.

Mitchell, R. K., B. R. Agle, and D. J. Wood, 'Toward a theory of stakeholder identification and silence: Defining the principle of who and what really counts', *Academy of Management Review*, vol. 22, no. 4, 1997, 853–86.

Mitchell, F., and S. P. Walker, 'Market pressures and the development of costing practice: The emergence of uniform costing in the UK printing industry', *Management Accounting Research*, vol. 8, no. 1, 1997, 75–101.

Mitchels, R. *Zur Soziologie des Parteiwesens in der modernen Demokratie. Untersuchungen über die oligarchischen Tendenzen des Gruppenlebens*, Leipzig: Verlag von Dr. Werner Klinkhardt, 1911.

Political Parties: A Sociological Study of the Oligarchial Tendencies of Modern Democracy. Kitchener: Batoche Books, 2001.

Morner, A. L., 'For SOHIO it was Alaskan oil: Or bust', *Fortune*, August 1977, 173–84.

Morris, P. W. G., *The Management of Projects*, London: Telford, 1994.

Morris, P. W. G. and G. H. Hough, *Preconditions of Success and Failure in Major Projects*, Oxford: Major Project Association, 1986.

The Anatomy of Major Projects: A Study of the Reality of Project Management. New York: John Wiley & Sons, 1987.

Morris, P. W. G., J. Pinto, and J. Söderlund, eds., *The Oxford Handbook of Project Management,* Oxford: Oxford University Press, 2012.

Morris, S., 'Cost and time overruns in public sector projects', *Economic and Political Weekly,* vol. 25, no. 47, 1990, M–154–68.

National Auditing Agency, *Investering vid statens järnvägar, sjöfartsverket och luftfartsverket – beslutsunderlag och statsmakternas styrning,* Dnr 1982:1168, Stockholm: Riksrevisionsverket, 1982.

Varför blev det dyrare? Kostnadsutvecklingen för statliga reformer, Dnr 1983:334, Stockholm: Riksrevisionsverket, 1983.

Infrastrukturinvesteringar: En kostnadsjämförelse mellan plan och utfall i 15 större projekt inom Vägverket och Banverket, RRV 1994:23, Stockholm: Riksrevisionsverket, 1994.

Vägverkets, Banverkets och länens förslag till infrastrukturinvesteringar åren 1998–2007 – en kvalitetsbedömning av beslutsunderlaget, Stockholm: Riksrevisionsverket, 1997.

Varför blev det dyrare? Kostnadsutvecklingen för offentlig försvarare, målsägandebiträde och offentligt biträde, Stockholm: Riksrevisionsverket, 2001.

National Audit Office, *North Sea Cost Escalation Study,* Department of Energy Paper No 7, London: Her Majesty's Stationery Office, 1976.

Nelson, R. R., 'The simple economics of basic scientific research', *Journal of Political Economy,* vol. 67, no. 3, 1959, 297–306.

'Uncertainty, learning and the economics of parallel research and development efforts', *Review of Economics and Statistics,* vol. 43, no. 4, 1961, 351–64.

Newcomb, H. T., *Railway Economics,* Philadelphia: Railway World Pub. Co., 1898.

Nofsinger, J. R., *The Psychology of Investing,* 5th edn., Upper Saddle River: Pearson Prentice Hall, 2016.

Nordlund, P., J. Åkerström, B. Öström, and H. Löfstedt, *Kostnadsutveckling för försvarsmateriel,* Report FOI-R-3213-SE, Stockholm: Totalförsvarets forskningsinstitut, 2011.

Oborne, P., *The Triumph of the Political Class,* London: Simon & Schuster, 2007.

Odeck, J., 'Cost overruns in road construction: What are their sizes and determinants?', *Transport Policy,* vol. 11, no. 1, 2004, 43–53.

Odeck, J., 'Do reforms reduce the magnitude of cost overruns in road projects? Statistical evidence from Norway', *Transportation Research Part A,* vol. 65, July 2014, 68–79.

Odeck, J., M. Welde, and G. H. Volden, 'The impact of external quality assurance of costs estimates on cost overruns: Empirical evidence from the Norwegian road sector', *European Journal of Transportation Infrastructure Research,* vol. 15, no. 3, 2015, 286–303.

Odenmar, U., *Kommunal budgetprocess och projektadministration för byggprojekt,* Malmö: Avdelningen för Byggproduktionsteknik, Lunds Tekniska högskola, 1983.

Ogunlana, S. O., *Accuracy in Design Cost Estimating*, PhD thesis, Loughborough University of Technology, 1989.

Olaniran, O. J., P. E. D. Love, D. J. Edwards, O. Olatunj, and J. Matthews, 'Chaotic dynamics of cost overruns in oil and gas megaprojects: A review', *International Journal of Civil, Environmental, Structural, Construction and Architectural Engineering*, vol. 9, no. 7, 2015, 889–95.

Oliveira S. J., M. C. Coutinho, and C. V. Martins, 'Forecasting errors in capital budgeting: A multi-firm post-audit study', *The Engineering Economist*, vol. 52, no. 1, 2007, 21–39.

Otoleva, P. and E. Snowberg, 'Overconfidence in political behavior', *American Economic Review*, vol. 105, no. 2, 2015, 504–35.

Ouchi, W., 'The conceptual framework for the design of organizational control mechanisms', *Management Science*, vol. 25, no. 9, 1979, 833–48.

Ouchi, W., and A. Berry, 'Control, organization and accounting', *Accounting, Organization and Society*, vol. 5, no. 2, 1980, 231–44.

Packard Commission, *A Quest for Excellence: Final Report to the President's Blue Ribbon Commission on Defense Management*, Washington DC, June 1986.

Parkinson, C. N., *The Law and the Profit*, London: John Murray, 1960.

Patanakul, P., Y. H. Kwak, O. Zwikael, and M. Liu, 'What impacts the performance of large-scale government projects?', *International Journal of Project Management*, vol. 34, no. 3, 2016, 452–66.

Peck, M. S. and F. M. Scherer, *The Weapons Acquisition Process: An Economic Analysis*, Boston: Division of Research, Graduate School of Business Administration, Harvard University, 1962.

Peng, T.-C., 'Overcapitalization and cost escalation in housing renovation', *New Zealand Economic Papers*, vol. 45, no. 1–2, 2011, 119–38.

Perrow, C. R., *Normal Accident: Living with High Risk Technologies*, New York: Basic Books, 1984.

'Organizing to reduce the vulnerabilities of complexity', *Journal of Contingencies and Crisis Management*, vol. 7, no. 3, 1999, 150–5.

'Complexity, catastrophe, and modularity', *Sociological Inquiry*, vol. 78, no. 2, 2008, 162–73.

Persky, J., 'Retrospectives: Cost-benefit analysis and the classical creed', *Journal of Economic Perspectives*, vol. 15, no. 4, 2001, 199–208.

Peterson, C., 'The future of optimism', *American Psychologist*, vol. 55, no. 1, 2000, 44–55.

Pham, M. T., 'Emotion and rationality: A critical review and interpretation of empirical evidence', *Review of General Psychology*, vol. 11, no. 2, 2007, 155–78.

Pickrell, D. H., 'A desire named streetcar: Fantasy and fact in rail transit planning', *Journal of the American Planning Association*, vol. 8, no. 2, 1990, 158–76.

Polanyi, K., *The Great Transformation: The Political and Economic Origins of Our Time*, New York: Rinehart & Company, Inc., 1944.

Pope, D., *Nuclear Implosions: The Rise and Fall of the Washington Public Power Supply System*, Cambridge: Cambridge University Press, 2008.

Postlewaite, A. and O. Compte, 'Confidence enhanced performance', *American Economic Review*, vol. 83, no. 5, 2005, 1536–57.

Powell, K., ed., *The Great Builders*, London: Thames & Hudson Ltd., 2011.

Prendergast, C., 'A theory of "Yes Men"', *American Economic Review*, vol. 83, no. 4, 1993, 757–70.

Prest, A. R., and Turvey, R., 'Cost-benefit analysis: A survey', *Economic Journal*, vol. 75, no. 300, 1965, 683–735.

Priemus, H., 'Decision-making on mega-projects: Drifting on political discontinuity and market dynamics', *European Journal of Transport and Infrastructure Research*, vol. 10, no. 1, 2010, 19–29.

Pruitt, S. W. and L. J. Gitman, 'Capital budgeting forecast biases: Evidence from the Fortune 500', *Financial Management*, vol. 15, Spring 1987, 46–51.

Przeworski, A., S. C. Stokes, and B. Manin, eds., *Democracy, Accountability, and Representation*, Cambridge: Cambridge University Press, 1999.

Pugh, P., *The Cost of Sea Power: The Influence of Money on Naval Affairs from 1815 to the Present Day*, London: Conway Maritime Press, 1986.

Pyszczynski, T., J. Greenberg, S., Solomon, J. Arndt, and J. Schimel, 'Why do people need self-esteem? A theoretical and empirical review', *Psychological Bulletin*, vol. 130, no. 3, 2004, 435–68.

Rabin, M., 'Psychology and economics', *Journal of Economic Literature*, vol. 36, no. 1, 1998, 11–46.

Reichelt, K. and J. Lyneis, 'The dynamics of project performance: Benchmarking the drivers of cost and schedule overrun', *European Management Journal*, vol. 17, no. 2, 1999, 135–50.

Remer, D. S. and H. R. Buchanan, 'The cost of doing a cost estimate', *Cost Engineering*, vol. 35, no. 3, 1993, 7–11.

'Estimating the cost for doing a cost estimate', *International Journal of Production Economics*, vol. 66, no. 2, 2000, 101–4.

Roberts, J., 'No one is perfect: The limits of transparency and an ethic for "intelligent! Accountability', *Accounting, Organizations and Society*, vol. 34, no. 8, 2009, 957–70.

Roberts, J., 'Organizational ignorance: Towards a managerial perspective on the unknown', *Management Learning*, vol. 44, no. 3, 2012, 215–36.

Ross, J. and B. M. Staw, 'Expo 86: An escalation prototype', *Administrative Science Quarterly*, vol. 31, no. 2, 1986, 274–97.

Ruttan, V. W., *Is War Necessary for Economic Growth? Military Procurement and Technology Development*, New York: Oxford University Press, 2006.

Sahlin-Andersson, K., *Beslutsprocessens komplexitet: Att genomföra och hindra stora project*, Karlshamn: Bokförlaget Doxa AB, 1986.

Sawhney, H., 'Dynamics of infrastructure development: The role of metaphors, political will and sunk investment', *Media, Culture & Society*, vol. 23, no. 1, 2001, 33–51.

Sawyer, J. E., 'Entrepreneurial error and economic growth', *Explorations in Entrepreneurial History*, vol. 4, no. 2, 1952, 199–204.

Schmidt, J. B. and R. J. Calantone, 'Escalation of commitment during new product development', *Journal of the Academy of Marketing Science*, vol. 30, no. 2, 2002, 103–18.

Schnee, J. E., 'Development cost: Determinants and overruns', *Journal of Business*, vol. 45, no. 3, 347–74.

Schonberger, R. J., 'Why projects are "always" late: A rationale based on manual simulation of a PERT/CPM network', *Interfaces*, vol. 11, no. 5, 1981, 66–70.

Schulz, W., 'Reconstructing mediatization as an analytical concept', *European Journal of Communication*, vol. 19, no. 1, 2004, 87–101.

Schultze, T., F. Pfeiffer, and S. Schulz-Hardt, 'Biased information processing in the escalation paradigm: Information search and information evaluation as potential mediators of escalating commitment', *Journal of Applied Psychology*, vol. 97, no. 1, 2012, 16–32.

Scitovsky, T., *The Joyless Economy: An Inquiry into Human Satisfaction and Consumer Dissatisfaction*, New York: Oxford University Press, 1976.

Sedikides, C., W. K. Campbell, G. Reeder, and A. Elliot, 'Self-serving bias in a relational context', *Journal of Personality and Social Psychology*, vol. 74, no. 2, 1998, 378–86.

Segelod, E., Kostnadsuppföljning med analys för Genastorp vattenkraftstation, Karlshamnsverkets första oljekraftverk samt för Barsebäcksverkets båda kärnkraftsaggregat, FE-rapport 187, Företagsekonomiska institutionen, Göteborgs Universitet, 1982.

Kalkylering och avvikelser: Empiriska studier av stora projekt i kommuner och industriföretag, Malmö: Liber, 1986.

'How to avoid cost overruns?', *Journal of General Management*, vol. 16, no. 4, 1991, 16–23.

'Explanations of project deviations', in I. Hägg and E. Segelod, eds., *Issues in Empirical Investment Research*, Amsterdam: North-Holland, 1992, pp. 262–82.

Renewal Through Internal Development, Aldershot: Avebury, 1995.

Resource Allocation in Divisionalized Groups: A Study of Investment Manuals and Corporate Level Means of Control, Aldershot: Avebury, 1996.

'Investments and investment processes in professional service groups', *International Journal of Production Economics*, vol. 67, no. 2, 2000, 135–54.

'Resource allocation in a few industries: Determinants and trends', *International Journal of Production Economics*, vol. 77, no. 1, 2002, 63–70.

'The cost of the Swedish nuclear waste program', *Progress in Nuclear Energy*, vol. 48, no. 4, 2006, 314–24.

Segelod, E. and L. Carlsson, 'The emergence of uniform principles of cost accounting in Sweden 1900-36', *Accounting, Business, and Financial History*, vol. 20, no. 3, 2010, 327–63.

Segelod, E. and G. Jordan, 'The use and importance of external sources of knowledge in the software development process', *R&D Management*, vol. 34, no. 3, 2004, 239–52.

Shane, S. A., *The Illusions of Entrepreneurship: The Costly Myths That Entrepreneurs, Investors, and Policy Makers Live*, New Haven: Yale University Press, 2010.

Shapira, Z. and D. J. Berndt, 'Managing grand-scale construction projects: A risk-taking perspective', *Research in Organizational Behavior*, vol. 19, 1996, 303–60.

Sharot, T., 'The optimism bias', *Current Biology*, vol. 21, no. 23, 2011, R941–5.

Shepherd, D. A., H. Patzelt, and M. Wolfe, 'Moving forward from project failure: Negative emotions, affective commitment, and learning from the experience', *Academy of Management Journal*, vol. 54, no. 6, 2011, 1229–59.

Shepperd, J., W. Malone, and K. Sweeny, 'Exploring causes of the self-serving bias', *Social and Personality Psychology Compass*, vol. 2, no. 2, 2008, 895–908.

Siemiatycki, M., 'Academic and Auditors: Comparing perspectives on transportation project cost overruns', *Journal of Planning Education and Research*, vol. 29, no. 2, 2009, 142–56.

Simon, H. A., *Administrative Behavior*, New York: The Macmillan Company, 1947.

'A behavioural model of rational choice', *Quarterly Journal of Economics*, vol. 69, no. 1, 1955, 99–118.

'Theories of decision-making in economics and behavioral science', *American Economic Review*, vol. 49, no. 3, 1959, 253–83.

'Making management decisions: The role of intuition and emotion', *Academy of Management Executive*, vol. 1, no. 1, 1987, 57–64.

'Bounded rationality in social science: Today and tomorrow', *Mind & Society*, vol. 1, no. 1, 2000, 25–39.

Simon, M., S. M. Houghton, and K. Aquino, 'Cognitive bias, risk perception, and venture formation: How individuals decide to start companies', *Journal of Business Venturing*, vol. 15, no. 2, 1999, 113–34.

Sleesman, D. J., D. E. Conlon, G. McNamara, and J. E. Miles, 'Cleaning up the big muddy: A meta-analytic review of the determinants of escalation of commitment', *Academy of Management Journal*, vol. 55, no. 3, 2012, 541–62.

Slemrod, J., 'Thanatology and economics: The behavioral economics of death', *American Economic Review*, vol. 93, no. 2, 2003, 371–5.

Smith, A., *The Theory of Moral Sentiments*, 6th edn., 1790, London: A. Millar, 1759.

An Inquiry into the Causes and Effects of the Wealth of Nations, London: W. Strahan; and T. Cadell, in the Strand, 1776.

Solomon, S., J. Greenberg, J. Schimel, J. Arndt, and T. Pyszczynski, 'Human awareness of mortality and the evolution of culture', in M. Schaller and C. S. Crandell, eds., *The Psychological Foundation of Culture*, Mahwah: Lawrence Erlbaum Associates, Inc., 2004, pp. 15–40.

Sovacool, B. K., D. Nugent, and A. Gilbert, 'Construction cost overruns and electricity infrastructure: An unavoidable risk?', *Electricity Journal*, vol. 27, no. 4, 2014, 112–20.

The Standish Group, *The CHAOS Report*, 1995.

Stangert, P., *Information, Uncertainty and Adaptive Planning*, Stockholm: FOA P Rapport C8392-M3, 1974.

'Adaptive planning and uncertainty resolution', *Futures*, vol. 9, no. 1, 1977, 32–44.

Statman, M. and T. T. Tyebjee, 'Optimistic capital budgeting forecasts: An experiment', *Financial Management*, vol. 13, Autumn 1985, 27–33.

Staw, B. M., 'Knee-deep in the big muddy: A study of escalating commitment to a chosen course of action', *Organizational Behavior and Human Performance*, vol. 16, no. 1, 1976, 27–44.

'The escalation of commitment: An update and appraisal', in Z. Shapira, ed., *Organizational Decision Making*, Cambridge: Cambridge University Press, 1997, pp. 191–215.

Staw B. M., and J. Ross, 'Understanding behaviour in escalation situations', *Science*, vol. 246, no. 4927, 1989, 216–20.

Stecklein, J. M., J. Dabney, D. Brandon, B. Haskins, R. Lowell, and G. Moroney, *Error cost escalation through the project life cycle*, Report JSC-CN-8435, Houston, TX: NASA Johnson Space Center, 2004.

Steinberg, G. M., 'Large-scale national projects as political symbols: The case of Israel', *Comparative Politics*, vol. 19, no. 3, 1987, 331–46.

Summers, R., 'Cost estimates as predictors of actual costs: A statistical study of military developments', in T. Marschak, T. K. Glennan, Jr., and R. Summers, eds., *Strategy for R&D*, Berlin: Springer Verlag, 1967, pp. 140–89.

Svedenstierna, E. T. and C. J. Lidbeck, 'Utdrag af byggnads-räkningen öfver Tunkarsbo nya masugn, år 1805', *Samlingar i bergsvettenskapen*, vol. 3, no. 1, 1811, pp. 44–9.

Svenson, O., 'Are we all less risky and more skillful than our fellow drivers?', *Acta Psychologica*, vol. 47, no. 2, 1981, 143–8.

Svensson, P., *Styrning av produktutvecklingsprojekt: En studie av förutsättningarna för planering av produktutvecklingsprojekt i några svenska verkstadsföretag*, Göteborg: Institutionen för Industriell organisation och ekonomi, Chalmers tekniska högskola, 1990.

Sverlinger, P.-A. M., *Managing Knowledge in Professional Service Organizations: Technical Consultants Serving the Construction Industry*, Gothenburg: Department of Service Management, Chalmers University of Technology, 2000.

Swedish Government Official Reports, *Spent Nuclear Fuel and Radioactive Waste: A Summary of a Report Given by the Swedish Government Committee on Radioactive Waste*, SOU 1976:32, Stockholm, 1976.

Kärnkraftens avfall: Organisation och finansiering, SOU 1980:14, Stockholm: Liber Förlag, 1980.

Översyn av lagstiftningen på kärnenergiområdet, SOU 1991:107, Stockholm: Allmänna förlaget, 1991.

Säkrare finansiering av framtida kärnavfallskostnader, SOU 1994:107, Stockholm: Fritze, 1994.

Säkrare finansiering av framtida kärnavfallskostnader, SOU 1994:108, Stockholm: Fritze, 1994.

Betalningsansvaret för kärnavfallet, SOU 2004:125, Stockholm: Norstedts Juridik, 2004.

Swedish Nuclear Waste Fund, Antagande om real avkastning på medlen i Kärnavfallsfonden inför avgiftsberäkningar m.m. för år 2004, Dnr KAFS 14–03, 2003.

Swedish Nuclear Fuel and Waste Management Company, Kärnkraftens slutsteg – Plan 82: *Plan för kärnkraftens radioaktiva restprodukter*, Stockholm: Svensk Kärnbränsleförsörjning AB, 1982.

Kärnkraftens slutsteg – Plan 83: *Plan för kärnkraftens radioaktiva restprodukter*, Stockholm: Svensk Kärnbränsleförsörjning AB, 1983.

Plan 1984: *Kostnader för kärnkraftens radioaktiva restprodukter*, Stockholm: Svensk Kärnbränslehantering AB, 1984.

Plan 2004: *Kostnader för kärnkraftens radioaktiva restprodukter*, Stockholm: Svensk Kärnbränslehantering AB, 2004.

Plan 2013. *Costs from and including 2015 for the radioactive residual products from nuclear power. Basis for fees and guarantees for the period 2015–2017*, Technical Report TR-14–16, Stockholm: Swedish Nuclear Fuel and Waste Management Company, 2014.

Sydow, J., G. Schreyögg, and J. Koch, 'Organizational path dependence: Opening the black box', *Academy of Management Review*, vol. 34, no. 4., 2009, 689–709.

Tang, M.-J., 'An economic perspective on escalating commitment', *Strategic Management Journal*, vol. 9, Summer 1988, 79–92.

Tchapga, F., *Overview and comparison of international practices on funding mechanisms*, Topical Session on Funding Issues in Connection with Decommissioning of Nuclear Power Plants, Paris: Nuclear Energy Agency and OECD, 2004.

Tiger, L., *Optimism: The Biology of Hope*, New York: Simon & Schuster, 1979.

Toda, M., 'Emotion and decision making', *Acta Psychologica*, vol. 45, no. 1–3, 1980, 133–55.

Tversky, A. and D. Kahneman, 'Judgment under uncertainty: Heuristics and biases', *Science*, vol. 185, no. 4157, 1974, 1124–31.

'The framing of decisions and the psychology of choice', *Science*, vol. 211, 30 January 1981, 453–8.

Tyebjee, T. T., 'Behavioral biases in new product forecasting', *International Journal of Forecasting*, vol. 3, no. 3–4, 1987, 393–404.

Unger, E. J., M. A. Gallagher, and E. D. White, III, 'R&D budget-driven cost and schedule overruns', *Journal of Cost Analysis & Management*, vol. 6, no. 1, 2004, 80–9.

Vaki, A., 'Human uniqueness and the denial of death', *Nature*, vol. 460, 6 August 2009, 684.

Wachs, M., 'When planners lie with numbers', *Journal of the American Planning Association*, vol. 55, no. 4, 1989, 476–9.

Waldman, M., 'Systematic errors and the theory of natural selection', *American Economic Review*, vol. 84, no. 3, 1994, 482–97.

Walsh, J. P. and J. K. Seward, 'On the efficiency of internal and external corporate control mechanisms', *Academy of Management Review*, vol. 15, no. 3, 1990, 421–58.

Wildavsky, A., 'The political economy of efficiency: Cost-benefit analysis, systems analysis, and program budgeting', *Public Administration Review*, vol. 26, no. 4, 1966, 292–310.

'If planning is everything, maybe it's nothing', *Policy Science*, vol. 4, no. 2, 1973, 127–53.

Williams, D. W., 'The politics of forecast bias: Forecaster effect and other effects in New York City revenue forecasting', *Public Budgeting & Finance*, vol. 32, no. 4, 2012, 1–18.

Williams, T., 'Assessing and moving on from the dominant project management discourse in the light of project overruns', *IEEE Transactions on Engineering Management*, vol. 52, no. 4, 2005, 497–508.

Wilson, R. M., and Q. Zhang, 'Entrapment and escalating commitment in investment decision making: A review', *British Accounting Review*, vol. 29, no. 3, 1997, 277–303.

Wittfogel, K. A., *Oriental Despotism: A Comparative Study of Total Power*, New Haven: Yale University Press, 1957.

Woodward, S. N., 'Performance in planning a large project', *Journal of Management Studies*, vol. 19, no. 2, 1982, 183–98.

World Nuclear Association, *The Economics of Nuclear Power*, Information Papers, London: World Nuclear Association, 2008.

Wramsby, G. and U. Österlund, *Svenska fastighetsinvesteringar inom EG 1987–1990: Investeringsbedömning, kreditbedömning och hyrespåverkande variabler*, Göteborg: Handelshögskolan vid Göteborgs Universitet, 1995.

Xia, W. and G. Lee, 'Grasping the complexity of IS development projects', *Communications of the ACM*, vol. 47, no. 5, 2004, 138–47.

Yates, J. F., J.-W. Lee, and H. Shinotsuka, 'Beliefs about over-confidence, including its cross-national variation', *Organizational Behavior and Human Decision Processes*, vol. 65, no. 2, 1996, 138–47.

Yen, C.-L. and C.-Y. Lin, 'The effects of mortality salience on escalation of commitment', *International Journal of Psychology*, vol. 47, no. 1, 2012, 51–7.

Zacharakis, A. L. and D. A. Shepherd, 'The nature of information and over-confidence on venture capitalists' decision making', *Journal of Business Venturing*, vol. 16, no. 4, 2001, 311–32.

Zardkoohi, A., 'Do real options lead to escalation of commitment?', *Academy of Management Review*, vol. 29, no. 1, 2004, 111–9.

Index